# Family Violence and Social Change in the Pacific Islands

The Pacific Islands have some of the highest rates of family violence in the world. Addressing the contemporary mutations of Pacific Island families and the shifting understandings of violence in the context of rapid social change, this book investigates the conflict dynamics generated by these transformations.

The contributors draw from detailed case studies in a range of Pacific territories to examine family violence in relation to the social, economic, and political situation of native populations as well as individual, collective, and institutional responses to the development of violence within and upon the family. They focus on vernacular understandings, conflicting social norms, the emergence of different types of violent patterns, the impact of violence on individuals and communities, and local attempts at mitigating or combating it. Combining ethnographic expertise with engaged scholarship, this volume offers a vivid account of ongoing social change in Pacific Island societies and a crucial contribution to the understanding of family violence as a social process, cultural construct, and political issue.

This book will appeal to scholars with interests in the sociology of violence and the family, Pacific studies, development studies, and the social and cultural anthropology of Oceania.

**Loïs Bastide** is Associate Professor of Sociology at the University of French Polynesia, where he is a member of the Équipe d'accueil Sociétés Traditionnelles Contemporaines en Océanie (EASTCO) research team. He is also Associate Researcher at the Maison des Sciences de l'Homme du Pacifique (MSH-P) and at the Institute of Sociological Research at the University of Geneva, Switzerland. His research interests include transnational migrations in Southeast Asia, the management of pandemics, public health crises, natural disasters, and violence in the family. He is currently coordinating a wide-ranging research programme on social change in French Polynesia at the MSH-P. He is the author of *Habiter le transnational: Espace, travail et migration entre Java, Kuala Lumpur et Singapour* (ENS, 2015).

**Denis Regnier** is Head of Humanities and Social Sciences and Assistant Professor at the University of Global Health Equity, Rwanda. He holds a PhD in social anthropology from the London School of Economics and has previously taught at the University of French Polynesia, where he is a member of the Équipe d'accueil Sociétés Traditionnelles Contemporaines en Océanie (EASTCO) and Associate Researcher at the Maison des Sciences de l'Homme du Pacifique (MSH-P). His research interests include the legacies of slavery in the Indian Ocean, the development of social essentialism in Madagascar, and social and public health issues in Africa and the South Pacific. He is the author of *Slavery and Essentialism in Highland Madagascar: Ethnography, History, Cognition* (Routledge, 2020).

# Routledge Studies in Family Sociology

This series presents the latest research on the sociology of the family, with particular attention to family dynamics, changing family forms and the impact of events in the life-course and societal transformation on family practices.

**Titles in the series**

**Father Involvement and Gender Equality in the United States**
Contemporary Norms and Barriers
*Richard J. Petts*

**Family Violence and Social Change in the Pacific Islands**
*Edited by Loïs Bastide & Denis Regnier*

# Family Violence and Social Change in the Pacific Islands

Edited by
Loïs Bastide & Denis Regnier

Routledge
Taylor & Francis Group

LONDON AND NEW YORK

First published 2023
by Routledge
4 Park Square, Milton Park, Abingdon, Oxon OX14 4RN

and by Routledge
605 Third Avenue, New York, NY 10158

*Routledge is an imprint of the Taylor & Francis Group, an Informa business*

*British Library Cataloguing-in-Publication Data*
A catalogue record for this book is available from the British Library

*Library of Congress Cataloging-in-Publication Data*
A catalog record for this book has been requested

ISBN: 978-0-367-70506-0 (hbk)
ISBN: 978-0-367-70507-7 (pbk)
ISBN: 978-1-003-14666-7 (ebk)

DOI: 10.4324/9781003146667

Typeset in Times New Roman
by Apex CoVantage, LLC

MAISON
DES SCIENCES DE L'HOMME
DU PACIFIQUE

# Contents

*List of contributors*       ix
*Acknowledgements*       xiii

**Introduction: family, violence, and social change in the Pacific Islands**       1
LOÏS BASTIDE AND DENIS REGNIER

1 **Settler violence, family, and whānau violence in Aotearoa New Zealand**       20
TRACEY MCINTOSH

2 **Placing the children: fostering native Hawaiian children in an American state**       37
JUDITH SCHACHTER

3 **Transferred children and the production of family violence in French Polynesia: social change and the adaptations of *fa'a'amura'a***       52
LOÏS BASTIDE

4 **Familialism and gender violence in New Caledonia families**       67
CHRISTINE SALOMON

5 **Naming violence: forms of economic violence in highland Papua New Guinea**       82
RICHARD EVES

6 **Culture-based counselling at the domestic violence shelter of the Sisters of the Anglican Church of Melanesia in the Solomon Islands**       95
XANDRA MIGUEL-LORENZO

7   Women-only households in Port Vila, Vanuatu: sites of
    social resistance                                              110
    DANIELA KRAEMER

8   From structural violence to family violence: insights into
    perpetrators' experiences in French Polynesia today           124
    MARIE SALAÜN, MIROSE PAIA, AND JACQUES VERNAUDON

9   'This is not *Vaelens*!': naming and reacting to physical abuse
    in a Vanuatu school                                            138
    ALICE SERVY

10  Quarrels, corporal punishment, and magical attacks:
    what is 'family violence' in Kiriwina?                         151
    LOUISE PROTAR

11  Contexts and levels of community violence in
    highlands Papua New Guinea                                     165
    PAMELA J. STEWART AND ANDREW J. STRATHERN

    Postface – analysing violence: lessons from a collective
    reflection                                                     178
    MICHEL WIEVIORKA

    *Index*                                                        183

# Contributors

**Loïs Bastide** is Associate Professor of Sociology at the University of French Polynesia, where he is a member of the Équipe d'accueil Sociétés Traditionnelles Contemporaines en Océanie (EASTCO) research team. He is also Associate Researcher at the Maison des Sciences de l'Homme du Pacifique (MSH-P) and at the Institute of Sociological Research at the University of Geneva, Switzerland. His research interests include transnational migrations in Southeast Asia, the management of pandemics, public health crises, natural disasters, and violence in the family. He is currently coordinating a wide-ranging research programme on social change in French Polynesia at the MSH-P. He is the author of *Habiter le transnational: Espace, travail et migration entre Java, Kuala Lumpur et Singapour* (ENS, 2015).

**Richard Eves** is Emeritus Professor with the Department of Pacific Affairs, Australian National University, Australia. His work deals with contemporary issues in Melanesia, with a particular focus on gender, violence, and the AIDS epidemic. He recently completed research on the Do No Harm project, which examined the relationship between women's economic empowerment and violence against women in the Solomon Islands and Papua New Guinea, and the project was funded by the Australian government through the Department of Foreign Affairs and Trade's Pacific Women Shaping Pacific Development Programme. He is currently completing an ethnography of contemporary Christianity in Papua New Guinea with a particular focus on the influence of Pentecostalism in New Ireland. He is a co-editor of *Making Sense of AIDS: Culture, Sexuality, and Power in Melanesia* (University of Hawai'i Press, 2008) and *Talking it Through: Responses to Sorcery and Witchcraft Beliefs and Practices in Melanesia* (Australian National University, 2015).

**Daniela Kraemer** is Post-Doctoral Research Fellow in Anthropology at The University of New Mexico, USA, and Instructor in Anthropology at Wilfrid Laurier University, Canada. Her research explores urbanity and social transformation, particularly in Port Vila, the rapidly growing capital city of Vanuatu. She is currently working on a monograph examining the reterritorializing practices of marginalized unemployed young men in urban Vanuatu.

**Tracey McIntosh**, MNZM, is Ngāi Tūhoe and is Professor of Indigenous Studies and Co-Head of Te Wānanga o Waipapa (School of Māori Studies and Pacific Studies) at the University of Auckland, New Zealand. She is also former Co-Director of Ngā Pae o te Māramatanga New Zealand's Māori Centre of Research Excellence. Her recent research focused on incarceration (particularly of Māori and Indigenous peoples) and issues pertaining to poverty, inequality, and social justice. She recognizes the significance of working with those that have lived experience of incarceration and marginalization and acknowledges them as experts of their own condition. She has a strong interest in the interface between research and policy.

**Xandra Miguel-Lorenzo** Xandra gained her Ph.D. in anthropology from the London School of Economics after conducting fieldwork in the Solomon Islands on the Sisters of the Church of Melanesia's response to domestic violence. She first researched domestic violence in Granada, Spain, while she held a research studentship as an undergraduate in the department of anthropology at the University of Granada. She has also volunteered in Bolivia, as a researcher-activist, for the organisation CIDEM and she has published an article about CIDEM's femicide archive. She currently works as a Safelives accredited independent domestic violence advocate for Solace Women's Aid in London and she is a Visiting Research Fellow in the anthropology department at the London School of Economics. She is a trauma-informed intersectional feminist practitioner.

**Mirose Paia** is a Lecturer in Polynesian Languages and Literature at the University of French Polynesia, France, where she is also a member of the Équipe d'accueil Sociétés Traditionnelles Contemporaines en Océanie (EASTCO) research team. Her research focuses mainly on Polynesian languages (codification, phonological, and grammatical description), translation issues, plurilingualism, educational practices, training of educational actors, and the creation of plurilingual environments. She is a native speaker of Tahitian.

**Louise Protar** holds a doctorate in sociology from the University of Paris Panthéon Sorbonne, France. Her doctoral research focused on the organization of work within the family in Kiriwina, an island in Papua New Guinea and one of the Trobriand Islands. Her research questions the logics of the division of labour, the representations of different forms of activity, kinship practices, and gender relations. She is currently interested in family practices in the Pacific region.

**Denis Regnier** is Head of Humanities and Social Sciences and Assistant Professor at the University of Global Health Equity, Rwanda. He holds a PhD in social anthropology from the London School of Economics and has previously taught at the University of French Polynesia, where he is a member of the Équipe d'accueil Sociétés Traditionnelles Contemporaines en Océanie (EASTCO) and Associate Researcher at the Maison des Sciences de l'Homme du Pacifique (MSH-P). His research interests include the legacies of slavery in the Indian Ocean, the development of social essentialism in Madagascar, and social and public health issues in Africa and the South Pacific. He is the author of *Slavery and Essentialism in Highland Madagascar: Ethnography, History, Cognition* (Routledge, 2020).

**Marie Salaün** is Professor of Social Anthropology and Vice-Dean of the Faculty of Societies and Humanities at the University of Paris, France. She is also a researcher at Unité mixte de Recherches Migrations et Société (URMIS) under the supervision of the University of Paris, Côte d'Azur University, the Institute of Research for Development, and the National Centre for Scientific Research. Her research explores sovereignty movements and decolonisation in the Pacific and the Americas, Indigenous issues, colonial and imperial history of the insular Pacific, public policies in colonial and post-colonial contexts, issues about scientific investigations in decolonisation contexts, and the adaptation of institutions to linguistic and cultural realities in the French overseas territories.

**Christine Salomon** is an anthropologist specializing in New Caledonia. Her research focuses on the transformations of gender relations, their articulation with social and political changes, and the interweaving of gender, ethnic, class, and age inequalities. She has worked on the increasing participation of Kanak women in public life, their questioning of gender violence, and their new judicial recourses as well as on the interactions between justice and custom. Her research encompasses the observation and analysis of forms of resistance to domination, whether deviations from norms, individual subversions, or collective protests.

**Judith Schachter** is Professor Emerita of Anthropology and History at Carnegie Mellon University, USA. Her research explores migration and international conventions, adoption and fosterage, life histories, and visual anthropology. Her publications include *Ruth Benedict: Patterns of a Life* (Chatto & Windus, 1983), *Kinship With Strangers: Adoption and Interpretations of Kinship in American Culture* (University of California Press, 1994), *A Town Without Steel: Envisioning Homestead* (University of Pittsburgh Press, 1998), *A Sealed and Secret Kinship: Policies & Practices in American Adoption* (Berghahn Books, 2002), and *The Legacies of a Hawaiian Generation: From Territorial Subject to American Citizen* (Berghahn Books, 2013). She is currently pursuing a project on Native Hawaiians in urban settings. She has also edited special issues of journals, including *Pacific Studies* and *The Asia-Pacific Journal of Anthropology*.

**Alice Servy** is Associate Professor in Anthropology at the University of Strasbourg, France, where she is also a member of the Societies, Actors and Government in Europe (SAGE) research centre. Her research in Oceania sheds light on the production and transformation of health and gender-related discourses and practices. Having previously focused on the prevention of sexually transmitted infections and on interpersonal violence in Vanuatu, she is currently working on inter-island and international medical evacuations of people diagnosed with cancer in French Polynesia.

**Andrew J. Strathern** and **Pamela J. Stewart** are a research team based at the University of Pittsburgh, USA, where they are Andrew Mellon Professor of Anthropology and Senior Research Associate in Anthropology, respectively. They are currently working on issues pertaining to sustainability, political change and violence, social justice, medical anthropology and global health issues, environmental changes, global warming, and the importance of ritual practices in general social life. Their fieldwork areas are the Pacific (particularly Papua New Guinea), Asia (with special reference to Taiwan, China, and Japan), and Europe (with special reference to Scotland and Ireland). They have published widely and have authored over 50 books and hundreds of articles, book chapters, and essays.

**Jacques Vernaudon** is Lecturer in Linguistics at the University of French Polynesia, France, where he is also Deputy Director of the Équipe d'accueil Sociétés Traditionnelles Contemporaines en Océanie (EASTCO) research team. His main fields of research are metalinguistic descriptions of Oceanic languages, digital humanities for Polynesian languages and culture, and the study of contemporary linguistic practices in language contact situations. He speaks Tahitian.

**Michel Wieviorka** is Director of Studies at the École des Hautes Études en Sciences Sociales, France. His main research deals with social movements, democracy, racism, anti-semitism, violence, and multiculturalism. He has served as President of the International Sociological Association (ISA, 2006–2010) and a member of the Scientific Council of the European Research Council (ERC, 2014–2019). He has been President of the Fondation Maison des Sciences de l'Homme (FMSH, Paris, 2009–2020). His books in English include *The Making of Terrorism* (University of Chicago Press, 1993), *The Arena of Racism* (SAGE, 1995), *The Lure of Anti-Semitism: Hatred of Jews in Present-Day France* (Brill, 2007), *Violence: A New Approach* (SAGE, 2009), and *Evil* (Polity Press, 2012).

# Acknowledgements

This volume has its origin in a research programme on family violence that was launched at the Maison des Sciences de l'Homme du Pacifique in Tahiti in 2018. A major goal of the project was to initiate a regional dialogue on the topic of family violence, a prevalent and increasingly scrutinized issue in Tahiti, like in many other societies of the Pacific. These initial efforts led to the organization of an international symposium titled 'Violences familiales et changement social dans les sociétés insulaires du Pacifique' (Family violence and social change in Pacific Islands societies), held in November 2019 at the University of French Polynesia. It gathered together francophone and anglophone sociologists and anthropologists, whose work provided a broad array of empirical case studies across the region and a plurality of analytical frameworks to address the issues at stake. The idea of publishing an edited volume was discussed during the symposium with some of the participants, and other scholars came on board at a later stage as we sought to extend our regional outreach. We are extremely grateful to all the contributors for their engagement, work, and patience during the editing process. We express our deepest thanks to Michel Wieviorka for accepting to write a postface to the volume.

We also thank the Maison des Sciences de l'Homme du Pacifique and its Founding Director, Eric Conte, for providing unfailing support to our project, and the University of French Polynesia for co-funding and hosting the symposium. Finally, we extend our gratitude to the Institut National de la Jeunesse et de l'Éducation Populaire (INJEP), at the French Ministry of National Education, which funded the first phase of our research programme in Tahiti.

# Introduction

## Family, violence, and social change in the Pacific Islands

*Loïs Bastide and Denis Regnier*

If intimate partner violence can be considered a proxy, Pacific Islands societies struggle with very high rates of family violence (World Health Organization, 2021). This volume looks at the phenomenon of family violence from the specific angle of the fast and far-reaching social change that has swept through the region – albeit at very different paces and in different forms – over the last decades. It aims at filling two gaps in the literature: first, it looks at family as a whole, rather than at a specific subtype of family violence – for instance, domestic or intimate partner violence – second, it treats both the family and violence as problematic categories in need of conceptual clarification. In doing so, we hope to generate new, sited knowledge about family violence and social change in the region. We also hope to bring new, original elements to the theoretical discussions on family and kinship on the one hand, and on violence on the other hand, in sociological and anthropological debates.

Indeed, one of the most enduring difficulties encountered by researchers investigating family violence across diverse cultures and societies is that neither the concept of 'family' nor that of 'violence' is easily circumscribed. Both words can mean very different things in English, and of course, their translation into other languages poses additional problems. Our goal in this introduction is to make a few comments on these long-debated and often-confusing concepts and to provide an overview of how the contributors to the volume, all of whom have extensive research experience in the Pacific Islands, have taken up the challenge of both writing about 'family violence' in the communities they study and explaining how fast social change, across the region, has affected or is affecting violent relations within the family domain. Violence in Pacific Islands families is not a new phenomenon, and the exact role of modernization processes in this social issue is an open debate. It could be argued, however, that it has not received the attention it deserves, despite important works noting in the early 1990s that domestic violence was prevalent in the South Pacific and that anthropologists had often ignored or overlooked it (Ayers Counts, 1990).

In this introduction, we start with some remarks on the anthropological and sociological study of the family, before introducing the volume's chapters. In the second part of our introduction, we briefly revisit the chapters to reflect on the thorny issue of defining violence and on the challenge of applying this concept to family relations and to social worlds where norms and values differ greatly.

DOI: 10.4324/9781003146667-1

## The family: anthropological and sociological perspectives

Anthropologist Claude Lévi-Strauss once suggested, wittily, that scholars of the family are either 'Verticals' or 'Horizontals' (Lévi-Strauss, 1986; see also Lévi-Strauss, 1983). Verticals consider society to be made up of nuclear families formed by a man, a woman, and their children. They argue that these 'core' families are grounded in biology: sexual attraction between the sexes as well as the instinct of reproduction and the instinct of caring for one's offspring provide evidence that this is the case. For them, all the other social links are derived or extended from 'primary' links, such as those between parent and child, between children born to the same parents, and between a man and a woman as parents of a child. For Verticals, according to Lévi-Strauss, descent is indeed the main given, and the reality of the family first and foremost consists in its continuity through time. From this point of view, the institution of the family consists in the linear fidelity that links generations together, and families are threads that are woven together to produce society.

Horizontals, by contrast, focus on the weft rather than the warp of the social fabric. They stress that, because of marriage prohibition rules, each family comes from the union of two other families, and therefore also from their splitting. For a family to be founded, there must be two families, each amputated from one of its members, as Lévi-Strauss puts it, and in turn, the children born in this family will have to leave it to found a new family. Society only allows nuclear families to last for a limited amount of time, on the condition that their members will be displaced, given, or rendered, so that others can build new families with them, before collapsing themselves. This perpetual back-and-forth movement, which disaggregates biological families, transports their elements to a distance and links them to other elements to form new families; it is what weaves transversal networks of alliance. For Horizontals, this is the main force that engenders social life.

Lévi-Strauss' own view, however, is that such a duality of perspectives is inherent to the institution of the family itself. Few social institutions pose such a large variety of problems and problems of such complexity, he explains, because of the dual nature of the family, which is grounded in biological necessities and constrained by society. Everywhere in the world, he argues, the family realizes a compromise between nature and culture. Yet, despite its natural roots, the family takes a great variety of forms across space and time, and therefore, for Lévi-Strauss, its study must always be approached empirically and never dogmatically. Even if the nuclear family seems to be frequent in past and contemporary societies, it does not respond to a universal need. Rather, the nuclear family represents a middle-way solution, a certain equilibrium between different possible formulas, which other societies have sometimes preferred. Yet even if there is no universal form of the family, says Lévi-Strauss, what we understand as 'family life' exists in all human societies.

This far too brief and incomplete summary of Lévi-Strauss' thoughts on the family allows us, for the sake of this introduction, to make three important points. First, since the family varies across space and time, we need to work with a very inclusive definition, such as the one recently proposed by historians retracing the world history of the family: 'families are small groups of people linked by culturally recognized ties of marriage or similar forms of partnership, descent, and/or adoption, who typically share a household for some period of time' (Maynes & Waltner, 2012, p. x). Second, since the family as an institution and 'family life' exist in all societies, albeit in a bewildering diversity of forms, and since they cannot be studied dogmatically, it is necessary to adopt an empirical approach to study all their aspects, including the aspect we call 'violence'. This aspect seems universal insofar as it is unlikely that we will ever find a society where one form of family violence or the other is unheard of, even though of course we will find that in a particular social and cultural context, with its idiosyncratic set of norms and values, *some* forms of family violence may be much less frequent than in other contexts, to the point that they may seem entirely absent – this would be the case, for example, in societies where physical punishment of children is rarely observed. Third, family violence can take place either vertically or horizontally, or it can radiate in both directions, as shown by some of the studies included in this volume. By vertical family violence, we mean violence against one's forebears or offspring, following direct descent lines, or against other members of one's descent group (descendants of common ancestors), including members who have been added to the group through adoption or fosterage. Vertical family violence in this sense includes violence against children or elders within the domain of what anthropologists traditionally call 'consanguinity', with the addition of relatives made by kin-making social practices referred to as 'fictive kinship' or 'relatedness' (Carsten, 2000). By horizontal family violence, we mean violence directed against spouses and affines, and by extension against sexual partners and their relatives. Horizontal family violence thus includes, predominantly, what is often called 'intimate partner violence' today.

Despite the existence of a multidisciplinary academic field studying the whole spectrum of family violence, mostly in the West and predominantly in the United States (Barnet, Miller-Perrin, & Perrin, 2011; Gelles, 2017; Wallace, Roberson, & Globokar, 2019), these different 'directions' of violence are often considered as separate social issues by the layperson or as separate objects of research by social scientists. Violence against children (most notably incest) and intimate partner violence, for example, are typically viewed as quite separate domains when it comes to violent behaviour within the family. It is one of the goals of this volume, by contrast, to view both vertical and horizontal forms of family violence from a holistic perspective, to show that instances of family violence must always be analysed as specific 'situations' in which violent behaviours can be directed at different types of relatives.

Lévi-Strauss' take on the family, outlined earlier, is that of an anthropologist. Anthropologists study families mostly through the lenses of kinship systems, terminologies, and practices, as well as through the lenses of marriage rules, preferences, and customs, which they have collected in non-Western societies and sometimes used as points of comparison when they turned their comparatist gaze back to their own society (see, e.g. Barnard & Good, 1984; Fox, 1967; Keesing,

1975). Perhaps one of the most important values of these studies is that they have shown the magnitude of the cultural variation existing around the world about what constitutes a family, and that the modern, Western idea of the nuclear family, as well as the norms and values that are often unconsciously associated with it, are only one way of thinking that has no more value than others. Indeed, cultural relativism is arguably both the hallmark and one of the most long-lasting contributions of anthropological studies of kinship.

Not all social scientists, however, have approached the family in such a way. Most notably, the sociological approach to the family has followed a path different from that of its anthropological counterpart. Jack Goody rightly notes that, in addition to the Levi-Straussian distinction between 'Verticals' and 'Horizontals', there has been an equally important distinction between anthropologists and sociologists in the way they have written about kinship and the family since the late 19th century (Goody, 1986). In contrast to most anthropologists, sociologists, following in the steps of Frédéric Le Play, Émile Durkheim, and other pioneers, have studied the modern forms of the family, and have analysed and questioned the rise and fall of the nuclear family model in industrialized societies. Much of their scholarship has consisted of documenting and explaining changes in family patterns. Their work has been concerned with issues such as the tensions between modern individualism and traditional forms of family, the family as a socializing institution, the fragilization of marriage, the construction of personal identity, and the relations between the modern state and the family, between labour and the family, between the family and social classes, and much more (cf. Singly, 2010; Segalen & Martial, 2013).

Although most contributors to this volume are anthropologists and sociologists, the reader will hardly find a description of kinship terminology or family life, or an analysis of change in family structures. The focus of the book is instead on family violence writ large: it deals with various forms of violence occurring in the family, as well as with the way other types of violence, such as colonial or structural violence, are impacting families. True to Lévi-Strauss' call to study the family empirically – as well as, we would add, the violent aspects of its 'life' – all the analyses presented here are based on extensive fieldwork and grounded in the cultural context of nation-states or small-scale societies of the Pacific Islands, where anthropologists have been studying kinship and the family for quite a long time (see, e.g. Jolly & Macintyre, 1989; Toren & Pauwels, 2015), and which are, like the rest of the region – and indeed the rest of the world – undergoing rapid social change (see, e.g. Dousset & Nayral, 2018).

## Violence on and within families: (post)colonial adoption and customary fosterage

Some of the contributions to this volume pay a great deal of attention to the impact of colonialism and postcolonialism on Indigenous families, and to the violence and alienation generated by state policies regulating adoption and by the transformations of customary practices of fosterage.

Tracey McIntosh (Chapter 1) shows that, in New Zealand, 'settler violence' confiscated land and resources from *whānau* (i.e. the extended families that are the primary economic units of Māori society), leading to a general impoverishment, and at the same time, denigrated Māori men and women for lacking control and discipline over their children. The latter attitude is still echoed today by non-Māori commentators, who tend to view the high level of violence in Māori families as a deficit in Māori culture, while most Māori hold that the high levels of violence are due to their cultural alienation provoked by colonization. McIntosh stresses that in the 20th century, many Māori families were broken apart through processes of state care and child uplift. Māori children have always been overrepresented in state care and abused at higher rates than their non-Māori peers. In addition, the use of adoption as a means of child uplift has significantly harmed Māori families. *Whāngai* (customary adoption) was common in pre-colonial Māori society, but it kept the adopted children close to the *whānau*. By contrast, the colonial practice of closed adoption severed the genealogical ties of many Māori children, who were predominantly placed in non-Māori homes and thus often alienated from their culture, history, and *whānau*.

Judith Schachter (Chapter 2) resonates with McIntosh's contribution and proposes a striking account of how control over 'where the children are' – that is, in which kinds of families foster children are placed – has become a struggle in the intricate relationship between an Indigenous people and an imperial government. She examines the cultural differences in assessing the appropriate 'place' for a child who is in an abusive or vulnerable position, and the contemporary situation and responses to the high number of Native Hawaiian children who fall into the limbo of 'placement'. When a native Hawaiian child enters the system of foster care of the American state of Hawai'i, she argues, decisions about his or her placement implicate Indigenous interpretations of relatedness and belonging that contrast or compromise with Western interpretations, in particular the principles and policies imposed by the United States through state and federal law. Potential tensions and normative conflicts arise because, even when a child is placed within a Native Hawaiian extended family (*'ohana*), the legal system forms a backdrop to customary understandings of the transfer of a child from one person to another. A brief historical analysis recalls that an adoption law was passed in Hawai'i, earlier than in the United States, mainly because 19th-century missionary wives watched with distress how Hawaiian children moved from one adult to another, seemingly without reason, signalling to the missionaries that there was a potential for abandonment, neglect, or abuse. Inheritance issues about traditionally fostered children (*hānai*) soon exposed the gaps in both law and custom, and led to debates over various issues, including concepts of kinship and family. The difference in meaning between adoption, understood as a legal contract, and *hānai*, understood as a custom that cements 'ties of friendship' and creates harmony and community, became increasingly significant. Of particular importance is the fact that, in the customary arrangement meant to ensure the well-being of children, a child maintains a connection to his or her birth family. The discussion of several cases by Schachter highlights the different options open to Native Hawaiians for the care and placement of children, because they can appeal to both custom and law, and they can emphasize both the extensive ties of kinship and 'friendship' and the stability and safety of an intact, preferably nuclear family. There has been, however, a historical failure to place Native Hawaiian children (largely overrepresented in the state's foster care system) in Native Hawaiian families, mainly because of a statewide scarcity of Native Hawaiian foster parents. Children placed with families from other communities and cultures are seen as experiencing traumatizing culture shock and symbolic violence. But why, asks Schachter, is there a shortage of Native Hawaiian fostering families? To become a foster parent, an individual has to fulfil criteria that diverge greatly from the customary criteria of love, reciprocity, and 'ties of friendship': they include participation in training sessions, adequate bedrooms and income, and criminal history checks for all adult members of the household. Such criteria potentially exclude a Native Hawaiian applicant who falls short of the material resource requirements and whose extended family ('ohana) includes kin whose records are not 'clean' by Western standards. The state foster care agency systematically tends to favour foster families with resources and to dismiss culture, family, and the requests of biological parents. From the perspective of Native Hawaiians, this is threatening their survival as an Indigenous people, because most foster children experience a loss of Hawaiian culture. Schachter ends her chapter by discussing resistance to the imposition of state and federal rulings for ensuring a foster child's place in a culturally appropriate family, as well as its relation to the struggle for a Hawaiian 'nationhood' (lāhui).

Loïs Bastide (Chapter 3) examines the links between mobility within families and family violence in French Polynesia, focusing, like Schachter, on the issue of foster children. His investigation, based on biographical interviews with victims and perpetrators of family violence, leads to a characterization of 'family universes' in which violent situations are likely to arise. When dealing with family violence, Bastide agues, it is necessary to come up with working definitions of violence and family, however difficult it is to agree on such definitions. As far as family is concerned, the analysis is conducted through the lenses of family ideology (conceived as a normative orientation towards family relations) and practical kinship (which sees family as an institution, a cognitive construct, and a relational practice). These perspectives allow the researcher to analyse family as a social entity always in the making, to account for fast social change impacting family life, and to deal with the empirical reality of family violence. Focusing on two structural levels of the 'family' (feti'i) – the 'ōpū feti'i (which includes all the descendants from an ancestral couple) and the 'ōpū ho'e (which is used, in its most frequent contemporary understanding, to refer to a couple and its descendants over two generations) – Bastide shows how these levels provide a family ideology defining rules of land tenure, inheritance, reciprocity, and obligations. Even though the two models are challenged by young generations' growing aspirations to emancipate themselves from their norms, values, and obligations, and form a petite famille ('small family', i.e. a nuclear family), they still have a strong normative value and continue to frame attitudes towards kinsmen and conceptions of family life. This is important, Bastide notes, because the fact that these two models encompass a much broader set of relations than in 'modern' and 'Western' nuclear families, mechanically increases the risk of violent occurrences that are viewed as 'family violence'.

Since individuals often activate family relations to respond to life events and circumstances, in a context of increasingly difficult access to monetary resources and weak public safety nets, the family can be viewed as constituting a type of 'social capital' – Bastide proposes calling it 'family capital'. French Polynesia is characterized by uneven development across its five archipelagos and 118 islands, and therefore, family capital is crucial to accessing economic and educational resources and opportunities located in a few centres, for the most part located on the island of Tahiti. Frequent spatial mobility is an intrinsic part of ordinary life in French Polynesia, but its cost is so prohibitive that the family (sometimes the *'ōpū feti'i* but more frequently the *'ōpū ho'e*) works as a 'migration infrastructure' allowing people to move along family networks. It is in this context that Bastide analyses the case of children who are 'transferred' following an ancient practice called *fa'a'amura'a*. Still widespread in French Polynesia, *fa'a'amura'a* has nonetheless undergone profound transformations, and emerging practices display a variety of new motives which go far beyond the ancient purpose of alliance-making and 'kinning'. The cases and data discussed by Bastide show that such 'transfers' are a crucial factor accounting for children's vulnerability to family violence.

## Violence against women: definition, naming, mitigation, and resistance

Christine Salomon (Chapter 4) addresses the issue of frequent violence against women and girls in New Caledonia and shows how different it is to conceptualize it in terms of gender violence, viewing it as a product of patriarchal domination in society (following a feminist perspective), or in terms of family violence, viewing it as a consequence of the dysfunction of the family (following a familialist perspective). Salomon's chapter nicely illustrates how 'the family' can be used as an ideology and how the forms of public action can greatly diverge depending on which perspective is used to frame the issue of violence against women. Familialism, as an ideology that puts priority on the family, is locally attractive, because violence often tends to be interpreted, somewhat similar to the situations described by McIntosh in New Zealand (Chapter 1) and by Schachter in Hawai'i (Chapter 2), as a failure of the contemporary Indigenous family – here, the Kanak family. In the case of New Caledonia, Salomon reports the frequent beliefs that moralization and a return to ancient, authoritarian family hierarchies and structures would provide a solution to the problem. Kanak women suffer more from gender violence than any other community in New Caledonia. Political responses to violence and recent feminicides, some of which are detailed by Salomon, have consisted of adding criminal mediation to prosecution. Mediation is not only advantageous to the perpetrators, Salomon stresses, but it also often leads to the victims feeling guilty. This shift is analysed as the adoption of a conservative familialist stance and as a backlash against Kanak women, who in the 1990s and 2000s have been successful in achieving abortion rights and political mandates, as well as better education and work opportunities. In contrast to that period, the Customary Senate has recently upheld patriarchal customs and native identity, the charter of the Kanak people even stating that 'Kanak society is a patriarchal society'. Salomon shows how divorce has become more cumbersome for Kanak women and how other juridical measures are being made more difficultly enforceable for women of 'customary status', that is, the particular 'native status' under which the Kanaks fall in New Caledonia.

Familialist ideology is deeply rooted in New Caledonia, Salomon argues. It dates back to the works of Protestant and Catholic missionaries in the 19th century. After the liberalization of values and claims for rights that accompanied the end of the *indigénat* regime in 1946 and the political radicalism of the 1960s, religious and traditionalist conservatisms, together with the nativist political movement, have hit back and succeeded, notably, in making customary unions an indissoluble 'sacrament' and proposing 'host families' and religious shelters that only provide a temporary respite for abused women, until they go back to their partner. Salomon shows that a renewal of feminist movements following the internationalization of the *Me Too* movement is discernible in today's New Caledonia, however, and concludes by stressing the weakness of 'institutional feminism', which avoids deviating from patriarchal norm and backward-looking custom.

Richard Eves (Chapter 5) focuses on economic violence as one of the many forms of violence suffered by women in Highland Papua New Guinea from their intimate male partners. Economic violence or abuse, he notes, often receives less attention than other forms of family violence, yet it is crucially important to examine it in its own right. Taking as a conceptual starting point the distinction between economic control (i.e. controlling women's ability to obtain, use, and make decisions about economic resources) and economic exploitation (i.e. taking women's income and withholding or restricting the funds they give to the family), Eves provides a detailed account of the outcome of interviews he conducted in two highland provinces, Jiwaka and Chimbu, where most women earn money through the informal economy (e.g. selling garden produce or cooked food), and others by selling livestock or coffee, or by filling roles in schools or churches. His research found that these women are subject to several forms of economic violence, which he describes in detail, showing that this violence spans the two broad types of economic control and economic exploitation. Men typically seek to control women's spending and financial decision-making, and sometimes they try to prevent women from income generation, thereby maintaining power over wives that is mainly due to a rigid gender hierarchy and to marriage practices, according to which the exchange of bride price is considered to give men absolute control over their wives.

Yet the most common form of economic exploitation, Eves argues, is demands for money by husbands who routinely pressure or bully their wives for their earnings and savings, often for their own spending on alcohol, marijuana, gambling, and other women. Men often do not consider contributing financial resources to the household to be their priority, and since they put themselves first, they sometimes view their wife's income generation as an opportunity to reduce their contribution to the household or opt out entirely. Polygynous marriages are also analysed in terms of economic violence, as Eves notes that often the first wife is abandoned, with the husband refusing to take any financial responsibility for the household and the children from the first marriage, and sometimes resorting to physical violence to drive the first wife away. The nexus between physical and economic violence, Eves argues, is strong, and so it must be recognized that economic violence is one part of a repertoire of violent behaviour aiming to achieve power and control in intimate relationships. He concludes by stressing the importance of recognizing the often-overlooked economic violence for what it is, and of naming it as a first step towards finding a solution to the problem.

Xandra Miguel-Lorenzo (Chapter 6) discusses the case of a shelter for abused women founded by Anglican Sisters in the Solomon Islands, and the counselling method they have developed to deal with and mitigate intimate partner violence. She shows that the Sisters' responses to domestic violence are influenced by *kastom* ('culture'), the State's criminal justice system, the Churches' canons, and international policies on women's rights. The Sisters allow women to remain 'relational beings', Miguel-Lorenzo argues, because when they stay at the shelter, they are placed under the Sisters' care and protection, just as if they were placed under the protection of a head of family. Yet, unlike what would happen if they were under the authority of a head of family, they can make their own decisions. Miguel-Lorenzo shows that by providing a 'foster Christian family', the Sisters fill the gap left by the women's families that have failed to protect them against violence from their partners. Such failures happen, she argues, because in the urban, multicultural context of Honiara people do not have easy recourse to their own *kastom* to stop domestic violence. Urbanization means that often the influential family members who could mediate conflict and control violence are absent. In addition, both Christian and customary ideas stress the subordination of women to their husbands, and marital arguments are considered normal unless the beatings result in the woman bleeding, in which case it is considered acceptable for her to seek refuge in the shelter, where the Sisters will offer her their particular type of counselling. Miguel-Lorenzo shows in some detail that this method is at the same time *kastom*-based, Christian, and community-based. The Sisters act as a foster family for women and lead counselling with both victims and perpetrators of violence, aiming at either reconciling couples or at least providing evidence that an attempt at reconciliation has been unsuccessful, so that the women can return to their own family. Unlike Salomon, who discusses the case of Christian shelters in New Caledonia (Chapter 4), Miguel-Lorenzo concludes that, in comparison with other options, the Sisters' shelter is the most effective alternative to mitigate intimate partner violence and abuse against women.

Daniela Kraemer (Chapter 7) examines the emerging trend of women-only households in Port Vila, Vanuatu, where some women, in a time of significant social and cultural change, are inventing new forms of living that enable them to resist gender-based family violence. Vanuatu has one of the highest prevalence of family violence in the world and Kraemer identifies three important socio-cultural factors for such violence: a reinterpretation of *kastom* ('tradition') based on the misinterpretation of Bible passages that justify men's right to physically discipline women, the introduction of a Western human rights discourse that makes men feel disempowered, and the female economic success in the booming hospitality industry that threatens masculine identity, because men are financially dependent on their wives, sisters, or daughters. Since gender-based family violence is frequent and prosecution of perpetrators is limited, it has become normal, Kraemer notes, even though there is a line between what is acceptable and what is not, for example, the rape of very young girls or acts during which blood is spilled, which are publicly condemned. Kraemer describes the histories of family violence experienced by three young women before they decided to leave with their children and set up a women-only household. There, they can make decisions about their lives, they feel safer, and a sense of independence comes with their economic self-sufficiency. Kramer analyses women-only households as sites of social resistance where women are prompting individual and social change. They can build the kind of life they want for themselves and their children through education and full employment. Women-only households are 'radical' in the sense that by living together, women are able to critique patriarchal dominance and innovate a solution for themselves, and they are 'political' in the sense that they are a symbol of women advancing the status of women in Vanuatu, in a context of rapid social and cultural change. The women-only house, Kraemer concludes, is a site in which women are negotiating and contesting their place in the world.

## Moral economies, local understandings, and factors of family violence

Marie Salaün, Mirose Paia, and Jacques Vernaudon (Chapter 8) draw from their research in the prisons of French Polynesia to give a striking account of the hiatus existing, in a postcolonial context marked by strong structural violence, between legal categories and the 'moral economies' (Thompson, 1971; Fassin, 2009) of the four inmates they portray, all of whom have a personal history of family violence. Three of them were imprisoned for murdering or raping their daughter or their partner, and the fourth was jailed for drug offences. As far as family is concerned, the analysis shows that these violent offenders share an idea of masculinity that relies on the capacity to resist structural economic violence and respond to it, sometimes by violent means. The place of a man, as husband or father, is measured in terms of his ability to provide for his 'little family' (i.e. the nuclear family, as opposed to the *fēti'i* – see Bastide's account in Chapter 3) and to protect it. This moral imperative may lead him, almost paradoxically, to seek violent control over his relatives. Salaün, Paia, and Vernaudon suggest that honour and personal quests for dignity were the main issues at stake in the criminal paths of their four interviewees, who make a distinction between the serious harm that one can cause to the family as a group and the harm – ultimately less serious, from the offenders' perspective – that can be caused to individuals, if they are members of that family. Echoing Salomon's analysis of familialist ideology in New Caledonia (Chapter 4), the authors suggest that the perpetrators have a specific ethos of 'amoral familialism', meaning that they limit their moral sense to their family, relatives, and friends, conceived as a network distinct from the rest of society. The four offenders, it is suggested, make a distinction between the law of the Republic and the law of the family, and choose to give precedence to the latter.

Alice Servy (Chapter 9) examines the local conceptions regarding the physical punishment of children, which is prohibited but nonetheless widespread in Vanuatu, and focuses on the specific context of a school in Port-Vila. In this school, many students and staff have kinship ties through consanguinity or affinity, and therefore, the relations of authority between teachers and students are intertwined with power relations based on classificatory kinship. In other words, there is a continuity between the family sphere and the school domain, both being conceived more broadly as the education domain. Knowing from previous research that the term *vaelens* ('violence') has been recently introduced and is rarely used in Port-Vila, Servy focuses her analysis on the use of other terms, like *kilim* ('hit') or *faet* ('fight'), to reach the conclusion that an act is referred to as *vaelens* not only on the basis of the physical pain (evidenced by marks left on the body) but also on the basis of the relational framework (if it involves family members or not) and the perception of the abuser's intentions (if it has an educational purpose or not). Schools, Servy contends, are places where many abusive interactions take place that contribute to organizing power relations between students, teachers, and sometimes outsiders, and within families. They perpetuate the idea that physical force is a legitimate tool for education, including in the family. Schools are also places where different conceptions of the acceptability and legitimacy of the use of physical force – defined by the normative frameworks of school, family, and law – are confronted and transformed through interactions.

Writing about Kiriwina Island in Papua New Guinea, Louise Protar (Chapter 10) describes practical aspects of 'the family' and examines the nature of conflicts between relatives. In a society where all people are connected by kinship ties, an analysis of family groups is necessary to shed some light on the sources of conflicts within the family. Protar's detailed observations show that quarrels take place most often at the intersection of family groups. In most cases, such disputes are limited to symbolic gestures and aggressive verbal exchanges, and do not lead to physical violence. But Protar then examines another type of social interaction within the family, which is by contrast characterized by outright physical violence, namely, the corporal punishment inflicted on children. She shows, however, that such punishment is never considered as violence in Kiriwina, since it is perceived as a legitimate educational tool. The last type of violent interaction within the family examined in this chapter consists of magical attacks, which are rarely analysed as family violence and yet are very relevant from an emic perspective. Protar describes a case of death that was unanimously explained as an assassination by distant relatives through magical attacks and concludes the chapter by stressing that the three types of family violence (family quarrels, corporal punishment, and magical attacks) are not thought of conjointly by Kiriwinians but only make sense as a separate and consistent domain in the sociologist's eye.

Pamela J. Stewart and Andrew J. Strathern (Chapter 11) provide a bird's-eye view of the macro-level factors that inflect patterns of violence at the domestic or family level in the highland societies of Papua New Guinea. Their analysis starts with an explanation of the 'triangle of violence' model, which sees violence as a relationship between perpetrators, victims, and witnesses, and has the merit of stressing the point that the legitimacy of an act always depends on the viewpoint of those involved. Stewart and Strathern then highlight the persistent resurfacing of fears in relation to witchcraft and sorcery, as well as the importance of rumours, which are often directed at disempowered women in the community. They provide an overview of factors conducive to gendered and family violence, which include the stressful experience of living in poor urban settlements with large numbers of unemployed migrants from rural areas, the increasing pattern of interethnic marriages where couples only have English or the lingua franca (*Tok Pisin*) to communicate, and the ill effects of new urban spaces on people. In addition, inter-group violence, Stewart and Strathern show, disrupts domestic relations in various ways. Finally, they note that the recent spread of the COVID-19 virus has further exacerbated domestic violence in Papua New Guinea.

## Social change, emerging forms of violence, and new conceptions of violent behaviours

The relationship between social change and family violence can work on two levels. On the one hand, contemporary processes of transformation across Pacific Islands societies alter the structural circumstances of family life and kinship. In doing so, they often render inherited forms of family organization ill-adapted or dysfunctional. The monetization of economic life, for example, puts a tremendous strain on traditional types of family solidarities based on non-monetary production and reproduction systems. Such tensions often generate conflicts and sustain the development of 'violent interactions' (Collins, 2008). On the other hand, con-temporary societies are connected to transnational social, cultural, political, and economic processes (Appadurai, 1996; Hannerz, 1996; Falzon, 2009; Marcus, 2009). They are increasingly exposed to heterogeneous social norms, values, and meanings, including new conceptions of the family and of violence. This in turn can transform the perception of existing family interactions. Bride price, or arranged marriages, for instance, are increasingly seen, perceived, and lived as a form of violence.

In their contribution, Stewart and Strathern (Chapter 11) illustrate the first type of change. They describe a highly 'compressed' (Kyung-Sup, 2010) process of societal transformation in Highland Papua New Guinea, where recent evolutions, such as urbanization, changes in residential patterns, inter-ethnic unions, tensions regarding livelihood, the monetization of economic life, and, more recently, social shocks, such as the COVID-19 crisis, have put traditional family structures under tremendous strain and generated new forms of violence in the family domain. Such transformations are also well explained by Eves (Chapter 5) when describing the effects of shifting gender roles on intimate partner violence within the household in Highland Papua New Guinea, and the tensions caused by the increasing role of women in the family monetary economy. Men in turn develop strategies to control women's economic and social empowerment by preventing their partners from income generation, controlling their spending, and limiting their budgetary decision-making capacity, seizing their income, or refusing to contribute to the household.

This context of deep social change and cultural displacement is also very salient in Schachter's piece (Chapter 2) on foster care in Hawai'i. Indigenous conceptions of relatedness among native Hawaiians contrast and conflict with the U.S. federal legal system and Western conceptions about family and kinship, as demonstrated in the case of the placement of 'at risk' native children by state social services. Such transactions take place in complex, unstable, and shifting arrangements between the increasing recognition of Indigenous rights and sovereignty, and the homogenous enforcement of U.S. federal regulations across the U.S. territory. This process is neither smooth nor peaceful. It unfolds at an institutional level but also in the individual practices of legislators, activists, birth and adoptive parents, legal professionals, and social workers. It is ridden with conflicts, misunderstandings, and difficult negotiations between disjunctive normative regimes. This process gives rise to uneasy, hybrid practices combining Western and native Hawaiian norms and values. It is seen as imposing a form of structural violence on native families and children.

Servy (Chapter 9) illustrates the second type of transformation – the shifting understanding of violence. She explains how advocacy work by international institutions and national authorities has promoted new conceptions of violence in Vanuatu. Through vernacularization and hybridization (Bhabha, 1994; Goodale & Merry, 2007, p. 348), violence, as a foreign concept, was appropriated and translated as *vaelens* and came to be associated with physical brutality *between kinsmen*. Local terms such as *kilim* continued to be applied to other forms of physical abuse. Indigenous concepts, representations, and perceptions of aggression or 'brutality' are being displaced and reworked in the context of transnational political processes.

Like Bastide (Chapter 3) and Protar (Chapter 10), Servy thus raises a thorny issue: violence is inextricably a descriptive and normative notion. A value judgement always needs to be made before we can qualify an act as violent and describe it as such. Our ability to distinguish between acceptable and unacceptable uses of force – for example between surgery and aggression – is conditional upon this preliminary moral stance: it allows us to isolate violence from other physical, verbal, or institutional practices. Qualifying an act as violent thus always implies both a description and a value judgement (Lenclud, Claverie, & Jamin, 1984; Michaud, 2018; Naepels, 2006; Wieviorka, 2009; see also Bastide's Chapter 3 in this volume). Because it is based on a value judgement, the definition of violence is thus inextricable from socially and culturally situated 'moral assemblages' and ethical practices (Zigon, 2010). It can only be appreciated from the perspective of a particular society or social group (Naepels, 2006). The historicity of violence also means that there can be no external (etic), de-contextualized, inter-contextual, least of all universal, definition of the notion. It is interesting to note that Servy refrains from using the English term 'violence', a defining label applied from the outside to vernacular practices. She prefers to use its translation as *vaelens* in Bislama, a national language of Vanuatu. Servy's chapter thus aptly stresses that the categorization of specific acts as violent is not merely a theoretical issue: it is also an empirical problem that needs to be investigated through careful inquiry, based on vernacular categories.

## Violence: moral entrepreneurs and power struggles

As illustrated by Servy, exogenous definitions of violence – such as those promoted by international organizations and non-governmental organizations (NGOs) – can work their way into specific societies and social groups by imposition, emulation, or 'interessement' (Akrich, Callon, Latour, & Monaghan, 2002), thus displacing and reworking vernacular conceptions. In Vanuatu, like in many other places, the recent emergence of violence as a new normative category thus results from the work of 'moral entrepreneurs' (Becker, 1963; Kaptein, 2019), namely NGOs, international organizations, politicians, activists, and other stakeholders. These interessement and vernacularization processes are anything but straightforward, however – violence becomes *vaelens*, as it fits into a new 'habitat of meaning' (Hannerz, 1996). They take place and introduce new stakes in a pre-existing social, cultural, and political milieu that is always 'thick', with different layers of meaning (Geertz, 1994). As a consequence, they support the constitution of new social and political coalitions, and the emergence of novel collective struggles. Such processes have been particularly well documented regarding gender violence in Papua New Guinea, for example, where the introduction of British common law, its institutionalization in the newly independent country, and the development of a market economy put pressure on Indigenous social norms and created new social and political struggles around issues of gender norms and relations (Jolly, Stewart, & Brewer, 2012).

Also writing about Vanuatu, Kraemer (Chapter 7) shows how the incremental alignment of national laws on the international human rights regime opens up new 'public arenas' (Céfaï, 2001). Imported definitions of family violence shed a new light on established family and kinship structure, now perceived as oppressive. New coalitions of actors constitute, push for, leverage, or contest this emerging normative regime. At a moment when ni-Vanuatu women's position problematizes traditional gender roles, including through their increasing participation in the economic sphere in a developing market economy, some of them seize these new normative and discursive repertoires to legitimate and push their struggle for autonomy, including through the development of 'women only' households. Conversely, many men feel diminished and threatened, and endorse a defensive, conservative position by invoking the sacrality of culture and *kastom* – custom in Bislama – to resist these changes and uphold traditional gender roles. The definition of violence is thus part and parcel of a larger struggle, where institutionalized power relations, including those between genders, are being re-negotiated.

Normative conflict between a 'foreign' legal system and vernacular social norms and values is also at the centre of Salaün, Vernaudon, and Paia's contribution on prisoners in Tahiti (Chapter 8). They show that the inmates' moral economies regarding violent behaviours in the family and their relation to other types of violence have little to do with 'tradition' or 'custom'. Rather, they are shaped by contemporary experiences of structural violence among the most disenfranchised people of French Polynesia. Such structural violence is a direct outcome of colonialism and the 'nuclear economy' generated by the French atomic bomb trials program, which had a lasting impact on the most vulnerable communities of the territory.

## Violence: public sociology and morality

Since it is used to categorize and delegitimize specific social behaviours, the concept of violence cannot be considered as analytically neutral and can never be used unproblematically to explain the transitive use of force on others. Basing our theories on a universal definition of violence would raise two major issues. First, it would delegitimate vernacular definitions of violence, which would be deemed at best naïve and inadequate, and at worst backward and oppressive. Second, it would run the risk of desensitizing researchers to the struggles involved in the very process of defining such a use of force as legitimate or illegitimate, and would obfuscate the associated power struggles led by social groups and communities. Endorsing such a universal definition would, paradoxically, place the researcher as a participant rather than an observer in these struggles.

Yet the positioning of researchers as moral entrepreneurs can also be constructed as an intentional and conscious commitment to a critical public sociology or anthropology (Burawoy, 2005; Borofsky, 2019) when they decide to side with marginalized groups in their fight for social and political recognition, for example, by promoting a particular set of norms and values – in the present case, a specific definition of violence within the family domain. Salomon (Chapter 4) engages in this kind of approach by taking a progressive and feminist stance on the issue of intimate partner violence in New Caledonia. She takes sides and stands with the social movements advocating for the emancipation of Kanak women, who strongly suffer from gender violence and are trapped between a lack of a real political commitment from a conservative government and the identity politics of a certain brand of Kanak activism, which promotes a return to customary gender norms.

Emerging definitions of violence result from these struggles, as much as they fuel them, as social and political movements exert a constant push for the recognition of marginalized social groups and uncover hitherto concealed or unseen structures of power and domination. Local struggles interact with transnational 'epistemic communities' (Haas, 1992) and are increasingly connected with transnational social movements (Khagram & Sikkink, 2002; Smith, Chatfield, & Pagnucco, 1998). Other transnational 'moral entrepreneurs', such as foreign state actors, international organizations, NGOs, and foreign aid institutions, also participate in collecting, producing, promoting, and circulating these new moral assemblages. All the chapters in the book testify, in one way or another, to this phenomenon in the Pacific Islands. As a result of these processes, 'violence' covers and qualifies an ever-broader set of social situations, institutions, and practices: from verbal violence to physical or sexual violence, from economic, institutional, or cultural, to structural, lateral, slow, or epistemic violence.

Salaün, Vernaudon, and Paia (Chapter 8) embrace such a heterogeneity. They leverage what we could call the 'adjectival dimension' of a multifaceted reality of violence (structural, cultural, or interpersonal violence) to show how these differ-ent forms can be articulated into a coherent causal framework and account for the generation of family violence in French Polynesia. In this model, interpersonal violence is seen as a by-product of large structural processes, as well as the result of deeply entrenched social inequalities.

McIntosh (Chapter 1) similarly proposes that in New Zealand, the violence against Māori citizens is a totalizing social experience, permeating all social structures and engulfing subjectivities. Under these circumstances, family vio-lence is contextualized as the by-product of an ongoing societal process of social and cultural marginalization. As a result, to understand the high prevalence of interpersonal violence within Māori *whānau* (extended families), we need to look at the dispossession of the Māori 'self' (Miller, 1980) as a multifaceted and all-encompassing experience of violence in a colonial context. McIntosh uses a multiplicity of definitions of violence to account for the heterogeneous forms of aggression inflicted on Māori as individuals and as a community. Like Salomon (Chapter 4), she shows that defining this multi-dimensional situation as violence is a way for researchers to take a political stance and embrace the fight for political, social, and cultural recognition of the Māori people.

## Cognitive sociology and the deconstruction of violence

Following Randall Collins (2008), Bastide (Chapter 3) adopts a very different approach. He seeks to circumscribe the most consensual, or least conflictual, definition of violence. He thus falls back on a hyper-restrictive definition, one where violence is understood as the intentional, and agonistic infliction of physical damage. This approach is another way of operationalizing the notion, by keep-ing it close to a very narrow set of practices in order to sharpen or restore its analytical value and avoid its 'metaphorization', which risks happening when the term is applied to an ever-increasing and arguably heterogeneous range of social phenomena.

The different approaches taken by the contributors to this volume thus stress the difficulty we face when we try to reach a consensual definition of violence for the purpose of social research. Reflecting on this difficulty and the proliferation of definitions, Michel Naepels suggests that we consider violence less as a concept than as a mere 'index of a field of experience which remains to be specified' (Nae-pels, 2006, our translation). We would like to suggest, in turn, that this conceptual deconstruction can be pushed a bit further. Following the work of Marie-Noëlle

Chamoux (1994), who has shown that many societies do not possess a vernacular equivalent to the concept of 'labour', we question the very idea that every society and culture possesses a semantic *analogon* to the concept of violence, that is, a single category of meaning capable of unifying the whole range of social experiences and practices related to the deviant, transitive use of force on others' bodies and subjectivities.

Protar's contribution (Chapter 10) usefully illustrates this point. In order to write her chapter, Protar explains, she had to revisit her fieldnotes from Kiriwina, in the Trobriand islands (Papua New Guinea), and look for entries on violent interactions. To be able to retrieve and collect all the relevant observations, she needed at least a working definition of violence. She quickly realized, however, that there was a discrepancy between her etic, working definition of violence and the perception of her informants. What she initially perceived as violence against children was considered locally to be an educational practice. In trying to delineate vernacular definitions, she then identified magical practices as a particular form of violence, considering that they entail the wilful, reprehensible infliction of bodily harm on others. The problem, however, is that subsuming these two types of aggression under the same category – that of violence – does not speak to vernacular conceptions at all. They are seen as two unconnected domains of practice. As we already noted, Servy (Chapter 9), facing a similar difficulty, tends to avoid using the term 'violence' and replaces it with 'brutality' to describe the transitive use of force, since she sees the term as being more axiologically neutral.

This complex analytical spectrum shows that the use of violence, as a concept, is always problematic and should be treated as such in social science. The various perspectives of the contributors indicate different positionings regarding this issue. Some engage in a form of public sociology and wilfully and self-consciously participate in the social struggle implied by the definition of social issues in the public sphere. As such, they are not mere observers: they become stakeholders. They use concepts of violence that aim at both producing analytical knowledge and promoting social justice. Others stick to what Raymond Boudon calls a 'cognitive sociology' (Boudon, 2019) and seek to separate the concept from its normative content. If we follow this latter path to its logical conclusions, however, we might well be led to asking ourselves: can violence be made into a scientific concept at all? Indeed, we would perhaps be better off trying to understand, in every society, how the use of physical force or moral coercion intersect with moral economies to produce morally acceptable or unacceptable social practices, rather than trying to seek *analogons* to Western conceptions of violence and universalize their value. Of course, these two perspectives – the analytical and the political (or normative) perspective on social sciences as a praxis – are not necessarily mutually exclusive. For instance, both dimensions can be fused, or they can be considered as two different stages in a social scientific practice, that is, an analytical moment leading to a political moment. The tension between these positions is at work, in one way or another, in all the contributions to this volume.

# References

Akrich, M., Callon, M., Latour, B., & Monaghan, A. (2002). The key to success in innovation part I: The art of interessement. *International Journal of Innovation Management*, *6*(2), 187–206. https://doi.org/10/br2kgf.

Appadurai, A. (1996). *Modernity at large: Cultural dimensions of globalization.* Minneapolis, MN: University of Minnesota Press.

Ayers Counts, D. (1990). Domestic violence in Oceania: Conclusion. *Pacific Studies*, *13*(3), 225–254.

Barnard, A., & Good, A. (1984). *Research practices in the study of kinship.* London: Academic Press.

Barnet, O., Miller-Perrin, O., & Perrin, R. (2011). *Family violence across the lifespan: An introduction* (3rd ed). Thousand Oaks, CA: Sage.

Becker, H. S. (1963). *Outsiders: Studies in the sociology of deviance.* New York, NY: The Free Press of Glencoe.

Bhabha, H. K. (1994). *The location of culture.* Abingdon, UK: Routledge.

Borofsky, R. (2019). *An anthropology of anthropology: Is it time to shift paradigms?* Kailua, HI: Center for a Public Anthropology.

Boudon, R. (2019). La théorie générale de la rationalité, base de la sociologie cognitive. In F. Clément & L. Kaufmann (eds.), *La sociologie cognitive* (pp. 43–74). Paris: Éditions de la Maison des sciences de l'homme. Retrieved from http://books.openedition.org/editionsmsh/14394.

Burawoy, M. (2005). Rejoinder: Toward a critical public sociology. *Critical Sociology*, *31*(3), 379–390. https://doi.org/10.1163/1569163053946237

Carsten, J. (Ed.). (2000). *Cultures of relatedness: New approaches to the study of kinship.* Cambridge: Cambridge University Press.

Céfaï, D. (2001). Les cadres de l'action collective: Définitions et problèmes. In D. Céfaï & D. Trom (eds.), *Les formes de l'action collective: Mobilisations dans des arènes publiques.* Paris: École des hautes études en sciences sociales.

Chamoux, M.-N. (1994). Sociétés avec et sans concept de travail. *Sociologie du travail*, *36*(1), 57–71.

Collins, R. (2008). *Violence: A micro-sociological theory.* Princeton, NJ: Princeton University Press.

Dousset, L., & Nayral, M. (Eds.). (2018). *Pacific realities: Changing perspectives on resilience and resistance.* New York: Berghahn.

Falzon, M. A. (2009). *Multi-sited ethnography: Theory, praxis and locality in contemporary research.* Farnham: Ashgate Publishing.

Fassin, D. (2009). Les économies morales revisitées. *Annales. Histoire, Sciences Sociales*, *6*, 1237–1266.

Fox, R. (1967). *Kinship and marriage: An anthropological perspective.* New York, NY: Penguin Books.

Geertz, C. (1994). Thick description: Toward an interpretive theory of culture. In T. S. Oakes & P. L. Price (eds.), *The cultural geography reader* (pp. 29–39). Abingdon: Routledge.

Gelles, R. (2017). *Intimate violence and abuse in families.* Oxford: Oxford University Press.

Goodale, M., & Merry, S. E. (Eds.). (2007). *The practice of human rights: Tracking law between the global and the local.* Cambridge: Cambridge University Press.

Goody, J. (1986). Préface. In A. Burguière, C. Klapisch-Zuber, M. Segalen, & F. Zonabend (eds.), *Histoire de la famille: Vol. 3. Le choc des modernités* (pp. 7–17). Paris: Armand Colin.

Haas, P. M. (1992). Introduction: Epistemic communities and international policy coordina-tion. *International Organization, 46*(1), 1–36.
Hannerz, U. (1996). *Transnational connections: Culture, people, places.* London: Routledge.
Jolly, M., & Macintyre, M. (1989). *Family and gender in the Pacific: Domestic contradic-tions and the colonial impact.* Cambridge: Cambridge University Press.
Jolly, M., Stewart, C., & Brewer, C. (Eds.). (2012). *Engendering violence in Papua New Guinea.* Acton: ANU Press.
Kaptein, M. (2019). The moral entrepreneur: A new component of ethical leadership. *Jour-nal of Business Ethics, 156*(4), 1135–1150. https://doi.org/10/gftq4j.
Keesing, R. (1975). *Kin groups and social structure.* Fort Worth, TX: Holt, Rinehart and Winston.
Khagram, S., Riker, J. V., & Sikkink, K. (2002). From Santiago to Seattle: Transnational advocacy groups restructuring world politics. *Restructuring World Politics: Transna-tional Social Movements, Networks, and Norms, 1,* 3–23.
Kyung-Sup, C. (2010). The second modern condition? Compressed modernity as internal-ized reflexive cosmopolitization: The second modern condition? *The British Journal of Sociology, 61*(3), 444–464. https://doi.org/10/c43nkr.
Lenclud, G., Claverie, E., & Jamin, J. (1984). Présentation: Une ethnographie de la vio-lence est-elle possible? *Études rurales, 95*(1), 9–21.
Lévi-Strauss, C. (1983). *Le regard éloigné.* Paris: Plon.
Lévi-Strauss, C. (1986). Préface. In A. Burguière, C. Klapisch-Zuber, M. Segalen, & F. Zonabend (eds.), *Histoire de la famille: Vol. 1. Mondes lointains* (pp. 9–16). Paris: Armand Colin.
Marcus, G. E. (2009). Multi-sited ethnography: Notes and queries. In M. A. Falzon (ed.), *Multi-sited ethnography: Theory, praxis and locality in contemporary research* (pp. 181–196). Farnham: Ashgate Publishing.
Maynes, M. J., & Waltner, A. (2012). *The family: A world history.* Oxford: Oxford Univer-sity Press.
Michaud, Y. (2018). *La violence.* Paris: Presses Universitaires de France.
Miller, D. L. (1980). *George Herbert Mead: Self, language, and the world.* Chicago, IL: University of Chicago Press.
Naepels, M. (2006). Quatre questions sur la violence. *L'Homme. Revue française d'Anthropologie, 177–178,* 487–495. https://doi.org/10.4000/lhomme.21787.
Segalen, M., & Martial, A. (2013). *Sociologie de la famille* (8th ed.). Paris: Armand Colin.
Singly, F. de. (2010). *Sociologie de la famille contemporaine* (4th ed.). Paris: Armand Colin.
Smith, J., Chatfield, C., & Pagnucco, R. (1998). *Transnational social movements and global politics: Solidarity beyond the state.* Syracuse, NY: Syracuse University Press.
Thompson, E. P. (1971). The moral economy of the English crowd in the eighteenth cen-tury. *Past & Present, 50,* 76–136.
Toren, C., & Pauwels, S. (Eds.). (2015). *Living kinship in the Pacific.* New York: Berghahn.
Wallace, H., Roberson, C., & Globokar, J. (2019). *Family violence: Legal, medical and social perspectives* (9th ed.). Abingdon: Routledge.
Wieviorka, M. (2009). *Violence, a new approach.* Los Angeles, CA: Sage.
World Health Organization. (2021). *Violence against women prevalence estimates, 2018.* Geneva: WHO Press.
Zigon, J. (2010). Moral and ethical assemblages: A response to Fassin and Stoczkowski. *Anthropological Theory, 10*(1–2), 3–15. https://doi.org/10.1177/1463499610370520.

# 1 Settler violence, family, and whānau violence in Aotearoa[1] New Zealand

*Tracey McIntosh*

## Contextualizing violence in settler states

The Māori experience of colonization is reflected in the experience of Indigenous peoples in other settler states who have also been systematically dispossessed and alienated by state policies and practices, and where they continue to be over-represented in every negative social indicator, including high rates of incarceration (McIntosh & Coster, 2017). The settler states have sought both to control Indigenous lives and to dispossess them of material and cultural resources in what Cunneen and Porter have called a process of 'immiseration' (2017, p. 669). Immiseration, in this instance, is the process of economic impoverishment through an organized system of racialized, state-controlled labour (Cunneen, 2013) and the related processes of cultural impoverishment. Redress and response to harm must capture the entirety of the context in which something harmful occurs. In reflecting on physical, sexual, psychological, emotional, and family violence, we must ensure that we address and seek to redress state, colonial/neo-colonial, legislative, structural, political, economic, cultural, religious, institutional, and collective violence (McIntosh & Curcic, 2020, p. 226). The latter are forms of systemic violence that often provide the context for the former. Legislative violence, for example, has both historical and contemporary cases where the impact of legislation on Indigenous peoples is marked. In many cases, legislative violence produces and reproduces economic impoverishment. The colonial state used legislative powers to alienate land and to punish (often by incarceration and other forms of detention) those original owners that sought to defend their lands and resources. Neo-colonial legislation has allowed the 'legal' removal of children from their families and too often has also attempted to remove their culture and identity.

Violence is multifaceted and can be incremental or explosive, unseen or overt. Nixon (2011) describes slow violence as 'violence that occurs gradually and out of sight, a violence of delayed destruction that is dispersed across time and space, an attritional violence that is typically not viewed as violence at all' (p. 2).

The concept of slow violence can be useful in looking at global problems, such as environmental degradation and climate change, but is also useful in understanding the impact of the violence of poverty, incarceration, and other entrenched

DOI: 10.4324/9781003146667-2

social issues. These social issues create the conditions for violence to occur within communities. Lateral violence can be understood as violence that is directed inwardly towards peers and family rather that at external adversaries and is an expression of deep social and personal dissatisfaction, particularly in marginalized communities (Wingard, 2010). Systemic violence is often the locus of trauma and the precedent to material deprivation that span generations. Systematic suffering (McIntosh, 2002) is the deliberate and planned delivery of processes that generate human and environmental suffering. Genocide and gross human rights abuses are extreme forms of systemic violence. Colonial violence has meant that the dispossession of land in one century has created the conditions for systemic racialized injustice and violence in the next. Shannon Speed (2019), in drawing on the experiences of incarcerated Indigenous migrant women in the United States, has argued that while interpersonal violence, criminal violence, and state violence are often understood as distinct dynamics, in fact, 'these forms [of violence] are inseparable, each bound to the other and mutually formative in the larger context in which they affect the women's lives' (p. 17).

Violence is a dominant characteristic of all forms of colonization. Its shape and configuration may differ, but it has been a feature of colonialism since its inception. Nancy Scheper-Hughes and Philippe Bourgois (2004) define violence as 'nonlinear, productive, destructive, *and* reproductive. . . . Violence gives birth to itself. So we can rightly speak of chains, spirals, and mirrors of violence – or, as we prefer – a continuum of violence' (p. 1).

For example, there is a recognition that someone who has suffered violence as a child and adolescence may be more inclined to draw on violence as a tool when experiencing frustration or in interpersonal conflict. Violence can be a learned behaviour, and it can be a strategy to resist further victimization (McIntosh & Coster, 2017). It can be used to attempt to control or dominate others. Violence generates more violence, both on micro-structural (everyday individual or small group interactions) and within macro-structural levels. As an intentional exercise of force or power, violence perpetuates pain through either physical force (physical assault), psychological manipulation (fear, anxiety, shame), social violence (stigma, social isolation), or political oppression (from direct police/ military violence to institutional violence). The last of these includes various forms of structural and symbolic violence through social institutions, including the criminal justice system. *Structural violence* can be identified through practices that embed poverty for Indigenous peoples and systematic colonization via dispossession of land and removal of the Indigenous economic base, culture, and livelihood, together with the generation of sites of confinement, such as youth homes, borstals, and native schools, and systemic deprivation of basic human rights (Mikaere, 2011; Stanley, 2016). *Symbolic violence*, on the other hand, appears as the result of systemic normalization and canonization to the degree where violence becomes misrecognized, taken for granted, and seen as something normal rather than as a form of violence and domination (Bourdieu, 2001; Bourdieu & Wacquant, 2001, p. 162). Consequently, this subtle violence becomes invisible even to its victims, especially because it colonizes everyday life, such as language, ways of thinking, and even lifestyle (McIntosh & Curcic, 2020). Thus, according to Scheper-Hughes and Bourgois:

> [v]iolence can never be understood solely in terms of its physicality – force, assault, or the infliction of pain – alone. Violence also includes assaults on the personhood, dignity, sense of worth or value of the victim. The social and cultural dimensions of violence are what gives violence its power and meaning.
>
> (2004, p. 1)

### Family and whānau violence[2]

Family violence is a prevalent issue among many Indigenous communities globally, and Aotearoa New Zealand is no exception to this. In Aotearoa, wāhine Māori, Māori women, are more likely than any other ethnic group to experience family violence. Two different studies found an extreme prevalence of family violence in Māori communities indicating rates of 57% and 80%, respectively, for lifetime violence among wāhine Māori[3] (Koziol-McLain et al., 2004; Koziol-McLain, Rameka, Giddings, Fyfe, & Gardiner, 2007). Rates of lifetime violence also indicate notable disparities between wāhine Māori and other women in New Zealand. While anywhere from one in two to four in five wāhine Māori experience violence, this rate drops to one in three for both Pākehā[4] (34%) and Pacific (32%) women (Fanslow & Robinson, 2010).

High rates of lifetime violence also correlate with high rates of family violence homicides for both Māori and non-Māori in New Zealand. Homicides due to family violence make up half of all homicides in Aotearoa New Zealand. Wāhine Māori are three times as likely to be victims of homicide as other women in New Zealand, and tamariki Māori[5] are 5.5 times more likely to be a victim of homicide (Family Violence Death Review Committee, 2014; Wilson, 2016). Inquiries into family violence homicide rates present valuable findings that forms of deprivation (socioeconomic, education, etc.) have a correlated relationship with family violence and homicide (Family Violence Death Review Committee, 2015).

Deprivation as a corollary of violence shapes the reality that the problem is more wide-ranging and complex than can be explained by simple, singular solutions. A holistic analysis of factors around family violence – including education, socioeconomic status, incarceration, and child services – indicates a structural environment that significantly disadvantages Māori within New Zealand society. In New Zealand, tamariki Māori achieve lower rates of National Certificate of Educational Achievement (NCEA) Level 2[6] recognition and tend to leave school earlier than peers in other ethnic groups, particularly those who are Pākehā and Asian (Bolton, 2017). These educational outcomes shape a Māori labour force that consistently has higher rates of unemployment as well as an over-representation in lower-paying occupations in Aotearoa New Zealand (Ministry of Business, Innovation and Employment, 2020). As Māori experience adverse educational and labour force outcomes as tangata whenua,[7] they are also grossly disproportionately incarcerated. While Māori make up 16% of Aotearoa New Zealand's population), they make up 50% of the prison population. This disparity is worse for wāhine Māori, who make up over 63% of the women's incarcerated population (McIntosh & Workman, 2017).

Structural inequities that contribute to increased rates of family violence are made all the more egregious by the unique relationship that Māori have with the Crown.[8] This is exemplified by the rights of tino rangatiratanga, defined as absolute and sovereign authority to rule (Mutu, 2019), and oritetanga, defined as equity, guaranteed in Te Tiriti o Waitangi,[9] the foundational treaty between Māori and the Crown (Wilson, 2016). All of these characteristics indicate a governmental and societal response that maintains ambivalence at best, and hostility at worst, towards te ao Māori[10] in New Zealand. An inability or unwillingness to help address structural issues faced by tangata whenua by service providers has the effect of reinforcing the neo/colonial society that has placed tangata whenua, both historically and presently, in a state of deprivation.

Understanding that Aotearoa New Zealand experiences high levels of family violence as a nation and further appreciation of the impact of disparities enables a recognition that whānau violence is not solely a 'Māori problem'. While wāhine Māori experience the highest rate of family violence of any ethnic group in Aotearoa New Zealand, they are by no means the exception. Indeed, the disparity between wāhine Māori and other ethnic groups experiencing violence should be a source of national shame and introspection. This is particularly important in this moment as New Zealand's future is rapidly becoming a Māori future – while one in four children born today are tamariki, this number will increase to one in three by 2038 (Te Puni Kōkiri, 2017).

## Historical record of family violence in Aotearoa New Zealand

The irony of focusing on Māori as the source of family violence in New Zealand is that the historical record of New Zealand recognizes this as largely an imported attitude and problem. As Cram (2001) notes, seminal pieces of Aotearoa New Zealand's history, including the signing of Te Tiriti o Waitangi, created an environment in which wāhine Māori were denigrated. This denigration was further proliferated by British settlers into the home, where early journals critiqued tāne Māori[11] for lacking control and discipline over both wāhine Māori and tamariki; indeed, there was concern over what was then seen as an overly indulgent and cosseted parenting of tamariki Māori (McCreanor, 1997). Rawiri Taonui (2010) notes that contemporary Pākehā commentators tend to argue that the high level of Māori child abuse, violence, and homicide is due to a deficit in Māori culture. Cultural-deficit explanations rely on 'master narratives' that encourage one-dimensional stereotypes of ethnic groups and promote the notion of collective cultural failure (Solórzano, Ceja, & Yosso, 2000, p. 27). Heather Came notes that these narratives are often not questioned by the dominant group, as they are considered self-evident and indeed 'natural and normal' (2012, p. 35). However, Māori tend to hold that the high levels of violence are due to the impact of colonization and that the origins of violence were largely due to cultural alienation. The Māori Family Violence in

Aotearoa report (Balzer, Haimona, Henare, & Matchitt, 1997) shows that there are links between the suppression of Māori knowledge and tikanga;[12] colonization and the imposition of Western beliefs and practices; and acts of violence in Māori families and broader collectives (Pihama, Cameron, & Te Nana, 2019, p. 17).

While the historical record recognizes the import of British attitudes about family violence, this same period of contact also created the conditions for New Zealand's violent colonial history. Physical and cultural violence have been documented in the settler states of Australia, Canada and the United States, and New Zealand. Early examples of this colonial violence include the New Zealand Wars, taking place between 1845 and 1872, and the invasion, confiscation, and occupation of Parihaka near Taranaki. Over 1,600 troops invaded Parihaka, which has come to symbolize peaceful resistance to military force, led by Te Whiti-o-Rongomai and Tohu Kākahi, to the confiscation of Māori land (O'Brien & Strongman, 2006). Both of these examples constitute historical examples of literal violence in relation to the seizure of land in Aotearoa New Zealand.

These examples of violence were further internalized in the 20th century, where many Māori families were effectively broken apart through large institutional processes of state care and child uplift. From a period ranging from the late 1940s through the 1980s, almost 100,000 children would enter state care in New Zealand. The Royal Commission of Inquiry into Abuse in Care Interim Report (2020) outlines a widespread and systemic bias towards placing tamariki into state care – by its own admission an outgrowth of Aotearoa's initial colonization. While tamariki have always been over-represented in state care institutions, an Oranga Tamariki Report (2019) also clearly indicates that tamariki have been abused at higher rates than their peers *within* state care. Not only do tamariki Māori make up 69% of children in care, they are far more likely to have experienced reported abuse while in care (Royal Commission of Inquiry, 2020). While the uplift of Indigenous children into state care is a global phenomenon, the recency of New Zealand to confront this past is stark, particularly considering how endemic the harm was and is. Statistician Len Cook estimates that by the late 1970s, 1 in 14 tamariki Māori, who were boys, were in state care (Royal Commission of Inquiry, 2020).

In addition to New Zealand's record of state care abuse, the use of adoption as a means of child uplift has significantly affected and harmed Māori communities. While adoption in Te Ao Māori was common prior to British colonization, the 1955 Adoption Act radically altered this framework. While whāngai, customary adoption, largely kept tamariki close to extended whānau, colonial practices of closed adoption largely severed the whakapapa, genealogical ties, of many tamariki (Hurihanganui, 2019). In a period from 1955 to 1985, roughly 45,000 children were involved in a closed adoption. Many of these tamariki would be placed into Pākehā homes. While state care and adoption have used different means, they have both contributed to the uplift of generations of tamariki from their communities. In doing so, these services – meant to help tamariki – have often alienated them from their culture, history, whenua, and whānau (Royal Commission of Inquiry, 2020). The systemic uplifting of children through a range of regulatory policies and practices and the ongoing impact on all aspects of te ao Māori is a stark example of structural and symbolic violence.

## Historical solutions, continual harm

These traumas, compounded by socio-economic, cultural, and educational discrimination, manifest as an identified ambiguous loss that serves to fracture whānau and extended Māori communities (Came, 2012). This sense of ambiguous loss of culture, community, and history presents the feeling of abnormal conditions – substance abuse, family violence, and high rates of incarceration – as a common status quo. A 2019 report from the *E Tu Wāhine, E Tu Whānau* project (Wilson, Mikahere-Hall, Sherwood, Cootes, & Jackson, 2019) noted that both wāhine Māori and tāne Māori experience these distorted views of both the roles of wāhine and tāne in the family environment, as well as the structure of both nuclear and extended families. As one member of the tāne focus group, Manaia, recounts in the report (p. 51):

> I was also brought up in a violent household, grew up with a lot of violence. And for me what I saw was that the perpetrator of the violence, who wasn't my real father, lacked a role model in his life so he didn't know how to be a father, how to be a husband, how to be any of those things. . . . I was violent myself. And that was just behaviour that I was mimicking that was role modelled to me, and I thought that was how you did things.

These cyclical conditions bear out on tamariki in family structures, further reinforcing negative patterns of individual, familial, and communal harm. Koziol-McLain et al. (2004, 2007) found that among wāhine Māori experiencing intimate partner violence, 60% of those going to an emergency provider, as well as 96% of those going to a Māori health provider, had children at home.

Yet, for all of the harm perpetrated historically by state care providers and adoption services, there continues to be a large disconnect between Te Ao Māori and these social services. As part of an inquiry by Manaakitia Ā Tātou Tamariki – Office of Children's Commissioner (2019), while tamariki Māori make up a quarter of Aotearoa New Zealand's children, they represent 69% of those in state care today. Indeed, while data from 2018 to 2019 show a reduction in the uplift of tamariki Māori, this follows a decade-long increase in the use of state custody for Māori children (Office of Children's Commissioner, 2019). At the same time, the trend line remains flat for non-Māori babies, thereby increasing the disconnect between its usage for Māori and non-Māori babies.

There is a clear irony to the usage of state custody and care, as its intended goal is to be an aid for all those in Aotearoa New Zealand. Instead, these processes, both historically and at present, intentional or not, commit grievous harm to tamariki Māori and by extension to Te Ao Māori itself. Of particular importance to this chapter is that wāhine Māori experiencing violence are often acutely aware of the harm that the state imposes upon them and whānau. This results in a dual process in which wāhine Māori must balance their experience of violence with concern for both basic living standards and possible intervention by Oranga Tamariki – Ministry of Children, the police, or other social services (Wilson et al., 2019).

Research indicates, in particular, the threat of involvement of social services, and their general unhelpfulness, as a large 'unseen fence' for wāhine Māori experiencing violence (Wilson et al., 2019). The earlier mentioned *E Tu Wāhine, E Tu Whānau* report (Wilson et al., 2019) notes also a high level of involvement with different social services. Of the women interviewed, just over 80% were involved with a social service, most having contact with the police and a significant number being contacted by Oranga Tamariki. The experiences recounted by wāhine often show the damage done by the way in which they have been treated by the state agencies. One of the participants, Maia, recounted an experience with a Oranga Tamariki worker who showed up, unannounced, with a summons for her unborn child and promptly left (p. 35):

> I recall the days where I've felt like a beaten-up dog on the ground, and I can tell you who made feel like that. It was a little Oranga Tamariki social worker. She rolled up to my house one day unannounced. I hadn't expected her. . . . She says, 'Oh these are for you [Maia], see you in court'. . . . Of all these years you know, even the things that I've had done, that [ex-partner]'s done to me, never have I actually been psychologically, emotionally and physically impaired as I had been from her.

The experiences identified in qualitative data speak to a larger ambivalence by New Zealand's government towards the experiences of wāhine Māori and create both an institutional and an individual cycle of harm.

## Movements of change

Māori communities have taken it upon themselves to create solutions that both advocate for their own self-determination or rangatiratanga[13] that give expression to their sovereignty and their collective and individual exercise of power and autonomy. This rangatiratanga is expressed on an individual level, as exemplified by wāhine Māori in both keeping themselves and their tamariki safe, as well as their whānau, hapū, and iwi,[14] who have established and implemented initiatives to protect their communities from different physical, mental, and cultural harms. This holistic approach identifies a more wide-ranging notion of safety that encompasses the connections of whakapapa, culture, and belonging to physical, mental, and emotional well-being for whānau Māori.

This culturally focused and connected approach represents a process in which the mana[15] of both an individual and a community is uplifted and in turn contributes to a healthy social ecosystem of whānau, hapū, and iwi. For Māori, a healthy social ecosystem is one where collective well-being is enhanced both materially and spiritually. There is also a deep relationship between personal and collective well-being with the well-being of the natural environment. To heal the impact of violence often requires a holistic approach, including recognizing the need for social, economic, and environmental justice. It is clear that there is an imperative that these approaches recognize the need to create the conditions for a just society that are culturally informed. Both wāhine and tāne Māori in the *E Tu Wāhine, E Tu Whānau* report (Wilson et al., 2019), noted that culturally focused services and teachings helped end cycles of abuse and helped develop emotional skills to heal both the individual and the community. For example, while many wāhine Māori interviewed for the report expressed negative feelings and experiences with social services, all those who worked with a kaupapa Māori[16] service provider noted a wider institutional feeling of being welcomed and heard in a non-judgemental space (Wilson et al., 2019, p. 34).

The experience of wāhine Māori also extends to tāne Māori as active contributors in breaking a cycle of violence. As evidenced by the report, culturally grounded services and connection helped tāne Māori to understand the roots of their offending and change course. Many tāne Māori in the report note experiences in understanding the necessary and dual roles of both tāne and wāhine Māori before colonization as important in their own healing (Wilson et al., p. 61). Healing with historical and social contexts can be an important component of decolonization. Not only does it expose the ramifications of history, but it more fully reveals traditional epistemology and associated practices. This in turn supports contemporary cultural approaches by grounding and legitimating such approaches. Drawing on cultural and decolonizing services also helped tāne Māori to find strategies that they could lean on to facilitate their individual healing of traumas, including the usage of karakia and other spiritual guides (Wilson et al., p. 61).

The contrast in the findings from reports of inquiry by both the state and outside groups identifies competing strategies for dealing with the current crisis of family violence in Aotearoa New Zealand. Whereas colonial approaches to family violence have addressed or address the singular problem, the institutional harm often committed by service providers is an affront to the mana of wāhine Māori. These experiences also lack the necessary context that recognizes family violence as a part of a larger system in which tangata whenua are largely disenfranchised and often culturally dislocated. Violence begets violence, and the colonization of Māori – and all it entails – has to be considered 'an extreme form of violence' (Kruger et al., 2004, p. 11).

## Healing whānau, addressing violence

Many Indigenous-specific programmes and models have arisen as a consequence of inadequate mainstream responses. Through colonization and the subsequent loss of cultural knowledge, identity, and practices, and the breakdown and dysfunction of whānau, hapū, and iwi, many cultural practices and values have been devalued and marginalized (Dobbs & Eruera, 2014, p. 29). Moreover, as Kruger et al. (2004) suggest, if whānau violence interventions continue to be delivered from a Pākehā conceptual and practice framework that isolates, criminalizes, and pathologizes individuals, nothing will change (Dobbs & Eruera, 2014, p. 29). For the past two decades, there has been a growing recognition of the need for a structural analysis of family violence, alongside the endorsement of the need for holistic Māori models of prevention and intervention.

Many of the interventions focus on trauma and healing. Historical trauma theory[17] has been explored to better articulate the impact of historical trauma events and the contribution of those events to the production of negative social indicators, including violence indicators. Historical trauma is the cumulative, multigenerational, collective experience of emotional and psychological injury in communities and in descendants (Brave Heart, 1999). It has been referred to as a 'soul wound' (Duran, Duran, Heart, & Horse-Davis, 1998). Historical trauma relates to the collective trauma experienced through 'massive cataclysmic' historical events that have been perpetrated intentionally by one group of people upon another (Pihama et al., 2014). Historical trauma theory encourages the development of understandings and healing frameworks that are cognizant of collective and historical Indigenous experience, particularly in regards to colonization and its impact. Such frameworks provide the context and starting place for identification of the pathways that will support recovery and healing (Pihama et al., 2019, p. 5). Healing as a decolonization process can be seen as a radical act. It can be used both as a form of activism in identifying the violence of colonialization and as a disruptor of the inter-generational transmission of social inequalities and trauma. It requires an understanding and awareness of the intergenerational impact of violence on whānau, hapū, and iwi that is embodied in the violence continuum (McIntosh & Curcic, 2020). Wirihana and Smith (2014) assert that the acknowledgement of historical trauma for Māori is critical to facilitate individual and collective healing and well-being. Identification of trauma is necessary but not sufficient. Healing must centre on Māori ways, ways of knowing, being, and acting. Trauma must be understood to have personal and political dimensions. For healing and restoration of mana to occur, there is a recognition of the need for decolonization at the personal, collective, and national level.

> Decolonisation is also multi-layered. Dealing with issues of systemic and institutional racism and underlying deficit understandings and assumptions is essential. Developing deeper understandings about the impact of colonisation is critical to providing knowledge about what constitutes healthy relationships, as a mechanism for the prevention of and intervention in whānau violence.
>
> (Pihama et al., 2019, p. 19)

## Case studies

The Amokura Family Violence Prevention Strategy (2005–2009) was an integrated, community-based initiative to address family violence in Northland (Tai Tokerau) New Zealand. It was led by the Tai Tokerau Iwi Chief Executives Consortium, made up of the Chief Executives of seven iwi authorities. It provided a whole of population approach to addressing family violence prevention and early intervention: research, education and promotion, professional development, and advocacy (Grennell & Cram, 2008).

The three fundamental tasks identified by the taskforce as underpinning a conceptual framework for achieving whānau well-being were to:

* dispel the misconception, at individual and collective levels, that whānau violence is normal, acceptable, and culturally valid;
* remove situations conducive to whānau violence to be perpetrated through education strategies that empower whānau, hapū, and iwi; and
* teach transformative practices based on Māori cultural imperatives that provide alternatives to violence.

(Dobbs & Eruera, 2014, p. 5)

The production of a whānau resource book called *Aroha in Action*[18] demonstrates a practical example of Amokura's work of strengthening well-being. This resource was produced to give whānau practical information and advice on:

* how to provide a safe and nurturing environment for all whānau members, especially tamariki;
* the impact of violence and abuse on whanau;
* ways to enact the belief that whānau violence is unacceptable and not culturally valid; and
* how to identify and to respond if violence has occurred.

(Dobbs & Eruera, 2014, p. 6)

The resource was for use by whānau, and governmental and non-governmental agencies that work with whānau. The project won a human rights award from the New York-based Leitner Center for International Law and Justice in May 2009. An evaluation undertaken by Di Grennell and Fiona Cram (2008) of the project found that across all four project sites (research, education and promotion, professional development and training, and advocacy), Amokura has met the objectives and often exceeded expectations. National and international recognition of the work of Amokura also endorsed the approach taken as being at the cutting edge of prevention and early intervention of whānau violence work. Yet despite this, the project was closed in 2011 after governmental funding was reallocated to frontline services as opposed to the continuation of funding for iwi-based community-led activities.

*E Tū Whānau* has been defined as a kaupapa Māori approach that seeks to eliminate all forms of violence in the home. It is strength-based, grounded in te ao Māori and leadership development; and it supports communities to identify and respond to their own priorities. The guiding principles of E Tū Whānau are: strong empowered whānau leading to strong and connected hapū and iwi; Māori-led solutions; reclamation of tikanga Māori; sanctity of the home and the use of Māori paradigms and conceptual frameworks (Māori Reference Group, 2013). In the most recent iteration of their strategic plan, they note that there are some things that only those in te ao Māori can do, other things, within a Tiriti of Waitangi framework, are the responsibility of government, and others demand a shared commitment. This provides the opportunity for Māori to lead in the solutions to address these issues with government support. It also recognizes that the key to success will be harnessing the strength of whānau across Aotearoa and taking action at the community level (E Tū Whānau, 2020). E tu Whanau is a place-based strategy focused on the whānau and the broader community. Whānau plans are a key element of the programme that set the aspirations and create whānau objectives in terms of education, health, and employment. Each whānau writes up their own plan and aspirations and monitors and demonstrates their own success. External indicators of success include a significant reduction of call to service from police for whānau violence, increased participation in education, reduction of truancy, and increased and sustained participation in employment and community activities. Within whānau, success indicators may include better communication strategies, anger management, shared leisure and cultural activities, and a sense of wellness.

In 2017, I was part of a larger team that carried out an evaluation of E Tū Whānau. As a part of that evaluation, I did a focus group with a group of people where E Tū Whānau had made a significant difference in their personal lives and in the life of the community. The focus group consisted of seven participants: six wāhine Māori and one tāne Māori. The tāne was in his late 50s, a father of two of the participants, an uncle by whakapapa or by custom to other participants, and a senior member of the Mongrel Mob.[19] The wāhine ranged in age from late 20s to early 40s. They were mothers and even grandmothers. All had blood ties or intimate relationship ties to the Mongrel Mob. All had strong connections to the community they lived in in the south of the North Island, and most continued to live locally.

This was a group of people whose relationship with government agencies had been poor. They had just come out of a protracted battle with a government housing agency where they had fought eviction and what they saw as the destruction of community. While it was acknowledged that the women themselves were not seen as being involved in criminal activity, the fact that they were 'associated' with Mongrel Mob gang members or had 'ongoing connections' meant that they and their tamariki had been effectively criminalized. As they note that they were not gang associated, they were gang related. The ongoing connections were with people with whom they have blood relationships, often paternal and fraternal ones, or intimate partnership relationships. They went through gruelling legal battles. Their relationship with agents of the state was based on a sense of mistrust and betrayal. They felt that they and their children had been condemned by state authorities. While they had seen how they were able to work together in solidarity and had seen the power of the collective, they were also suffering ongoing hurt by the struggle and the outcomes of their struggle.

E Tū Whānau was introduced to them by people they trusted who were from gang backgrounds, with whom they had longstanding, even familial, relationships. When E Tū Whānau was introduced, they were captivated and responsive to the concept. From the outset, they recognized that it allowed them the ability to see themselves as agents of change. For some of them, given their experience with agents of the state, the idea that E Tū Whānau could support them becoming more self-governing and taking responsibility for themselves and their community was very attractive. One of the women who has strong leadership qualities said that she was the 'water tester'. If it felt right with her, she could test it, and if she felt it could work for all of them then she would promote it and expect them to commit to the kaupapa. The other women all recognized her leadership and commitment. One of the strong elements of E Tū Whānau is role modelling change and success. The programme seeks to identify and support and provide resources for those that are seen as being Kahukura. *Kahukura* was chosen as the term to describe leaders of change within iwi, hapū, and whānau.

Growing up in gang whānau meant that they had a strong sense of the collective, but while they recognized that they were Māori, they did not have a strong sense of what that meant or an appreciation of Māori culture. One of the women said that when her father had talked to her about the early days of the Mongrel Mob in the 1970s, she realized that for him, as for many of the other men, it was easier to be a gang member than it was to be Māori. For those men, their experience of marginalization, racism, and state care had shaped who they were. This had then had an impact on her own development. Her father was already a patched member when she was born, and she has lived with Mongrel Mob all of her life. She reflected on the role that education has played in her journey with E Tū Whānau:

> At the Wānanga we were kept asking who are we, who had shaped us? Made me think about the Mongrel Mob being my family. All these questions of who shaped you, who made you what you are today. Well I can say my mum and dad but I had to be real to myself as I have lived with the Mongrel Mob my whole life. Every single day, in my house every day. Just because they are known to others as bad that is not the view I had and I was sheltered from a lot of the bad stuff. So I am going to say that Mongrel Mob shaped me. That is the truth, they are not just Mongrel Mob they are your family. Helping me be the person I am today. E Tū Whānau are a part of that too.

In the focus groups, the issue of explicitly addressing violence came up rarely. Much of the focus was on creating the conditions of change that could allow whānau to flourish. This was one of the positives they saw in a strength-based approach that sought to identify and build upon the collective strengths of the whānau. While violence elimination was the goal, this was seen to be best achieved by creating an environment that was conducive to positive interaction. Within the focus group, the participants explained flourishing as being able to self-determine their future through identifying their needs and aspirations in their whānau plans and then being supported through the programme to realize them. Education, sustained employment, and community participation were key to this and were the main focus of discussion. However, it was accepted that violence, as a victim or as a perpetrator, had been experienced differentially within the group. Some had suffered violence, all had witnessed violence, and some had used violence.

Though there was only one man in the group, he noted that the young women present had influenced his views on violence and he was trying to keep his hands to himself. His discussion on violence spoke to man-on-man violence, which he saw as disciplinary, retaliatory, or defensive in nature. While he still felt that there could be justification for certain types of violence, he said that he was far removed from the days when violence was his way in the world. What was noticeable in this exchange was how open the discussion was and how the women felt very comfortable giving their own views and offering dissenting views from his, even though they afforded him every respect. This was their way of walking the talk of E Tū Whānau.

One of the women spoke of how E Tū Whānau had completely changed the way she thought about violence. She had suffered a lot of violence in her home as a child and as a young woman and adult. She had also used a lot of violence against others. She felt remorseful for those that she had hurt but recognized the great gains she was making in living a life without violence. All others in the group gave her support and encouragement during this discussion and noted that, for them, she was the one who had made the greatest changes in her life since becoming part of E Tū Whānau.

There was a recognition of the barriers that work against a full expression of E Tū Whānau. Living under conditions of community deprivation and scarcity can sap strength and resolve. Every day struggles were experienced by most of these women and for the people of their community. Income stability and food security were still not achievable for all. Misuse of drugs and alcohol and methamphetamine addiction were serious concerns. The inter-generational reach of the prisons and the subsequent narrowing of opportunities were evident. Ongoing marginalization, even in educational institutions, due to their being gang whānau was still experienced. At the government agency and government policy level, a focus on gang desistance rather than a focus on supporting and enabling educational and work opportunities was seen as counter-productive. The participants did not minimize the challenges to create violence-free, healthy whānau but felt that if the foundations for meaningful education and jobs were there, then the conditions would be ripe for whānau to flourish. They had great belief in themselves and what could be achieved. For them, E Tū Whānau was an expression of self-determination and community sustainability and flourishing.

## Reflections

While violence remains a significant issue for communities, there is a commitment within these communities and among service providers and state agencies to redress harm and to work towards different forms of collective safety and security. Within communities, it is recognized that the solutions towards ending whānau violence are about contextualizing harm within a framework that recognizes the problem without demonising or diminishing Māori whānau. It demands practices of care and connection, including ensuring that individuals are supported in reconnecting to their whakapapa, whenua, and culture. This wider approach seeks to enhance the mana of wāhine, tane, and tamariki Māori and surround them with support and care instead of further isolation or marginalization. This shift in thinking proposes both an attitudinal and a practical shift for both service providers and the wider society. While violence in the domestic sphere is not unique to Māori communities, solutions proposed by whānau recognize the power of their culture to transform the problem of family violence. Envisioning this future is the whakatauki *kia whakatōmuri te haere whakamua* – I walk backwards into the future with my eyes fixed on the past.

## Notes

1 Aotearoa was originally used as a name for the North Island of New Zealand. It is now commonly used as the Māori name for New Zealand.
2 Whānau is the extended family of a family group understood as the primary economic unit of traditional Māori society. In contemporary Māori society, whānau can be multilayered, flexible, and dynamic. It includes physical, emotional, and spiritual dimensions and is based on whakapapa (genealogy).
3 Māori women.
4 New Zealander of European descent/White New Zealander.
5 Māori children.
6 NCEA Level 2 is one of the three National Certificates of Educational Achievement designed to recognize the general achievement of 16- to 19-year-old learners. It is a New Zealand government objective to increase the rates of young people, particularly Māori and Pacific students, achieving NCEA Level 2.
7 Denoting Maori, people of the land/Indigenous people.
8 The Crown refers to the Executive of the New Zealand (Government). It is the successor of the British Crown and Queen Victoria who was, alongside Māori, a party to the Treaty of Waitangi (Tiriti o Waitangi). The Crown is the inheritor of the obligations that the Queen took on in 1840 at the signing of the treaty.
9 There were two versions of the treaty: one written in English and one in Māori. Nearly all te Māori chiefs signed the Māori version. There are some distinct differences in the two versions: see Claudia Orange (2015). Māori recognize Tiriti o Waitangi.
10 The Māori world comprising Māori ways of knowing, being, and doing.
11 Māori men.
12 Cultural system of values and practices that shapes relationships with the social, physical, and spiritual worlds.
13 Right to exercise authority in an individual and collective sense. Chiefly authority.
14 The iwi (tribe) is the largest of the groups that form Māori society. Each iwi is made up of various hapū (clan or descent groups). Hapū in turn are made up of whānau groups.
15 Defining mana is difficult. Mana can speak to prestige, authority, control, power, and influence. It can also reference a spiritual force. Mana gives a person the authority to lead and to fully participate in the life of the collective. Mana can be both enhanced and diminished by social forces and social agents.
16 Kaupapa Māori refers to a Māori approach that draws on Māori principles and incorporates the knowledge, skills, attitudes, cultural practices, and values of Māori society.
17 Historical trauma theory is a relatively new concept used in public health. The premise of this theory is that populations historically subjected to long-term, mass trauma – colonialism, slavery, war, genocide – exhibit a higher prevalence of disease even several generations after the original trauma occurred (Sotero, 2006).
18 Love in Action.
19 The Mongrel Mob is an organized gang that is predominantly made up of Māori members. They have a network of more than 30 chapters and are particularly active in small and semi-peripheral towns in Aotearoa New Zealand.

## References

Balzer, R., Haimona, D., Henare, M., & Matchitt, V. (1997). *Maori family violence in Aotearoa*. Wellington: Te Puni Kokiri.

Bolton, S. (2017). *Educational equity in New Zealand: Successes, challenges and opportunities*. Wellington: Fulbright New Zealand.

Bourdieu, P. (2001). *Masculine domination*. Palo Alto, CA: Stanford University Press.

Bourdieu, P., & Wacquant, L. (2001). Neoliberal newspeak: Notes on the new planetary vulgate. *Radical Philosophy, 105*(Jan).

Brave Heart, M. Y. H. (1999). Oyate Ptayela: Rebuilding the Lakota nation through addressing historical trauma among Lakota parents. *Journal of Human Behavior in the Social Environment, 2*(1–2), 109–126.

Came, H. (2012). *Institutional racism and the dynamics of privilege in public health* (Doctoral dissertation). University of Waikato, Hamilton, New Zealand.

Cram, F. (2001). Ma te wa e whakaatu mai: Time will tell. *Feminism & Psychology, 11*(3), 401–406.

Cunneen, C. (2013). The race to defraud: State crime and the immiseration of Indigenous people. In J. McCulloch & E. Stanley (eds.), *State crime and resistance* (pp. 99–113). London: Routledge.

Cunneen, C., & Porter, A. (2017). Indigenous peoples and criminal justice in Australia. In A. Deckert & R. Sarre (eds.), *The Palgrave handbook of Australian and New Zealand criminology, crime and justice* (pp. 667–682). Cham: Palgrave Macmillan.

Dobbs, T., & Eruera, M. (2014). *Kaupapa Māori wellbeing framework: The basis for whānau violence prevention and intervention*. New Zealand Family Violence Clearinghouse, Issue Paper 6. Auckland: University of Auckland.

Duran, E., Duran, B., Heart, M. Y. H. B., & Horse-Davis, S. Y. (1998). Healing the American Indian soul wound. In *International handbook of multigenerational legacies of trauma* (pp. 341–354). Boston, MA: Springer.

E Tū Whānau. (2020). *E Tū Whānau: Mahere Rautaki framework for change*. Wellington, New Zealand: Ministry of Social Development.

Family Violence Death Review Committee. (2014). *Fourth annual report: January 2013 to December 2013*. Retrieved from www.hqsc.govt.nz/assets/FVDRC/Publications/FVDRC-4th-report-June-2014.pdf

Family Violence Death Review Committee. (2015). *Fifth annual report: July 2014-June 2015*. Retrieved from www.hqsc.govt.nz/assets/FVDRC/Publications/FVDRC-activities-report-Jun-2015.pdf

Fanslow, J. L., & Robinson, E. M. (2010). Help-seeking behaviors and reasons for help seeking reported by a representative sample of women victims of intimate partner violence in New Zealand. *Journal of Interpersonal Violence, 25*(5), 929–951.

Grennell, D., & Cram, F. (2008). Evaluation of Amokura: An indigenous family violence prevention strategy. *MAI Review, 2*, Article 4.

Hurihanganui, T. A. (2019). *How closed adoption robbed Māori children of their identity*. Retrieved from www.rnz.co.nz/national/programmes/insight/audio/2018703334/how-closed-adoption-robbed-maori-children-of-their-identity

Koziol-McLain, J., Gardiner, J., Batty, P., Rameka, M., Fyfe, E., & Giddings, L. (2004). Prevalence of intimate partner violence among women presenting to an urban adult and paediatric emergency care department. *The New Zealand Medical Journal (Online), 117*(1206).

Koziol-McLain, J., Rameka, M., Giddings, L., Fyfe, E., & Gardiner, J. (2007). Partner violence prevalence among women attending a Maori health provider clinic. *Australian and New Zealand Journal of Public Health, 31*(2), 143–148.

Kruger, T., Pitman, M., McDonald, T., Mariu, D., Pomare, A., Mita, T., Maihi, M., & Lawson-Te Aho, K. (2004). *Transforming whanau violence: A conceptual framework* (2nd ed.). Wellington, New Zealand: Ministry of Māori Affairs.

Māori Reference Group for the Taskforce for Action on Family Violence. (2013). *E Tu Whānau programme of action for addressing family violence 2013–2018*. Wellington, New Zealand: Ministry of Social Development.

McCreanor, T. (1997). When racism stepped ashore: Antecedents of anti-Maori discourse in Aotearoa. *New Zealand Journal of Psychology*, *26*(1), 36–44.

McIntosh, T. (2002). *Death in the margins: Riding the periphery* (Unpublished Ph.D. thesis). University of Auckland, Auckland, New Zealand.

McIntosh, T., & Coster, S. (2017). Indigenous insider knowledge and prison identity. *Counterfutures*, *3*, 69–98.

McIntosh, T., & Curcic, M. (2020). Prison as destiny? Descent or dissent? In L. George, A. N. Norris, A. Deckert, & J. Tauri (eds.), *Neo-colonial injustice and the mass imprisonment of Indigenous women* (pp. 223–238). Cham: Palgrave Macmillan.

McIntosh, T., & Workman, K. (2017). Māori and prison. In A. Deckert & R. Sarre (eds.), *The Palgrave handbook of Australian and New Zealand criminology, crime and justice* (pp. 725–735). Cham: Palgrave Macmillan.

Mikaere, A. (2011). *Colonising myths-Maori realities: He rukuruku whakaaro*. Wellington: Huia Publishers.

Ministry of Business, Innovation and Employment. (2020). *Māori labour market*. Retrieved from www.mbie.govt.nz/dmsdocument/11844-maori-in-the-labour-market-june-2020-quarter-pdf

Mutu, M. (2019). The treaty claims settlement process in New Zealand and its impact on Māori. *Land*, *8*(10), 152.

Nixon, R. (2011). *Slow violence and the environmentalism of the poor*. Cambridge, MA: Harvard University Press.

O'Brien, G., & Strongman, L. (Eds.). (2006). *Parihaka: The art of passive resistance*. Wellington: Victoria University Press.

Office of the Children's Commissioner. (2019). *State of care: Supporting young people on remand to live successfully in the community*. Retrieved from www.occ.org.nz/assets/Uploads/ShortReport-May2019-Pages2.pdf

Oranga Tamariki. (2019). *Safety of children in care*. Retrieved from www.orangatamariki.govt.nz/assets/Uploads/About-us/Performance-and-monitoring/safety-of-children-in-care/2018-19/Safety-of-children-in-care-Annual-Report-2018/19.pdf

Orange, C. (2015). *The treaty of Waitangi*. Wellington: Bridget Williams Books.

Pihama, L., Cameron, N., & Te Nana, R. (2019). *Historical trauma and whānau violence*. New Zealand Family Violence Clearinghouse, Issue Paper 15. Auckland: University of Auckland.

Pihama, L., Reynolds, P., Smith, C., Reid, J., Smith, L. T., & Nana, R. T. (2014). Positioning historical trauma theory within Aotearoa New Zealand. *AlterNative: An International Journal of Indigenous Peoples*, *10*(3), 248–262.

Royal Commission of Inquiry into Abuse in Care. (2020). *Tāwharautia: pūrongo o te wā -Interim report*. Retrieved from file:///Users/tmci005/Downloads/Abuse-in-Care-Volume-One.pdf

Scheper-Hughes, N., & Bourgois, P. (2004). Introduction: Making sense of violence. In *Violence in war and peace: An anthology*. Oxford: Blackwell.

Solórzano, D., Ceja, M., & Yosso, T. (2000). Critical race theory, racial microaggressions, and campus racial climate: The experiences of African American college students. *Journal of Negro Education*, *69*(1/2), 60–73.

Solórzano, D. G., & Yosso, T. J. (2002). Critical race methodology: Counter-storytelling as an analytical framework for education research. *Qualitative Inquiry, 8*(1), 23–44.

Sotero, M. (2006). A conceptual model of historical trauma: Implications for public health practice and research. *Journal of Health Disparities Research and Practice, 1*(1), 93–108.

Speed, S. (2019). *Incarcerated stories: Indigenous women migrants and violence in the settler-capitalist state*. Chapel Hill, NC: UNC Press Books.

Stanley, E. (2016). *The road to hell: State violence against children in postwar New Zealand*. Auckland: Auckland University Press.

Taonui, R. (2010). Mana tamariki: Cultural alienation: Māori child homicide and abuse. *AlterNative: An International Journal of Indigenous Peoples, 6*(3), 187–202.

Te Puni Kōkiri. (2017). *Building a future for whanau*. Retrieved from file:///Users/tmci005/Downloads/tpk-bim-english-2017.pdf

Wilson, D. (2016). Transforming the normalisation and intergenerational whānau (family) violence. *Journal of Indigenous Wellbeing, 2*(2), 32–43.

Wilson, D., Mikahere-Hall, A., Sherwood, J., Cootes, K., & Jackson, D. (2019). *E tū wāhine, e tū whānau: Wāhine Māori keeping safe in unsafe relationships*. Auckland: AUT Taupua Waiora Māori Research Centre.

Wingard, B. (2010). A conversation with lateral violence. *International Journal of Narrative Therapy & Community Work, 1*, 13–17.

Wirihana, R., & Smith, C. (2014). Historical trauma, healing and well-being in Māori communities. *MAI Journal, 3*(3), 197–210.

# 2 Placing the children

## Fostering native Hawaiian children in an American state

*Judith Schachter*

'Hawaiians are 20% of the population but about 50% of the kids in the system', claims a recent article in *Ka Wai Ola*, the Office of Hawaiian Affairs (OHA) newspaper (Fernandez-Akamine, 2019, p. 11). The story is not new: Native Hawaiians have seen a rise in the numbers of children at risk for several decades, the outcome of drug and alcohol abuse, domestic violence, and homelessness. Perceptions of risk and of safety vary. My chapter examines the complex impact of cultural differences in assessing the appropriate 'place' for a child who is in an abusive or vulnerable situation. Such complexity influences the decisions made by child welfare workers, by lawyers and judges, and, not least of all, by individuals whose concern about a child intersects with the options available to Native Hawaiians in an American state.[1] An examination of child placement in Hawai'i brings further insight into 'the potential tensions and normative conflicts between the social, cultural and legal domains' and highlights how 'institutional definitions may contradict or support individual perceptions' (Bastide & Regnier, 2023).

After a brief history of child-related custom and law in Hawai'i, I focus on the contemporary situation and on responses to the high number of Native Hawaiian children who fall into the limbo of 'placement'. Foster care, a public transaction in an American state, brings Western concepts of harm and of safety as well as of family and of kinship into decisions about a child's 'place'. I argue that when a Hawaiian child enters the system, decisions about his or her placement implicate Indigenous interpretations of relatedness and belonging that contrast or compromise with Western interpretations. In Hawai'i, the act of moving a child occurs in the context of principles and policies imposed by the United States through state and federal law. Even when a child is placed within the extended family (*'ohana*), the legal system forms a backdrop to customary understandings of the transfer of a child from one person to another.[2]

The system of foster care is neither static nor immune to the pressures of individual actors, particular cases, and changes in state and federal rulings. In Hawai'i, the Department of Human Services (DHS) oversees the Child Welfare Services Branch (CWS), which is directly responsible for placement decisions. As a state agency, DHS is subject to the 1978 constitutional mandate to preserve and protect 'Hawaiian culture and tradition', a phrase that absorbs and responds to a history of conquest by the United States. At the same time, DHS depends on funding from

DOI: 10.4324/9781003146667-3

federal government agencies that have to adhere in their policies to an array of anti-discrimination laws. The ensuing regulations often rest uneasily with Hawaiian cultural interpretations of harm and abuse, of safety and well-being.

Sovereignty movements of the last four decades further complicate the interaction between state and federal agencies. Competition over control of 'where the children are' then becomes a struggle over what nationhood means and how it is accessed under the U.S. constitution. Consequently, Hawai'i offers a potent example of the bearing of foster care practices on the intricacies of the relationship between an Indigenous people and an imperial government.[3] In such a highly fraught political context, official acknowledgement of 'ancient Hawaiian cultural traditions' is a lightning rod for the future of a people as well as for the fate of individual children (Partners in Development Foundation, 2020a). Behind the broad issues lies the daunting fact of a child in harm's way, and urgency determines the application of both custom and law.

Following an analysis of particular cases, I conclude with a discussion of resistance to the imposition of state and federal rulings on Native Hawaiian practices for ensuring a child's place and cultural identity. One effort involved the introduction of a bill to the state legislature to establish a Hawaiian Child Welfare Act on the model of the 1978 Indian Child Welfare Act (ICWA). The ICWA grants jurisdiction over child placement to tribal courts, based on the sovereignty granted to tribes by the U.S. government.[4] The Hawaiian bill died in the legislature, but its terms suggest a feasible redesign of placement practices to reflect cultural interpretations of a child's well-being. At the same time, recent acts passed by the federal government impose a more definitive Western interpretation of harm, safety, family, and kinship on state foster care systems. Around the fulcrum of foster care, then, lie issues of sovereignty, cultural autonomy, and the right of a people to decide the fate of younger generations.

## Brief background

The story begins in the early 19th century with the arrival of missionaries from the United States. Soon after they settled, missionary wives watched with distress as Hawaiian children moved from one adult to another – seemingly without rhyme or reason and without any hint of permanence. Their husbands, influential in government, persuaded Kamehameha III to draft a constitution on the American model. While the constitution did not discuss domestic relations, statutes immediately following did. By 1841, earlier than the United States, Hawai'i passed an adoption law stating that every transfer of a child should be recorded and signed before a judge in Honolulu.[5] Inheritance cases exposed the gaps in both law and custom. According to law, an adopted child has the right to inherit only when the right is formalized in a contract or a will. According to custom, a *hānai* child has the right to inherit only when a parent explicitly states her intention regarding property. Disputed cases came to court, where judges asked whether the social acquisition of parenthood creates the same responsibilities and rights as the biological parent–child relationship.

Such cases embroiled judges in discussions of nature and culture, of the 'best interests' of a child, and of the meaning and demonstration of parenthood. Debates over the concepts of child, parent, family, and kinship flourished (see Modell [Schachter], 2008).

At the end of the 19th century, the recently deposed queen published *Hawaii's Story by Hawaii's Queen* (1898). The book is Lili'uokalani's testament to the survival of the *lāhui*, a Hawaiian collectivity, despite the overthrow of a kingdom. She begins with an account of her 'adoption' at birth. 'Immediately after my birth I was wrapped in the finest soft *tapa* cloth, and taken to the house of another chief by whom I was adopted'. She adds: 'In speaking of our relationship, I have adopted the term customarily used in the English language, but there was no such modification recognized in my native land'. The term adoption, she implies, refers to a legal contract and not to a custom that cements 'ties of friendship'. Writing for English-speaking readers, she does not use the Hawaiian term *hānai*, but her account provides a description of the custom as well as its purpose: creating harmony and community (Lili'uokalani, 1990 [1898], p. 4).

The near synonymity of the terms adoption and *hānai* has beleaguered placement policies and practices for over two centuries, and is still a factor in decisions made about securing a child from harm, abuse, and abandonment. At the same time, as Kauanui points out in another context, concepts evolve, subject to political and generational shifts.

> How do we bridge that conceptual gap between languages and worldviews (Western and Hawaiian but also between generations) when attempting to understand and articulate what our *kupuna* [grandparent generation] were discussing or portraying in regard to gender and sexuality? The understanding of these concepts has evolved over time not only because language and culture are dynamic but also due to the introduction of new practices and misinterpretations that may gain a foothold.
>
> (Kauanui, 2018, p. 162)

In the case of adoption and *hānai*, changes in meaning reflect dynamic as well as conflicting cultural interpretations of what is 'good' for the child.

The sourcebook on Hawaiian tradition, *Nānā I Ke Kumu*, defines *hānai* as 'a child who is taken permanently to be reared, educated and loved by someone other than natural parents' (Pukui, Haertig, & Lee, 1972, vol. 1, p. 49). The entry goes on to state that in the traditional arrangement, the child maintains a connection to her birth family; she knows her ancestry, her ethnic background.[6] In Hawai'i knowing one's ancestry is an economic as well as a psychological issue. Under U.S. law, ancestry is reduced to race, coded as blood. A 50% blood quantum grants an individual access to Hawaiian homestead land and to other benefits, like health care and education. But 50% is only one definition; genealogy provides another, as does self-identification as Native Hawaiian. The range of possibilities diversifies the *lāhui* Lili'uokalani hoped to sustain, and it complicates the implementation of a culturally sensitive placement.

*Hānai* represents a customary approach to ensuring the well-being of a child, but reference to tradition does not provide a clear mode of action to workers who must abide by state laws and federal policies. At the same time, for decades, Native Hawaiian children have been disproportionately represented in the foster care system, a circumstance that raises questions of discrimination and failure to acknowledge conditions created by two centuries of colonization. A 2016 exposé in the *Honolulu Advertiser* drew on (and fuelled) perceptions of discrimination in the system (Perez, 2016). Accumulating criticism led DHS to hire a cultural specialist in 2017 and to encourage representation of Native Hawaiians in the Child Welfare Services branch; currently, Native Hawaiians and part Hawaiians comprise 29% of employees.[7] Neither of these factors ensures the application of custom to decisions made about the place of a Native Hawaiian child. Nor do those facts erase the experience of Native Hawaiians, who perceive the removal and re-placement of children as transgressing cultural interpretations of well-being.

## Determining a child's place

One evening Don was driving home from his job at Pearl Harbour when he heard sirens and saw lights behind him. The officers pulled him over, accusing him of 'abducting' two children in his household. Don had taken the children in at the request of their mother, a friend. A few years later, the mother changed her mind and complained to officials. The police took the children into custody. Don contacted a social worker from Child Protective Services (the former title of CWS) who argued, in court, that Don met the criteria for a good parent and the biological mother, homeless and addicted, did not.[8] Don and his wife Maria qualified on the basis of Western criteria: a nuclear family whose head earned a stable income and whose other children were well cared for.

Some years later, an elder (*kupuna*) asked Don and his wife to care for the infants born to his 14-year-old granddaughter. They agreed and made the transfer permanent in a court adoption. The original request, informal and in the context of an existing relationship, included the presumption of care for the children as well as the acknowledgement of ties of kinship between the adults who arranged the transfer. This replication of an 'ancient' custom, however, did not erase doubts Don and Maria had about its permanence. Faced with the possibility that the mother would change her mind (as happened in the earlier case), Don and Maria signed a legal contract. The case illustrates Don's dual role as a native Hawaiian and as an American citizen, and his equal respect for the weight of custom and the power of law.[9]

When Don's adolescent son's girlfriend gave birth to a daughter, Don brought the infant home. While the form mimicked the ancient custom in which a paternal grandparent raises his son's first child, the circumstances reflected structural disadvantages experienced by Native Hawaiians in an American state. Don exploited the custom to relieve the pressures on his son, a Native Hawaiian who lacked the benefits of education or a steady job. In drawing on custom, Don also took advantage of the prescribed acknowledgement of 'Hawaiian culture' in the 1978 state constitution. At the same time, he linked the custom to a Western interpretation of the basis for a child's well-being. By calling her his *keiki hānai*, Don made clear that she would be assured of love, care, education, and, significantly, permanence.

I cite the three cases to suggest the options available to *kanaka maoli* (Native Hawaiians) in contemporary Hawai'i for the care and placement of a child. These options also recall the argument that Bastide and Regnier make about the difficulty of defining 'violence', especially within a family context. In none of the three cases did violence appear as an infliction of bodily damage; all three cases, however, demonstrate the 'symbolic violence' represented by the perceived danger and damage to a child who remains in a particular domestic situation. Don used both custom and law to validate an arrangement that promised security and permanence to the children. Each of his five children avoided a foster care system whose failings are partly measured by an American emphasis on the stability and safety of an intact, preferably nuclear family.

'Native Hawaiian children [are] placed in foster homes more than any other single ethnic group', a 2004 article in the *Honolulu Advertiser* notes (Viotti, 2004), without exploring the reasons in high rates of substance abuse, disease, and poverty in the Native Hawaiian population (*Native Hawaiian Data Book*, 2019, p. 3; Mokuau, 2002, p. 83). The emphasis falls specifically on the fact that 'about half the children in foster care are of native Hawaiian ancestry'. The then-director of DHS, Lillian Koller, adds: 'Over 40 percent of them are placed in homes that are safe but not of the same cultural and ethnic background'. The article reported a grant of nearly $800,000 from the federal government 'to recruit 144 more Native Hawaiian foster parents over the next three years and to find other ways to help the children in their care' (Viotti, 2004). DHS contracted with the nonprofit Partners in Development Foundation (PIDF) to fulfil the goal.[10]

Fifteen years later, the OHA newspaper, *Ka Wai Ola*, published an issue that reveals how little has changed, both in numbers and in the failure to place Native Hawaiian children in Native Hawaiian families. An article titled 'Pehea Nā Keiki?' ('Where are the children?') confronts the problem of those numbers and explicates their bearing on the state of the Native Hawaiian population are both the source of and solution to the problem (Look, Trask-Batti, Agres, Mau, & Kaholokula, 2013, *passim*). 'The need for foster care is the result of complex social problems rooted in poverty and substance abuse and fueled by depression and hopelessness'. The statement in 'Pehea Nā Keiki?' frames the policies of PIDF, which is 'dedicated to drawing upon the ancient Hawaiian cultural traditions to meet the current challenges facing today's Hawaiian population'. Through Hui Ho'omalu, a group whose mission is 'to protect and shelter' Native Hawaiian children, PIDF develops programmes 'to better meet the needs of Hawai'i's children in foster care'. The term 'cultural traditions', however, does not provide a precise guideline to a social worker charged with respecting a child's 'culture' in the placement decision. Moreover, in the contemporary context, interpretation of a cultural tradition entangles with multiple sources of identity as 'Hawaiian'.

The staff of PIDF is aware of the complexities attached to its (well-meaning) argument. Since entry into foster care often results from the report or evidence of abuse, the choice of a placement has to be immediate; there may not be time to match child and family, whatever the criteria. Beyond issues of time and urgency lies the problem of a state-wide scarcity of Native Hawaiian foster parents. 'Without enough Hawaiian Resource families, when Hawaiian *keiki* are removed from their homes by the Department of Human Services (DHS)', continues the *Ka Wai Ola* article, 'they are placed with Resource Families from other communities and cultures'. The outcome evokes a version of violence: 'These traumatized *keiki* often experience culture shock on top of everything else' (Fernandez-Akamine, 2019, p. 12).

In a setting where *hānai* has historical significance and where children have moved from adult to adult for generations, why is there a shortage of Native Hawaiian fostering families? 'Foster care can be mentally and emotionally draining', a former foster child remarked to the *Ka Wai Ola* reporter. 'Taking on the *kuleana* [responsibility] of foster care can seem overwhelming', commented a foster parent for the same article (Fernandez-Akamine, 2019, p. 13). While these statements are undoubtedly true – especially given the stringent conditions experienced by Native Hawaiians – another reason stands behind these emotion-based explanations. In order to become a foster parent, an individual has to fulfil criteria that diverge from placement based on love, reciprocity, and 'ties of friendship' (Lili'uokalani, 1990 [1898], p. 4).

The PIDF recruiting programme is titled HANAI, 'Hawai'i Assures Nurturing And Involvement' (Partners in Development Foundation, 2020b). The criteria, however, obscure the custom: participation in six training sessions, adequate bedrooms, and an income that covers household expenses. In addition, all adult members of the household must pass 'a criminal history clearance, a child abuse and neglect background check, and a sex offender registry check' (Partners in Development Foundation, 2020b). While reasonable (and mandated by federal policies), the criteria potentially exclude a Native Hawaiian applicant whose *'ohana* includes kin whose records are not 'clean' by Western standards. An arrest for selling marijuana, for example, stains a person's record and imposes an alien 'bad apple' disqualification on everyone in the household.

The acronym HANAI also reflects a statutory effort to validate Native Hawaiian custom.

> The term *'hanai* relative' means an adult, other than a blood relative, whom the court or department has found by credible evidence to perform or to have performed a substantial role in the upbringing or material support of a child, as attested to by the written or oral designation of the child or of another person, including other relatives of the child.
>
> (Child Protective Act, 2016, § 587A-4, A-9)

The statute does not predict the outcome of placement decisions.

> The CWS caseworker is required to make every effort possible to place your child with safe relatives, kin, *hanai*, or family friends, who can meet the licensing requirements as special-licensed resource caregivers for your child. CWS understands that it may be less traumatic for children to be placed with relatives, kin, or family friends, especially those in the same, familiar community.
>
> (*A guide to child welfare services*, September 2020, p. 9)

But, as I discovered in a recent custody case, discretion rests with the state agency and ultimately with family court.

Julia asked me to testify to her *hānai* status in her petition to become the permanent guardian of two children in foster care. Her goal was eventually to adopt the children. CWS disputed her qualifications on the basis of her unauthorized visits with the foster family, and the case went to court. Julia's lawyer brought my expert testimony, along with other documents, to verify Julia's relationship to the children. While the judge granted her *hānai* status, in a second hearing, he denied her petition for guardianship. He judged the foster family to be better equipped economically and socially to raise the children, without referring to the ethnic identification of either of the parties.

'CPS simply goes on favoring foster families with resources – the principle they follow without regard to persons, to culture, to the family', remarked a social worker about an earlier case in which the children remained in a foster family. He criticized the CPS decision for its dismissal of culture, family, and the requests of the biological parents. His remarks also indicate his conviction that the threat is more than individual: placement of Native Hawaiian children in non – Native Hawaiian families threatens the survival of Hawaiians as an Indigenous people.

Mei-Ling, a parent, described to me her experience of 'losing' children to foster care at a time when she had no job and miscellaneous adults – maybe kin, maybe not – crowded into her household. 'With CPS taking kids, you have a hard time for [sic] to get them back'. She cited her qualifications for raising native Hawaiian children. 'I am 75% Hawaiian', she said, 'And I own the homestead house', the latter attesting to her Hawaiian ancestry.[11] 'My *tutu* lady [grandmother] talk to us in Hawaiian', she added, citing the resource language is for establishing cultural identity. But her resources were not enough; when last I heard, Mei-Ling's children remained in foster care.

While Julia, Mei-Ling, and the social worker did not refer explicitly to the loss of *kanaka maoli* sovereignty represented by the institutional decisions, the state's favouring of economic and structural considerations over cultural ones speaks to that outcome. At the heart of the matter is the persistently high number of Native Hawaiian children in the foster care system and the socio-economic disadvantages Native Hawaiians face in the American context. Variable definitions of abuse and neglect as well as of well-being and belonging exacerbate the situation, conceptual gaps that are particularly fraught for an Indigenous people in the 21st-century United States.

## Relationships: political and cultural

According to a Hawai'i State Statute, a child in foster care has the right 'To be treated fairly and equally and receive care and *services that are culturally responsive*' (italics mine).[12] Ideally, the right would be met by placing a Hawaiian child in a Hawaiian foster family.

Obstacles include the shortage of Native Hawaiian foster families, the goal of securing permanence, and, last but not least, the policies of federal government agencies that provide funding to state foster care programmes.

In its foster care issue, *Ka Wai Ola* draws on individual cases to prove the significance of culture in placement. A former foster child is quoted: 'If Hawaiian families are able to help foster kids keep connected to their culture it could mean everything. For me that was the missing link'. In conventional terms, Billie-Ann Bruce is a success – well educated and employed – yet she experiences a loss of Hawaiian culture: none of her foster parents shared her Hawaiian identity. She plans to become a foster parent and to transmit Hawaiian values to Native Hawaiian children in her care. A case a few pages later illustrates such an outcome. 'It feels good to give a Hawaiian child Hawaiian cultural experiences and raise her with Hawaiian values', said a parent about fostering and then adopting the child of a drug-addicted mother (Fernandez-Akamine, 2019, pp. 11, 14).

Like Mei-Ling, many native Hawaiian parents dispute the state's calculation of risk and decry its approaches to securing a child's well-being. That social workers share these perspectives was apparent at a staff meeting I attended at the Wai'anae Coast Comprehensive Health Center.

The meeting opened with a discussion of the spread of drug addiction in that part of O'ahu, populated largely by native Hawaiians. Marvin, a staff member, analysed the situation. 'The problems here are from poverty, not a cultural thing'. While he attributed the problem of addiction to structural inequities and the marginalization of a native population, he brought the solution home to the Hawaiian family and a tradition of caretaking. 'But the solutions can be Hawaiian', he concluded, 'the family taking everyone in, taking care'. He did not refer specifically to child abuse and neglect, instead extending *hānai*, the term colloquially applied to children, to include anyone in trouble. In Marvin's analysis, the solution was more important than the legislative definition of abuse and neglect.

In 1974, the federal government passed the Federal Child Abuse Prevention and Treatment Act (CAPTA). The act

> defines child abuse and neglect as, at a minimum, 'any recent act or failure to act on the part of a parent or caretaker which results in death, serious physical or emotional harm, sexual abuse or exploitation . . . or an act or failure to act which presents an imminent risk of serious harm'.

Hawai'i statutes do not range far from the federal definition. '"Child abuse or neglect" means the acts or omissions' by anyone responsible for the child, 'which have resulted in harm to the physical or psychological health or welfare of a child under age 18' or in potential harm (Child Abuse, 2011, § 350–1). Federal guidelines and state laws require that investigators assess the child's circumstances, a task that leaves much to individual discretion regarding the source of a child's well-being.

Caught between state law and federal guidelines, CWS workers are also expected to 'uphold ancient Hawaiian cultural traditions' in their decisions. Yet history shows how those traditions have been misinterpreted by outsiders, do-gooders, and experts. The legacy of the missionary viewpoint remains two centuries later, in an assumption that moving a child from one adult to another signals abandonment, neglect, or potential abuse. Reference to *hānai* indicates that these are not random moves, casual decisions, or disregard for the child. Under pressure to remove a child from harm, however, interpretations embedded in cultural differences may clash. Parents, CWS workers, activists, and politicians confront the resulting dilemma in several ways. A brief discussion of those approaches brings me to my conclusion.

## Native Hawaiian Child Welfare Act

At a CWS meeting I attended, several participants suggested that the best way out of the dilemma was to forego federal funding and the accompanying guidelines. While the assertion that those guidelines downplay Native Hawaiian culture gained sympathy, the consensus of the meeting was that federal funding had to be accepted if Hawaiian children are to be protected from harm and abuse. Foster care is expensive and the state cannot bear the costs alone.[13]

A more global approach considers control over child placement practices a 'right' due Native Hawaiians as an Indigenous people. This approach requires a delicate negotiation of U.S. acts barring race-based programmes. Funding for programmes addressing educational and health disparities, for example, scrupulously characterize Hawaiians as an Indigenous people and not a race. Under that principle, federal services should recognize the right of Native Hawaiians to determine the fate of Native Hawaiian children. According to the UN Declaration on the Rights of Indigenous Peoples, Indigenous people 'shall not be subjected to any act of genocide or any other act of violence, including forcibly removing children of the group to another group' (UN Declaration on the Rights of Indigenous People, 2007, Article 7 [2]). But the problem for Native Hawaiians is twofold: first, the congressional attribution of 'unique status' does not in fact acknowledge an Indigenous people but rather a group to whom the United States bears a trust relationship; and second, although Native Hawaiians understand themselves as a nation (*lāhui*), they have no representation which is recognized by the United States. The result is denial of autonomy in placement decisions.

On 28 January 2015, State Senator Maile Shimabukuro, representing Wai'anae, introduced a bill, 'Relating to Native Hawaiian Children', to the State Senate.[14] SB

992 proposes the creation of a Native Hawaiian Child Welfare Act that 'establishes the Na Kupuna Tribunal and grants it exclusive jurisdiction over child custody proceedings involving native Hawaiian children' (Relating to Native Hawaiian Children, 2015).

The bill opens by declaring

> that it is the policy of this State to protect the cultural and traditional interests of native Hawaiian children and to promote the stability and security of native Hawaiian families by . . . [e]stablishing standards for the removal of native Hawaiian children from their families and the placement of these children in *hanai* or *lawe hanai* homes that will reflect the unique values of native Hawaiian culture.
>
> (Relating to Native Hawaiian Children, 2015)

The bill was modelled on the ICWA, a long-debated act designed to grant tribes control over the placement of Native American children. Like the ICWA, SB 992 holds that decisions about the placement of a child should be in the hands of those whose collective survival depends on the continuity of generations. The Association of Hawaiian Civic Clubs (AHCC), a century-old guardian of native traditions, testified in support of the bill and agreed to become a Na Kupuna Tribunal partner on behalf of Native Hawaiian children. 'The AHCC is painfully aware of the multitude of problems that beset our Native Hawaiian families and that we are singularly set up to access cultural, genealogical, and nonprofit as well as governmental support for native based experiences' (Kalili, 2015).

Members of the legislative Committees on Hawaiian Affairs and Human Services and Housing accepted SB 992 into discussion, with deletions (Hawai'i Government Committee Reports). The deletions eliminate the two parts that describe Hawai'i's relationship to the U.S. federal government, that establish an independent tribunal, and that attribute 'special status' to native Hawaiians. Part I reiterates congressional responsibility for 'the protection and preservation of native Hawaiians and their resources', adding 'that there is no resource that is more vital to the continued existence and integrity of native Hawaiians than their children'. Part II provides a parsimonious definition of native Hawaiian: 'any person who is a linear descendant of the people who exercised sovereignty in Hawaii prior to 1778' as well as any community eligible for 'special programs and services provided by the United States to native Hawaiians because of their status as native Hawaiians' (Relating to Native Hawaiian Children, 2015).

On 22 January 2016, the Hawai'i state legislature declared SB 992 'dead'. Opposition to the bill from Republican and Libertarian, family lawyers and adoption attorneys, politicians, and social workers dominated the debate. Arguments included the threat a tribunal poses to legislative sovereignty, the problematic definition of 'Native Hawaiian', and the misleading model of tribal governance. The points were publicized in the sympathetic *Hawaii Free Press*. The article pointed out the 'devastating results' of petitioning for 'the transfer of proceedings involving a native Hawaiian child from any other state to its jurisdiction'. Even more 'devastating' was the establishment of a tribunal on the model of the ICWA, which would turn Native Hawaiians into 'a fake Indian tribe'. Finally, the granting of special rights to Native Hawaiians under the proposed tribunal is presented as discrimination bordering on racism (Walden, 2015). 'The preference, as applied, is granted to Indians not as a discrete racial group, but, rather, as members of quasi-sovereign tribal entities' (*Morton v. Mancari*, 1974). Even with the softening marked by '*kupuna*', the term for grandparent, arguments against the Na Kupuna Tribunal triumphed.

In a compromise, legislators established a working group composed of organizations and individuals concerned with the condition of Native Hawaiian children and specifically with the proportionately high number in foster care. The group came under the supervision of 'the Hawaii State Legislature's Keiki Caucus', and 'Na Kupuna Tribunal' was replaced by 'Legacy Coalition', a religiously based grandparent group whose concern is the well-being of children (Standard Committee Report SR 105). The Legislative Keiki Caucus focuses on 'the education, health and well-being of children in Hawai'i. The Zero to 3 Court specializes in cases of abused or neglected infants and toddlers by providing judicial oversight and social services' (Yoshioka, 2019). The Keiki Caucus takes all children in Hawai'i under its aegis, denying Native Hawaiian children any special consideration. DHS and its Child Welfare Division retain responsibility for providing Native Hawaiian children with 'culturally sensitive services', as mandated by statute.

Debates over SB 992 in 2015 and 2016 publicized the links between child placement and broader conceptual and political issues. Subjects of discussion included the distinction between race and indigeneity under U.S. law, the postcolonial condition that leads to the disproportionately high number of Native Hawaiian children in foster care, and the ongoing controversy over the meaning and implementation of nationhood. While the bill died, those subjects continue to thrive.

## Conclusion: a call to action

In February 2018, President Donald Trump slipped a foster care provision into the year's Bipartisan Budget Act. Barely noticed outside Congress (and maybe even inside Congress), the title of the legislation is 'Family First Prevention Services Act'. The act intends to limit foster care placements by providing help to families 'through the provision of mental health and substance abuse prevention and treatment services, in-home parent skill-based programs, and kinship navigator services'.[15] The euphemistic 'navigator services' means that placement with kin will be carefully monitored and qualifications as foster parent rigorously imposed.

According to a Pew Trust report,

> The law will place a burden on extended family members who are raising grandchildren, nieces and nephews outside of foster care. That's because 'kinship caregivers' won't be eligible for foster care payments under the new law'.
>
> (Wiltz, 2018)

The hairbreadth difference in language is a large difference in practice; a caregiver is not the same as an officially approved foster parent.

> The CWS caseworker is required to make every effort possible to place your child with safe relatives, kin, hanai, or family friends, who can meet the licensing requirements as special-licensed resource caregivers for your child'.
> (*A guide to child welfare services*, September 2020, p. 9)

Yet my encounters show that many of the named will not or cannot be licenced – creating the shortage PIDF bemoans.

The crux of the matter is the intertwining of crucial funding with guidelines that violate Native Hawaiian cultural traditions. The Family First Act weakens the state extension of *hānai* by effectively transforming a kin-based arrangement into a bureaucratic contract. *Hānai*, in other words, is no longer the exchange Lili'uokalani lovingly described in her book but the appointment of a 'resource parent' by an expert. The brunt of Family First, however, does away with foster care entirely (or lessens it as much as possible) by privileging the role of a nuclear family, the Western model of safety and permanence.[16] A child who is removed should, in the best-case scenario, be returned to his or her biological parent, implicitly a mother; federal funding under the act provides for parent 'training'.[17] Without damning reunification policies, it is still important to note the ways in which such policies transgress the very culture that, under the 1978 constitution, CWS workers are pledged to uphold. In a circular narrative, the act harks back to the early 19th-century missionary critique that moving a child from adult to adult destroys an essential biological bond between parent (mother) and child. But the Hawaiians acted otherwise. As a PIDF member put it, 'child fostering by *'ohana* or a family friend is the best-case scenario for children removed from their homes' (Fernandez-Akamine, 2019, p. 12).

Neither the death of a state legislative bill nor the agenda of a Trump presidency ended protest or stymies efforts to take control of the placement of Native Hawaiian children. 'Native Hawaiians are natural advocates, especially for things like children', said Jonathan Kay Kamakawiwo'ole Osorio, who adopted a foster child and who is, not incidentally, a scholar of the Hawaiian nation. His statement appears in the *Ka Wai Ola* foster care issue, in a section subtitled 'A Call to Action for the *Lahui*'. The subtitle unmistakably attaches the care of children to the vigour and resilience of a nation – the *lāhui*. 'My vision is that Hawaiians will just stand up and say, okay, we are going to fulfill the *kuleana* [responsibility] that we've always had: the care of our children' (Fernandez-Akamine, 2019, p. 13).

Often relegated to the literature on kinship, foster care displays the acute conflict between custom and law that evolves over centuries of contact between an Indigenous people and an imperial state. A system for placing children, in other words, provides insight into the 'fast and multidimensional transformations' that affect and challenge all contemporary Pacific Islander societies today. In the particular case of Hawai'i, foster care policies and practices also bring up the longstanding problem of Indigenous rights in the United States. Do Native Hawaiians have the 'right' to insert culture into foster care practices given the 'precarious position' the group holds as an Indigenous people (Kauanui, 2005)? As long as both state and federal law side-step the rights of the Indigenous people of the Hawaiian archipelago, the fight for control over child placement will depend on the voices of those directly involved in the system – those who embrace the *kuleana* bequeathed by former generations.

The 'Call to Action for the *Lahui*' does not die, and neither does the meaning of *lāhui* as nationhood. The word is a reminder that foster care is not simply an individual moment or a single court case, but rather a deeply entrenched reference to autonomy and to being a 'nation' even without the institution of an independent governing entity. An analysis of foster care and child placement practices reveals both the pressures on a changing Pacific Island that is an American state and the unresolved problem of an increasing number of native children whose circumstances place them in the way of harm.

## Acknowledgements

My first thanks go to Loïs Bastide and Denis Regnier for inviting me to participate in the volume. I benefited enormously from the close reading done by my colleagues Noah Theriault, Barbara Yngvesson, and Mikaela Wolf-Sorokin. As always, Albrecht Funk did first, last, and middle readings, and I am grateful for the time he took. The errors are, of course, my own.

## Notes

1 Native Hawaiian with an uppercase 'N' refers to all persons of Hawaiian ancestry regardless of blood quantum. I have used the capital 'N' except where the reference is clearly to Hawaiians who meet the 50% blood quantum definition.
2 The *'ohana* is composed of biological kin as well as those persons who become family members through a social (constructed) relationship.
3 The problem of 'taking children' has received less attention in the Hawaiian case than in the cases of Aboriginal populations, American Indians, and Blacks in the United States. Explanations lie in the history of Hawaiian-US relationships and, until recently, the downplaying of American imperialism as enacted through control over children.
4 'Under ICWA, all child welfare court proceedings involving Native American children must be heard in tribal courts if possible, and tribes have the right to intervene in state court proceedings. ICWA also established specific guidelines for family reunification and placement of Native American children'. www.masslegalservices.org/system/files/library/Brief%20Legislative%20History%20of%20Child%20Welfare%20System.pdf
5 Often considered the first adoption law in the United States, the 1851 Massachusetts law included discussion of inheritance, the entailments of an adoptive contract, and parental responsibilities. But formal requirements had appeared a decade earlier in the Hawaiian statute.
6 At the end of the 20th century, adoption reformers in Hawai'i referred to *hānai* in demanding that full knowledge of his or her biological background be provided to an adoptee.
7 By self-report. The next highest group is Japanese and Okinawan, at 19%.
8 I do not know the ethnicity of the CPS social worker.
9 Don meets the 50% blood quantum.

10  On 1 September 2006, the PIDF was awarded a master contract from DHS to create and implement innovative strategies to better meet the needs of Hawai'i's children in foster care as well as the Resource Families who care for them. https://humanservices.hawaii. gov/ssd/home/child-welfare-services/pidf-contract/
11  She had proved her 50% Hawaiian blood quantum.
12  The statute continues:

> and free from discrimination based on race, ethnicity, color, national origin, ancestry, immigration status, gender, gender identity, gender expression, sexual orientation, religion, physical and mental disability, pregnant or parenting status, or the fact that the child is in foster care.
>
> (Child Protective Act, 2016)

13  States get reimbursed for foster care through funding provided by Title IV-E of the Social Security Act, and that money can be used only for foster care, adoption, or family reunification.
14  In 2007, HB 1895, with the same title, was introduced in the State House of Representatives but not passed.
15  The full paragraph reads: 'The purpose of this subtitle is to enable States to use Federal funds available under parts B and E of title IV of the Social Security Act to provide enhanced support to children and families and prevent foster care placements through the provision of mental health and substance abuse prevention and treatment services, in-home parent skill-based programs, and kinship navigator services'. According to Pew, it 'will force states to overhaul their foster care systems by changing the rules for how they can spend their annual $8 billion in federal funds for child abuse prevention'.
16  This is also, of course, a cost-saving measure.
17  DHS celebrates National Reunification Month every year; http://humanservices.hawaii. gov/?s=foster%20care&type=network&searchblogs=1,2,3,4,5,8

## References

Bastide, L., & Regnier, D. (2023). *Family violence and social change in the Pacific Islands.*
Child Abuse, Hawaii Revised Statute § 350–1 (2011).
Child Protective Act, Hawaii Revised Statute §§ 587A-4; 587A-9; 587A-3 (2016).
Fernandez-Akamine, P. (2019). "Exceptional Resilience," "Pehea Nā Keiki?" and "Ka 'Ohana Osorio". *Ka Wai Ola, 36*(12), 11–15.
*A guide to child welfare services.* (2020). Honolulu, HI: State of Hawaii Department of Human Services.
Kalili, D. (2015). *Ka Nuhou – The news, a weekly digest.* Retrieved from http://piilani.org/ aloha/wp-content/uploads/2015/04/Gmail-AHCC-Ka-Nuhou-April-12-2015.pdf
Kauanui, J. K. (2005). Precarious positions: Native Hawaiians and federal recognition. *Contemporary Pacific, 17*(1), 1–27.
Kauanui, J. K. (2018). *Paradoxes of Hawaiian sovereignty: Land, sex, and the colonial politics of state nationalism.* Durham, NC: Duke University Press.
Lili'uokalani. (1990 [1898]). *Hawaii's story by Hawaii's queen.* Honolulu, HI: Mutual Publishing.
Look, M. A., Trask-Batti, M. K., Agres, R., Mau, M. L., & Kaholokula, J. K. (2013). *Assessment and priorities for health & well-being in Native Hawaiians & other Pacific peoples.* Honolulu, HI: Center for Native and Pacific Health Disparities Research.
Modell [Schachter], J. (2008). "A relationship endeared to the people": Adoption in Hawaiian custom and law. *Pacific Studies, 31*(3/4), 211–231.

Mokuau, N. (2002). Culturally based interventions for substance use and child abuse among Native Hawaiians. *Public Health Reports, 117*(1), 82–87.

*Morton v. Mancari*, 417 U.S. 535 (1974).

*Native Hawaiian Data Book.* (2019). Honolulu, HI: Office of Hawaiian Affairs. Retrieved from http://hhdw.org/office-of-hawaiian-affairs-2019-native-hawaiian-data-book/

Partners in Development Foundation. (2020a). *Foster care: It's our kuleana.* Honolulu, HI: PIDF.

Partners in Development Foundation. (2020b). *Hui ho'omalu.* Honolulu, HI: PIDF.

Perez, R. (2016, January 10). Hawaiians at risk: Keiki locked in cycle of foster care system. *Honolulu Advertiser*, p. 1.

Pukui, M. K., Haertig, E. W., & Lee, C. A. (1972). *Nānā I Ke Kumu (Look to the source).* Honolulu, HI: Queen Liliʻuokalani Children's Center.

Relating to Native Hawaiian Children, Hawaii SB 992. (2015). Retrieved from https://legiscan.com/HI/text/SB992/id/1093189

Standard Committee Report No. 1202. (2015, April 1). Retrieved from www.capitol.hawaii.gov/session2015/CommReports/SR105_sd1_sscr1202_.pdf

United Nations Declaration on the Rights of Indigenous People (2007).

Viotti, V. (2004). Retrieved November 11, 2020, from http://the.honoluluadvertiser.com/article/2004/Nov/10/ln/ln16p.html

Walden, A. (2015, February 17). SB992: Creates tribal judiciary, places 12,000 Hawaiian children at risk. *Hawaii Free Press*, p. 1.

Wiltz, T. (2018). *This new federal law will change foster care as we know it.* Retrieved from www.pewtrusts.org/en/research-and-analysis/blogs/stateline/2018/05/02/this-new-federal-law-will-change-foster-care-as-we-know-it

Yoshioka, W. (2019, January 30). Hawaiʻi Legislative Keiki Caucus: Year of the child. *Hawaii Public Radio*. Retrieved from www.hawaiipublicradio.org/post/hawaii-legislative-keiki-caucus-year-child#stream/0

# 3 Transferred children and the production of family violence in French Polynesia

## Social change and the adaptations of *fa'a'amura'a*

*Loïs Bastide*

According to the available data, French Polynesia has the highest rate of family violence in France and its overseas territories (Clanché, 2017, pp. 154–156). This seems in line with what we know about other Pacific Islands societies, where a high prevalence of domestic violence has been consistently documented over the past 10 years (Heard, Fitzgerald, Whittaker, Va'ai, & Mutch, 2020). In the case of French Polynesia, however, this is all the more striking, because the *fenua* ('country') is also remarkable for having one of the lowest rates, at the French national level, of interpersonal violence outside the household.

In this chapter, we draw on our ongoing fieldwork to shed some light on this paradox. To understand family violence and its prevalence in French Polynesia, we posit that a few identifiable social processes are at play in the many forms of violence taking place within the family. Family violence, we contend, is a coherent social phenomenon with its own underlying dynamics, distinct from other forms of violence.

Here, we focus on one aspect of our findings: the relationship between mobilities within the family – particularly frequent in the *fenua*, where individuals typically move many times between different households during their life course – and violence within the family. Mobility, in turn, cannot be understood without taking into consideration the dynamics of migration between the islands and archipelagos of the territory,[1] which is in large part due to a very unbalanced geography of development.

To explore the relationship between mobility and family violence in French Polynesia, we highlight the specific situation of children who are raised, cared for, or fostered by adults other than their biological parents, either permanently or during a given period of time. As we shall see, the transfers of filiation – a common social practice in the region – lay the groundwork for the development of heightened forms of vulnerability. These children provide a particularly telling example of the relationship between mobility and violence in the French Polynesian context.

We start this chapter with a brief presentation of our research methodology before introducing a working definition of our two main concepts: violence as a social process, and the family as a social unit. In the following section of the

DOI: 10.4324/9781003146667-4

chapter, we propose to approach the contemporary French Polynesian family through the lenses of 'practical kinship' (Bourdieu, 1972, p. 151; Weber, 2005). The fourth section elaborates on the relationship between family and spatial mobilities, stressing the importance of social capital. In the last part, we discuss the case of the transferred child as an analytical figure, which allows us to explain the relationship between mobility within the family and family violence.

## Some remarks on methodology

The data upon which this chapter is based were collected for an ongoing research programme on family violence in French Polynesia, launched at the Maison des Sciences de l'Homme et du Pacifique in early 2018.

This material consists of 43 in-depth biographical interviews (life stories), with 37 different respondents. With these interviews, we aimed at capturing individual 'careers' (Abbott, 1997; Becker, 1963; Goffman, 1971) of family violence. They were carried out with victims, but also with perpetrators, we often met in jail. Interviewees were recruited through advertisements in the local press, through our contacts at non-governmental organizations (NGOs), and at the two penitentiary centres in Tahiti, as well as emails to university students.

Our current sample includes 31 victims (5 having themselves, on occasion, exerted violence within their family) and 6 perpetrators (among them, 5 can also be considered victims of family violence). We interviewed 26 women, all mainly victims, and 11 men, among whom 6 were mainly perpetrators and 5 can be considered as both victims and perpetrators.[2] The median age of our respondents was 27, with all of them having ages between 19 and 58 at the time of the interview.

These interviews gave us a picture of what we could call different 'family universes'.[3] Indeed, the individual narratives offered rich descriptions of a broad set of situations of family violence, beyond individual cases, as our respondents dug into their family life and retrieved memories of violent situations and relationships.

Since direct observation of family violence was impossible, we triangulated these data with press reports on family violence, starting from the 1980s, as well as with observations of court hearings in Papeete. We were thus able to map the gradual emergence of family violence as a public issue in French Polynesia, and to document the arguments and justifications exchanged by the plaintiffs, the accused, and witnesses, in the context of judiciary trials. Provided we anonymized the data, an NGO also granted us access to its archives, which consist of individual files of homeless people in the urban area of Papeete and its surroundings. Thanks to these additional sources, we were able to confront the findings from interviews with other types of data, rife with many occurrences of family violence.

## Family and violence: a conceptual note

When dealing with family violence, most institutions and, perhaps more astonishingly, many academic works either fail to define both violence and family or only define violence, treating family as a self-evident category. This has the (somewhat exorbitant) advantage of making comparisons across regions, countries, and cultures seem unproblematic. However, the value of such comparisons is, at best, poor, since they put on an equal footing highly heterogeneous family configurations, which shape distinctive social contexts for violence. These differences in family configurations, in turn, can directly influence the way family violence is recorded and quantified. Dealing with family violence thus requires accounting for the distinctive boundaries and relational economies of family and kinship across social groups, and devising a working definition of violence. Let us first turn to the definition of violence.

## *Violence*

Violence is notoriously difficult to define from a social science perspective (Naepels, 2006). Part of the difficulty comes from its inherently normative aspect. Violence is often viewed by both lay persons and critical thinkers as a social pathology in need of a remedy (Wieviorka, 1998). At best, violence is considered as a necessary evil, justified under specific circumstances – as a weapon against oppression, in the context of war or resistance struggles, in the case of self-defence, or as a power of coercion exclusive to the state (Weber, 2003). Furthermore, violence has been increasingly used to qualify a wide range of social phenomena and processes. Notions such as 'verbal violence', 'symbolic violence', and 'structural violence' have been developed to account for social patterns whose relation to the infliction of physical damage is thin.

In order to turn the notion of violence into an actionable analytical concept, we need to do two things. First, we must isolate its analytical content from its normative content. In social analysis, norms and values can be studied, but they cannot be used as an analytical device. As we will see, this is not an easy task, since violence, as a label applicable to certain actions, always involves a moral or an ethical stance. Second, it is necessary to restrict the concept to a consistent and homogenous set of empirical facts. If we fail to do so we risk weakening its analytical value.

To isolate the analytical content of violence and restrict its concept to homogenous facts, we follow Randal Collins' micro sociological approach to violence, conceived as the infliction of physical damage (Collins, 2008). We do so even though we acknowledge that many forms of physical harm cannot be equated with violence if they are not socially 'labelled' as such (Becker, 1963; Lemert, 1973). For instance, cutting through the skin in the context of a street feud, a surgical act, or as part of scarification practices does not hold the same social meaning (Bastide, 2020; Protar, this volume). To qualify as violence, an act needs to be carried out with the primary goal of inflicting harm. We thus choose to define violence as the agonistic, intentional, and socially unacceptable infliction of bodily damage. This brings us back to the issue of normativity, since the boundaries between socially acceptable (or even valued) bodily harm and an act defined as a violent assault ultimately depend on value judgements based on social norms, which are specific to particular societies and cultures (Collier & Lakoff, 2005; Zigon, 2010).

Consequently, we assume that the distinction between violent and non-violent acts is always a situated, empirical question, since it cannot be made in abstract terms but only from a given moral (and social) position.

We also follow Collins' radical empirical approach, which considers that the most significant factors of violence are not to be found in social structure, nor in individual psychologies (or character). In his view, violence is a situational outcome. Its roots lay in the interactional dynamics between those who participate in the violent event (see also Stewart & Strathern, 2002, and this volume). Violence thus needs to be analysed at this very level, the situation, or in other words at the level of unfolding, sited social interactions.

Collins insightfully observes that violence, as a social action, is always difficult (Collins, 2008, p. 20). Indeed, it goes against the 'natural' dynamics of social interactions, which tend to drive participants towards a shared emotional entrainment, cooperation, and solidarity. Understanding violence therefore means understanding the properties of violent situations, that is, the properties of social interactions in which the social inhibition of violence is overcome and violence is unleashed. In our case studies, these violent situations are structured by their embeddedness in family relations in the sociocultural context of French Polynesia. Our goal is thus to identify the social and cultural factors which fuel the proliferation of violent interactions within families in the territory.

## *Family*

It goes without saying that families in the Pacific Islands have undergone dramatic changes and transformations since the first contacts with Westerners, as demonstrated also by other contributors in the current volume (McIntosh, Strathern, Reids). In the *fenua*, these shifts occurred against the backdrop of evangelization, colonization, and the more recent extension of capitalist relations across the five archipelagos. Unfortunately, there is a dearth of research on these issues. The most extensive anthropological studies of kinship and family in French Polynesia were conducted 50 years ago (Ottino, 1972; Panoff, 1965), and since then little research has been carried out, with the remarkable exception of Tamatoa Bambridge's study on land tenure in the Australes archipelago (Bambridge, 2009). Moreover, Ottino's work, for example, used a structuralist framework, with a strong orientation towards abstract models. While his book remains an extremely valuable documentation of kinship in Rangiroa, it unfortunately provides an idealized (or reified) view of family structures. A key part of our research, by contrast, consists in exploring some of the contemporary configurations of French Polynesian families through the conceptual lenses of 'practical kinship' (Weber, 2005) and 'family ideology' (Singly, 2017), with the aim of capturing the current context of family violence.

Family ideology consists of a set of socially legitimate ways of relating to, and conceiving of, the family and family ties, through consensual semantic categories, shared social norms, and values. As such, it provides an idealization of actual family practices, which tend to be more flexible and adaptive to pragmatic circumstances (Protar, 2020). Practical kinship, on the other hand, refers to the idea that family life exceeds this consensual, symbolic construction in many ways. To understand practical kinship, that is, actual family relations and practices, Florence Weber (2005), drawing on the work of Pierre Bourdieu, proposes to consider three different conceptual layers when we look at family as an empirical object. First, she suggests considering kinship as a normative category based on a shared *name*. At a second level, kinship is to be considered as a specific network of relations, where biological ties play a key role. Both these analytical levels constitute what we have just called 'family ideology'. Finally, the family is *actually* constituted through daily interactions among people who consider themselves as relatives. The family is thus an institution (a set of norms and values), a cognitive construct (a way of perceiving the social), and a relational practice. From this perspective, it can not only be considered as a substantive category, but it must also always be treated as a social entity in the making. Consequently, it has to be analysed as un unfolding process, accomplished and negotiated continuously through the activation and reworking of specific family relations. Because it encompasses these three levels, the practical kinship approach is a good theoretical tool to deal with family life (and family violence) as an empirical reality, and even more so in a context of fast social change, since it allows us to look at its constant adaptation to evolving circumstances, both as an ideology and as a praxis.

## From the *feti'i* model of family relations to practical kinship

In his study of Rangiroa, the largest Atoll of the Tuamotu archipelago, Ottino identified different levels of organization in kinship structures (Ottino, 1972). For the sake of our argument, we will focus on two of them: the *'ōpū feti'i* and the *'ōpū ho'e*.

The *'ōpū feti'i* includes all descendants from a common couple, or ancestor. It defines kinship in its largest extension. The *'ōpū ho'e*, however, is more restrictive, since it consists, in its broader understanding, of siblings, their children, and grandchildren. The term can be used more restrictively to encompass a single couple and its descendance over two generations – children and grandchildren. In anthropological terms, it is a cognatic (bilateral or undifferentiated) descent group, or 'stock' – a ramage. The individual is thus included in a large set of kinship relations: since kinship is bilateral, one belongs to both her paternal and maternal *'ōpū feti'i* and *'ōpū ho'e*. Given the large number of individuals in an *'ōpū feti'i*, many of its members never interact in meaningful ways. Conversely, the *'ōpū ho'e* is where most sustained social interactions take place, not least because it is tightly associated with land tenure and inheritance. These issues bring relatives together on a regular basis, and often in conflictual circumstances (Bambridge, 2009).

In addition to delineating the scope of interpersonal relations in the context of family ties, the *feti'i* model of family relations, as a family ideology, defines the rules organizing social interactions among its members – forms of reciprocity and redistribution, mutual expectations, and obligations. Importantly, *'ōpū ho'e* relatives are expected to show solidarity with each other. A branch of a *'ōpū opu ho'e* living in Tahiti, the most developed island of French Polynesia, may be asked to host children from relatives living in more remote locations, for example, because the children have to move to Papeete to attend high school. Such a demand is difficult to reject without risking one's social reputation and status, not only in the family but also in the broader community.[4]

These expectations are, however, increasingly threatened by imported family models. Traditional family norms, values, roles, and obligations are challenged by a growing aspiration, among the younger generation, to emancipate from the broader family (conceived as *'ōpū feti'i* or *'ōpū ho'e*) and to form a *petite famille* ('small family'), a model corresponding to the nuclear family as the main locus of family interactions and practical kinship. Despite ongoing social changes, however, the *feti'i* model of kinship organization (*'ōpū feti'i* and *'ōpū ho'e*) still has a strong normative value, even though its traditional material base, founded on co-residence (Ottino, 1970), has for the most part vanished, at least in the case of the *'ōpū feti'i*. As a family ideology, it continues to frame individual and collective attitudes and conceptions towards family life.

Regarding family violence, two things are worth stressing: first, the set of relations encompassed by the *'ōpū ho'e* and even more so by the *'ōpū feti'i* is much broader than in typical 'Western' families, where family ties are much more focused on the conjugal – or nuclear – family. This in itself probably increases mechanically the risks of violent occurrences. Second, mutual expectations, reciprocity, and obligations within the family context are both more tightly defined and more imperative in French Polynesian families than in the 'relational family' model, most common in the West (Singly, 2017), where they appear increasingly idiosyncratic.

As a bundle of social ties and a set of rules of interactions, the *feti'i* model can thus be seen in terms of a latent relational field, available to the individuals when they face life circumstances – it shapes situational affordances (Gibson, 1977). In these circumstances, everyone within the *'ōpū feti'i* thus interacts with a subset of relatives: some family members tend to seek greater autonomy from the broader family context, while others rely more intensively (or often) and/or extensively (with a greater set of kin) on family resources. By mobilizing family ideology (the *feti'i* model of mutual obligations and solidarity) in the context of his or her lineage, every member of the *feti'i* 'performs' family relations by nurturing specific interactions and delineating the perimeter of practical kinship. We thus use the phrase 'practical kinship' to describe the social ties that are activated among all possible family relations.

## Family relations, spatial mobility, and social capital

Practical kinship thus results from the many ways individuals deal with family relations. This, in turn, is partly determined by the fact that they rely on the family, under its different possible configurations (*petite famille, 'ōpū ho'e*, and *'ōpū feti'i*), to respond to specific life events and circumstances. In this respect, the family can be viewed as constituting a 'social capital' (Forsé, 2001; Lallement,

2006) – which we could call 'family capital' and which can play out in many ways, in relation to all sorts of situations. This capital plays a major role in a context where livelihood increasingly depends on market relations – in a now established market economy, one where many individuals suffer from poor access to monetary resources (ISPF, 2015) and weak public safety nets, families thus often play a critical role in supporting individuals.

In French Polynesia, a striking aspect of this family capital relates to the critical importance of spatial mobility in structuring contemporary, individual existences. The *fenua* is characterized by its extreme spatial scattering. It occupies an area roughly the size of Europe (5.5 million square kilometres), with only 4,167 square kilometres of emerged land, spread across 118 islands. In addition, it is plagued by a deeply unbalanced geography of development, as most public services, amenities, jobs, and economic opportunities are in Tahiti and almost entirely contained within Papeete's urban area. The imperative of accessing these highly centralized resources – school and health services, the job market, administrative services, cultural and consumer goods, etc. – or dealing with family matters causes most people to move to or from Tahiti at a certain point – momentarily, repeatedly, or permanently. Mobility between other islands is also frequent.

Many respondents within our sample recounted that they left their childhood household for schooling, sometimes as early as in early secondary school. Some of them were, as children, successively under the care of different relatives, moving along family networks. As young adults, some had moved back and forth several times, either to look for jobs in Tahiti, in search of the 'good life' in Papeete, or to work elsewhere – for example, in pearl farms. Others had also moved to take ownership of a piece of family property, or to live with a partner from another island.

Spatial mobility is integral and critical to the ordinary, individual life course in French Polynesia. It also comes at a prohibitive cost, especially for transportation and lodging.[5] To mitigate these costs, the *'ōpū feti'i*, most often in the more limited relational context of the *'ōpū hoe'e*, operates as an efficient 'migration infrastructure' (Xiang & Lindquist, 2014) by allowing individuals to move along family networks, thus circumventing the economic burden of spatial mobility. Because *'ōpū ho'e* are shaped by norms of mutual support and hospitality, they play a key role in facilitating and framing mobilities across the archipelagos. Since *'ōpū ho'e* are almost always spread across different islands, they facilitate access to spatially scattered resources. As a result, the high spatial mobility which is characteristic of French Polynesia tends to overlap with mobilities within the family. It thus keeps individuals in situations of close economic and/or residential (inter)dependency on the family (maternal or paternal *feti'i* or in-laws).

This is in stark contrast with contemporary 'Western' families, where adulthood tends to constitute a biographical 'turning point' (Abbott, 1997) for the individual. Young adults are expected to reach financial and residential autonomy and to found their own, autonomous family unit, in the form of a new nuclear family. Individuals subsequently tend to nurture elective social ties with a number of selected relatives beyond the conjugal household (Singly, 2017), in a context where family solidarities have been replaced by public safety nets.

In contemporary French Polynesia (as in the broader 'Polynesian world'), family resources play a greater role in organizing individual social trajectories. Moreover, this process of individual emancipation with regards to the family is not expected or valued. In fact, it is quite the opposite: individuals are strongly expected to remain in the domain of the *feti'i*. Individuals therefore live in much closer association with their *feti'i* in terms of practical kinship. This results in both more intense (or frequent) and more extensive relations with other family members. It also involves a persistent dependency throughout the life course on the family as a critical provider of resources. This greater dependency on family resources shapes a context for family violence. In particular, it defines specific forms of vulnerability for those who are most reliant on family material and immaterial (i.e., symbolic, moral, and affective) support.

## Mobility, family, and vulnerability: the case of transferred children

Spatial mobility thus illustrates most strikingly the strong dependency of the individual vis-à-vis family resources. As it entails moving between households within the *feti'i*, it carries a high risk of generating violent behaviours. Indeed, such arrangements are often based on necessity rather than choice, on the part of both the moving individual and the receiving household, often in a context of scarce material resources, or even deprivation. As a result, it increases pressure on livelihood, and it feeds interpersonal tensions (Taerea & Bastide, 2022). Thus, our argument does not focus on migration itself. Rather, spatial mobility is worth exploring to the extent that it sheds a crude light on a more fundamental property of family life in the *fenua*: the high degree to which family members depend on family resources among many Polynesian families, as well as the high rates of mobility within the *feti'i*. In turn, dependency, as a typical form of social relation, shapes a favourable terrain for the development of violent relations (Collins, 2008, pp. 134–155; Memmi, Cousin, & Lambert, 2019). We now turn towards *fa'a'amura'a* – the transfer of children between parental households – as an extreme form of family mobility – the transfer of filiation – and of dependency – considering that children are particularly *dependent* on their parents for the fulfilment of their biological, symbolic, moral, and affective needs.

### Fa'a'amura'a as a social institution

The social organization of families thus generates structural positions of vulnerability vis-à-vis violence. To explore this issue, we focus on 'adopted'[6] children whose social situation combines a high dependency regarding the fulfilment of their basic needs, with a radical form of family mobility – the transfer of filiation relations – which often entails deep social, affective, and material uncertainties.

In French Polynesia, as in many societies across Oceania, the adoption of children is an old social practice, well attested since the first encounter with European sailors in the 18th century. In Tahiti, this practice is known under the name of

*fa'a'amura'a,* which refers to the act of 'nurturing' or 'feeding' an infant. Historically, this type of transaction seems to have been a very important institution. It
was an integral part of 'kinning practices' (Howell, 2003) – practices intended to
generate or support kinship ties – to broaden or strengthen the links, alliances,
and solidarities within or between *feti'i* (Asselin, 2020; Panoff, 1970). This social
transaction was a crucial way of dealing with issues of alliance, land tenure, and
inheritance.

In practice, the *fa'a'amura'a* involves transferring a child from the filiation,
care, responsibility, and authority of his or her biological parents to those of a
relative or relatives, most often a grandparent, an aunt, or an uncle from either
ramage (paternal or maternal). The initiators of the transaction can be the biological parents, the receiving household, or, today, the child herself who sometimes takes shelter in another household within the *feti'i.* When a demand for a
child (or a child to be born) is expressed by legitimate relatives, rejecting this
demand can be exceedingly difficult for the natural parents. Unlike the French
legal adoption system, the *fa'a'amura'a* does not involve the severing of biological ties. The inclusion of a child in her new filiation is additive rather than
substitutive. As far as inheritance is concerned, the child can thus be legitimately
seen as belonging to both sides – the lineages of her biological *and fa'a'amu*
parents (Asselin, 2020).

In contemporary French Polynesia the *fa'a'amura'a* is still widespread. A recent
survey conducted by a research team from the French National Institute of Demographic Studies (INED) found that at the age of 45, 12% of women had given a
child away. Moreover, 20% of women between 55 and 59 and 24% of women
between 70 and 74 declared having *fa'a'amu* children to care for (Sierra-Paycha,
Lelièvre, & Trabut, 2018). This apparent continuity of a traditional practice results
in part from the fact that the terminology is somehow deceitful: the word is often
used as an unproblematic Tahitian equivalent for adoption and is applied to situations which differ, sometimes radically, from the 'historical' *fa'a'amura'a* (for a
similar issue in the context of Hawai'i, see Schachter, this volume). This apparent continuity should not hide the fact that the practice has undergone profound
transformations.

Two important shifts occurred that concern the reach of the *fa'a'amura'a* and
its purpose. First, today children can be adopted outside of their biological parents'
*feti'i,* as in the case of French Polynesian children adopted by European families.
Second, the transfer of children now widely exceeds the practical domain of 'kinning' and alliance-making, as it can respond to a much broader array of reasons.
To grasp this variety, Jean-Vital de Monléon (2002) proposed a typology of the
reasons behind adoption in contemporary French Polynesian families. In addition
to its traditional purpose, adoption is now being used as an alternative to family
planning – reducing a couple's number of children. It is also an answer to conjugal
issues when, for example, children from a previous union are entrusted to their
biological grandparents. It is a response to social and economic pressure, in the
context of a market economy, when giving a child away alleviates situations of
economic or social distress.

Our data show that this typology can in fact be extended ad libitum: motives behind the transfer of a child appear highly circumstantial, and the rationales behind adoptions are heterogeneous (Benjamin, Chang, & Steele, 2019). To what extent is it still appropriate to speak of *fa'amura'a* to account for such diverse practices? Notwithstanding these shifts, the legacy of the traditional institution appears threefold. First, there remain highly flexible forms of transfer of filiation, characterized by the continuity of biological ties to the child and a substantial reversibility of the adoption relationship, since the adopted child can often reintegrate into her original household. Second, and critically, there is still a strong social (and cultural) legitimacy associated with such transfers despite their plural forms. Eventually, *fa'amura'a* also pervaded the legal system. French Polynesia is indeed characterized by a de facto legal pluralism with regards to adoption. Its law, based on French law, tolerates *fa'a'amura'a* as a Polynesian custom, thus opening a space where adoption is much easier and more flexible, socially and legally, than it is in the rest of France (Asselin, 2020).

Beyond de Monléon's typology, it seems more illuminating to think of these varied practices of child transfer in French Polynesia as a plastic social resource – a socially and legally legitimate means – since it opens a broad transactional space around the mobility of children that is specific to the *fenua*. This space is available to biological parents and to their relatives and can be used in many different ways according to the specific affordances and necessities of life circumstances (Bastide, 2020). It can take many different forms. At one end of the spectrum, it can be implemented through the French legal system, thus involving the permanent relinquishing of parental rights, and sometimes the severing of all social relations with biological parents. At the other end, it can be closer to fosterage (Isiugo-Abanihe, 1985), such as when a child is temporarily entrusted to another family and reintegrates into his or her biological parents' household at a later stage (Asselin, 2020).

Given these transformations, we prefer to keep the term *fa'a'amura'a* to describe transactions closer to the traditional form, and to speak of 'child transfer' to account for this variety of emerging practices, which can be permanent, transient, and reversible, and can respond to increasingly varied needs and motives but nevertheless remain connected to the traditional form of adoption, including in terms of their social acceptance.

### Child transfer and family violence

In our sample, 11 respondents were or had been transferred as children, under diverse circumstances. For instance, Germaine, a woman in her forties, had been placed in her grandmother's household after the separation of her parents. Taina, in her 30s, was left with her maternal grand-aunt in Bora Bora by her mother, who did not feel ready to raise a child at a time when she was planning to separate from her partner (Taina's biological father) and live with her new lover. Thierry, 31, was placed under the care of his grandparents by the will of his mother, to strengthen his position in the order of succession within her *'ōpū ho'e*. Heihere (21) and Maina (27), two sisters, were placed under the care of one of their mother's cousins by social services. Germaine and Heihere each gave a child to European couples because of social and economic hardship.

If we shift the perspective from an individual point of view to the broader vantage point of the nuclear family, then it appears that most of our interviewees have had a close experience of child transfer, albeit under different circumstances. Herenui, a 23-year-old woman, adopted her sister's daughter. Hina, 26, was a *fa'a'amu* child and adopted her nephew. Hanaiti's (32) sister was adopted, like Françoise's (22). Vahiana's (33) parents gave four of their children for adoption. In a few families of our sample, the *fa'amura'a* thus concerns several members of a nuclear family, as in the case of Heihere, Maina, Raina, Thierry, and others.

Among our 42 interviewees (38 belonging to families with a distinctive Polynesian heritage), 27 of our respondents thus closely experienced child transfer in one form or another, at the giving or the receiving end of the transaction, within the boundaries of their nuclear family. Research on homeless people recently conducted in Papeete by Yasmina Taerea (Taerea & Bastide, 2022) also shows an overwhelming over-representation of such histories of child mobilities. In a sample of over 200 homeless individuals, pluri-mobilities within the family and unstable social inscriptions within the *feti'i* seemed to be the norm. About half of these people also suffered from family violence, most often as victims.

Of course, both these samples (our own and Taerea's) are highly specific: our respondents were recruited with regard to their background in a violent family context, and family issues play an important part in framing homelessness. In the general population, child transfer usually takes place in safe circumstances for the child, who receives adequate care and does not suffer from moral wounds entailed by a feeling of abandonment, as shown by many testimonies.[7] Nonetheless, our results, in line with consistent reports by social workers, do show that such mobilities are a crucial factor of vulnerability to family violence.

This relationship between child transfer and family violence can be captured and analysed in relation to two important dimensions. First, this type of transaction often provides motives for violence. For instance, the arrival of a non-biological child sometimes triggers the hostility of the couple's biological children, who might be worried about the redistribution of parental care and affections, or succession rights. When adoption is forced upon the receiving household, given the difficulty of rebuking such a demand within the *feti'i*, or at least in the *'ōpū ho'e*, the animosity against the transferred child can also involve the *fa'amu* parents. This was the case for Heihere, Maina, and Taia. These three sisters were adopted by one of their mother's cousins in Tahiti. They suffered multiple forms of physical violence and abuse from their adoptive parents and siblings. They were also assigned household chores, taking on the entirety of reproductive labour within the family. The fate of Mahana, a 28-year-old woman, was similar. Entrusted to a maternal cousin by her biological parents while she was still a baby, she too suffered severe forms of violence within the household and was put to work by her adoptive mother when she was 12, helping her in her paid work as a cleaner at a private school.

The second dimension refers to the fact that child transfer also supplies means for violence. Indeed, for the adopted child, the transfer frames a condition closely resembling 'close domination' (Memmi et al., 2019), which results from (1) continuous, (2) physical (face-to-face) co-presence (3) in a closed or semi-closed space (the home), (4) with very limited interactional 'backstage' (intimacy). In the case of transferred children, the domination is reinforced by a constitutive state of deep dependency regarding the fulfilment of their primary material, social, and affective needs. Because *fa'a'amura'a* typically involves young children or infants, the transaction between biological parents and the receiving household can even take place before parturition. Taken together, these factors provide caregivers with a ubiquitous power over the child.

The combination of the potential conflicts surrounding adoption – the motives for violence – and the structural vulnerability of non-biological children within the household – the means for violence – shape child transfer as a social condition (and institution) particularly prone to the development of what Randal Collins calls 'violence against the weak' (Collins, 2008, pp. 134–155). This type of violence develops under circumstances of strong relational asymmetry, combined with demanding social expectations – responsibilities – from the caregiver to the person under his or her responsibility. When child transfer is forced upon the receiving household (through the conjuring of the relational norms of *fa'amura'a*), this responsibility can be experienced as an undue yet unescapable burden, thus founding the abusive relationship with the adopted child.

When the relationship turns sour, the dependency of a child on his or her caregivers facilitates the 'relational work' (Bastide, 2020), which is necessary to sever the victim's relationships beyond the household, thus producing sufficient social isolation to allow the full development of violence. This is illustrated by the case of Mahana, whose adoptive parents sent her to school at the other end of Tahiti. She spent three hours a day commuting between the family house and her school. This effectively prevented her from developing social relations with 'outsiders'. In Heihere's case, her adoptive father supervised all her phone calls to her biological mother, to make sure that the two sisters' ordeal in their new household was kept secret.

Contemporary forms of child transfer, rooted in *fa'a'amura'a*, as a social institution and as a specific position within the family, can motivate the development of violent relationships, and supply the tools necessary to install, organize, and perpetuate such relations within the household.

## Conclusion

The case of transferred children sheds light on the process of transformation of the Polynesian family, as a social arrangement, under the effect of deep and thorough social change, especially since the late phase of 'compressed modernization' (Kyung-Sup, 2010) triggered by the development of the French military nuclear programme in French Polynesia in the 1960s (Lextreyt, 2019). The lasting legacy of the *fa'amura'a*, in a context of pluralization of child transfer practices, captures this historical experience – the persistence and transformation of inherited social patterns, in the context of a booming market economy and an increasing state presence and increasing state interventions over the past 60 years.

Based on our definition of violence as an interactional outcome, the situation of the transferred child also highlights how specific social and cultural arrangements, in French Polynesia and within contemporary Polynesian families, tend to shape situations conducive to the development of violent interactions. The lasting importance of family capital, in an institutional context marked by an increasingly pervasive market economy and fragile social safety nets, creates situations of strong dependency towards the *feti'i*. This dependency, in turn, frames deeply asymmetrical power relations and creates situations of vulnerabilities to violence.

In this perspective, family violence thus appears as a by-product of a singular trajectory of modernization, rather than as a cultural heritage, as it is too often understood to be.

## Notes

1  French Polynesia comprises five distinct archipelagos.
2  Statuses regarding violent acts can be complex and entangled: victims can also be perpetrators, at the same time or diachronically (Bastide, 2020).
3  It is important to note here that we sometimes interviewed people from the same family and couples, so we got a little less than 36 'family universes'.
4  In view of our own research, such 'efficient' relations of mutual obligations seem to remain mostly within the boundaries of the *'ōpū opu ho'e*. However, the sample is too small to draw meaningful conclusions.
5  In 2016, cost of living was 39% higher in French Polynesia than in France, while GDP per capita stood at 52% of the national level. The territorial purchasing power thus barely reached 37% of the level in Metropolitan France (Dropsy & Montet, 2018, p. 10).
6  We will come back to the term 'adopted' to show that it is too restrictive.
7  See, for instance: www.faaamu.com/blog/

## References

Abbott, A. (1997). On the concept of turning point. *Comparative Social Research, 16,* 85–106.

Asselin, A.-J. (2020). *Défis et enjeux aujourd'hui pour les familles et les professionnels des services sociaux de Polynésie française* (Master's thesis). Université de Laval, Laval, QC, Canada.

Bambridge, T. (2009). *La terre dans l'archipel des Australes: Étude du pluralisme juridique et culturel en matière foncière (Pacifique Sud).* Pirae: Au vent des îles.

Bastide, L. (2020). *Les violences familiales en Polynésie française: Entrer, vivre et sortir de la violence.* Paris: INJEP.

Becker, H. S. (1963). *Outsiders: Studies in the sociology of deviance.* New York, NY: The Free Press of Glencoe.

Benjamin, T., Chang, D. F., & Steele, M. (2019). A Qualitative study of "fa'a'amu" kinship care experiences in Tahiti. *Adoption Quarterly, 22*(3), 173–198.

Bourdieu, P. (1972). *Esquisse d'une théorie de la pratique; Précédé de trois études Kabyles.* Paris: Librairie Droz.

Clanché, F. (2017). *Insécurité et délinquance en 2017: Premier bilan statistique*. Paris: Interstat, Ministère de l'Intérieur.

Collier, S. J., & Lakoff, A. (2005). On regimes of living. In A. Ong and S. J. Collier (eds.), *Global assemblages: Technology, politics, and ethics as anthropological problems* (pp. 22–39). Hoboken, NJ: Wiley-Blackwell.

Collins, R. (2008). *Violence: A micro-sociological theory*. Princeton, NJ: Princeton University Press.

de Monléon, J.-V. (2002). Document sans titre. *Bulletin Amades*, 52. Retrieved September 29, 2021, from http://journals.openedition.org/amades/894

Dropsy, V., & Montet, C. (2018). Croissance économique et productivité en Polynésie française: Une analyse sur longue période. *Economie et Statistique*, *499*, 5–27.

Forsé, M. (2001). Rôle spécifique et croissance du capital social. *Revue de l'OFCE*, *76*, 189–216.

Gibson, J. J. (1977). The theory of affordances. In R. E. Shaw & J. Bransford (eds.), *Perceiving, acting, and knowing*. Hilldale, NJ: Lawrence Erlbaum Associates.

Goffman, E. (1971). *Asylums: Essays on the social situation of mental patients and other inmates*. Harmondsworth: Penguin.

Heard, E., Fitzgerald, L., Whittaker, M., Va'ai, S., & Mutch, A. (2020). Exploring intimate partner violence in Polynesia: A scoping review. *Trauma, Violence, & Abuse*, *21*(4), 769–778.

Howell, S. (2003). Kinning: The creation of life trajectories in transnational adoptive families. *Journal of the Royal Anthropological Institute*, *9*(3), 465–484.

Isiugo-Abanihe, U. C. (1985). Child fosterage in West Africa. *Population and Development Review*, *11*(1), 53–73.

ISPF. (2015). *Etude budget des familles 2015: Polynésie française*. Papeete: ISPF.

Kyung-Sup, C. (2010). The second modern condition? Compressed modernity as internalized reflexive cosmopolitization. *The British Journal of Sociology*, *61*(3), 444–464.

Lallement, M. (2006). Capital social et théories sociologiques. In M. Lallement & A. Bévort (eds.), *Le capital social: Performance, équité et réciprocité* (pp. 71–88). Paris: La Découverte.

Lemert, E. M. (1973). Beyond mead: The societal reaction to deviance. *Social Problems*, *21*, 457.

Lextreyt, M. (2019). Les années CEP (1963–2004). In E. Conte (ed.), *Une histoire de Tahiti des origines à nos jours* (pp. 273–311). Papeete: Au vent des îles.

Memmi, D., Cousin, B., & Lambert, A. (2019). Servir (chez) les autres: Pérennité et mutations de la domination rapprochée. *Actes de la recherche en sciences sociales*, *230*(5), 109–119.

Naepels, M. (2006). Quatre questions sur la violence. *L'Homme*, *177–178*, 487–495.

Ottino, P. (1970). Les fare tupuna ou "maisons de famille" en Polynésie orientale. *Homme*, *10*(2), 45–58.

Ottino, P. (1972). *Rangiroa: Parenté étendue, résidence et terres dans un atoll polynésien*. Paris: Éditions Cujas.

Panoff, M. (1965). La terminologie de la parenté en Polynésie. Essai d'analyse formelle. *L'Homme*, *5*(3), 60–87.

Panoff, M. (1970). *La terre et l'organisation sociale en Polynésie*. Paris: Payot.

Protar, L. (2020). *Produire le genre, fabriquer la parenté : Ethnographie du travail domestique et horticole à Kiriwina* (Doctoral dissertation). Université Paris 1, Paris, France.

Sierra-Paycha, C., Lelièvre, E., & Trabut, L. (2018). *Le fa'a'amura'a: Confier et recevoir un enfant en Polynésie Française*. Papeete: ISPF.

Singly, F. de (2017). *Sociologie de la famille contemporaine*. Malakoff: Armand Colin.

Stewart, P. J., & Strathern A. J. (2002). *Violence: Theory and ethnography*. London, New York: Continuum.

Taerea, Y., & Bastide, L. (2022). *Errance et pratiques spatiales des sans domicile fixe en Polynésie française*. Research report, Maison des sciences de l'Homme du Pacifique, Ministère des Solidarités et de la Famille (unpublished), Papeete.

Weber, F. (2005). *Le sang, le nom, le quotidien: une sociologie de la parenté pratique*. La Courneuve: Aux lieux d'être.

Weber, M. (2003). *Le savant et le politique : Une nouvelle traduction*. Paris: La Découverte.

Wieviorka, M. (1998). Le nouveau paradigme de la violence. *Cultures et Conflits, 29/30*, 9–57.

Xiang, B., & Lindquist, J. (2014). Migration infrastructure. *International Migration Review, 48*, S122–S148.

Zigon, J. (2010). Moral and ethical assemblages: A response to Fassin and Stoczkowski. *Anthropological Theory, 10*(1–2), 3–15.

# 4 Familialism and gender violence in New Caledonia families[1]

## Christine Salomon

In New Caledonia, violence against girls and women has long attracted the attention of the media. As early as 2004, statistical figures were objectifying the breadth of the issue, and female Caledonians have repeatedly taken to the streets to push for political action on the matter. However, it is only in 2020 that the *Congrès*, the country's deliberative assembly, elevated this social problem into a public issue, a 'cause Pays' (national cause), by inviting competent authorities to prioritize the creation of emergency shelters and of institutional support and integration systems, among other things.[2]

With the internationalization of the *Me Too* movement, reporting to law enforcement has increased dramatically,[3] to the point where every instance of rape and feminicide reported in the media sees people taking to the streets: many women have thus protested not only in Nouméa, the capital city, but also in rural municipalities. During one of these marches in Houaïlou, where the second feminicide of New Caledonia in 2019 had taken place, Anne-Marie Kede, the Kanak president of the *Fédération des groups de femmes* (Federation of Women's Groups), declared:

> Violence is becoming all too common: violence, rapes, barbaric actions, abuses. These acts do not result in an adequate response, neither in our societies nor from public authorities. Our outrage is not limited to a day or to a passing demonstration. We demand answers and guarantees of immediate change in the accomplishment of the tasks of all the stakeholders and authorities whose mission is to take care of the cases of the women who have been assaulted, and to prosecute the perpetrators harshly.[4]

To denounce once more the 'deafening silence of institutions in facing this extremely severe situation', a feminist collective in Nouméa, *Femmes en colère* (Angry Women), which brings together Caledonian women of various origins, organized a gathering in front of the place where the president of the newly appointed government was delivering his general policy discourse.[5]

In his discourse, this Caledonian politician of European and Tahitian descent framed the issue of violence as 'being mostly perpetrated within the family sphere [and] laying the ground for juvenile criminality'. He did not introduce this topic in the section of his speech concerned with 'women recognition', but

DOI: 10.4324/9781003146667-5

rather while developing a chapter titled 'protecting persons and property'. The only new announcement was the creation of a 'dedicated commission within the Caledonian family council'.[6] While in previous legislatures 'intra-family violence' had been treated as a specific issue in the broader category of violence 'against women', which fell under the 'women's issues' sector, during the distribution of appointments within the new government, dominated by the loyalist right, it was recategorized as 'intra-family violence' and relocated under the 'family, disability and animal welfare' sector.[7]

Grasping the issue in terms of violence against women or in terms of intra-family violence is obviously not without consequences. Indeed, both terminologies involve different concepts, definitions, and institutional answers (Lieber & Roca i Escoda, 2015). The view, built on the sociological fact that most victims are women and girls, and that violence is related to their gender, tends to consider partner violence or violence committed by another relative – as well as violence committed by a stranger in the public space – as a mechanism of social control. As such, it is seen as both a product and a tool of patriarchal domination which permeates society. In this conceptual framework, public action aims at delegitimizing gender violence socially by deconstructing sexist stereotypes; at the individual level, it aims at helping and housing victims as well as punishing perpetrators. Conversely, conceptualizing the issue in terms of intra-family violence eliminates, or at least dilutes, the structural dimension of violence as the expression of a social relationship of domination. Violence is problematized as a dysfunction of the family as an institution whose norms and roles are not questioned. This vision translates into actions aiming at restoring family relations or the conjugal bond, including through mediation programmes. In New Caledonia, violence often tends to be interpreted as a scourge inherent in the contemporary Kanak family and seen as testimony to its flaws – as does juvenile delinquency – with the underlying idea that moralization and a return to the ancient, authoritarian structures of supervision of the Kanak world might reduce it.

The following text, primarily focused on the Kanak community, sheds light on the ways in which the forms of public action – or inaction – diverge according to their framing in a feminist or in a familialist perspective. After exposing the scale of gender violence, I go on to analyse the characteristics of feminicides perpetrated over the last few years by looking at the claims of their perpetrators as a testimony of conjugal and marital norms, which legitimate the use of violence by men to subdue their intimate partners. I follow by presenting the many ways this issue has been treated, by analysing the various political responses that occurred over the last 15 years in the political context of New Caledonia. In this old 'settlement colony',[8] which is currently engaged in a process of decolonization and where independentists have been fighting against loyalists since the 1970s, a new nativist political perspective is appearing. Without questioning the status of the country as a French territory, it promotes a political and juridical differentialism based on the restoration of customary Kanak authorities and a particularly conservative brand of familialism, rooted in missionary history, with a strong hostility towards divorce. Thus, within the Kanak community, a tension

appears between the yearning for a neo-tradition on one side and the reassess-
ment of gender relations and conjugality on the other.

## A multi-ethnic context

An island part of Melanesia first settled more than 3,000 years ago, New Caledonia
has been a French territory since 1853. Successive waves of immigrants have
added to the native Kanak population – convicts from France and Algeria, free
European settlers, indentured labourers from Asia and Oceania who came during the colonial period to work in the colony's nickel mines, and, more recently,
migrants from Polynesia and metropolitan France who began settling in the late
1960s. Today, the archipelago has a population of 271,407 (2019 census). Kanaks
and Kanak Métis[9] make up 43% of the total population, Europeans and European
Métis 31%, Polynesians and Polynesian Métis 12% (of whom 10% originate from
Wallis and Futuna, and 2% are of Tahitian descent).

New Caledonia is split between three provinces: North, South, and Loyauté
Islands. Kanaks represent the vast majority of the population in the *Province Nord*
(Northern Province, where 18.4% of the total Caledonian population resides) and
virtually the whole population of the Loyauté Islands (6.8% of the total Caledonian
population). Europeans and other communities live essentially in the *Province Sud*
(Southern Province), where greater Nouméa is located, which contains over half
of the total Caledonian population.

Despite real progress resulting from the proactive socioeconomic readjustment
policy agreed upon after the civil war of 1984–1988 and despite the beginning of
the decolonization process, social inequalities and inequalities between communities remain stark: Kanaks and Polynesians are still mainly concentrated in the
lower social segments in terms of education, work, and income, while Europeans –
born in New Caledonia or, even more so, immigrants from France – occupy better
positions (Gorohouna & Ris, 2017; Ris, 2013).

However, communities are not closed universes. Cross-relations are old and have
increased following the social and political disruptions of the last several decades.
Nevertheless, an important difference between Kanaks and non-Kanaks has per-
sisted since the colonial period: Kanaks fall under a particular juridical 'native status'
(except for those who make a claim before a court to shift to common law), which
today is called the 'customary status'. This status of 'customary right' confers only
to men specific property rights on 'customary land' (land located in the 'indigenous
reservations' of the colonial period), while courtrooms with customary assessors[10]
for family matters (divorce, child custody, and support) and property issues refer to
all Kanaks, whether men or women, under the term 'customary status'.

## Women: a non-homogenous category in relation to violence

Protests against sexual and physical violence against women are not new. In the
early 1980s, radical young feminists in the Kanak nationalist movement actively
engaged in this fight, refusing to be 'the left behinds of independency' (Salomon,

2017a). After the Kanak uprising of 1984–1988 and the agreement passed between the independentists, the loyalists, and the French government to reduce the inequalities affecting the Kanaks, important social transformations in the life of Caledonian women[11] resulted in the development of this movement of denunciation. This dynamic was supported by the creation of two associations dedicated to combating violence against women, one focused on sexual violence and the other on intimate partner violence. This configuration proved conducive to the launch, in 2002–2003, of a general female population survey on violence against women that aimed to measure the phenomenon. As elsewhere, the results showed that gender violence affects all social segments and communities, albeit in different proportions. Kanak women – mostly those in rural areas – were most impacted, given that 34% of them declared they had experienced physical violence and 17% said they had experienced at least one rape or rape attempt.[12] In contrast, European women, whether born in New Caledonia or not, were affected by the same types of violence at rates of 8% and 1.7%, respectively. Polynesian women – who, distinctively from their Kanak counterparts, are almost all urban dwellers – appear to stand in an intermediate position. Of course, the particular exposition of Kanak women results not only from very unequal gender norms but also from social factors, which include a combination of poverty, less access to material, social, and symbolic resources, and a colonial history of 'brutalization' of social relations, including between genders (Salomon & Hamelin, 2008).[13]

The gap between communities is particularly pronounced with regard to couple and family life. Within couples, the rate of physical violence among Kanaks – 32% – turns out to be four times higher than it is among Europeans. Partner rapes are also twice as frequent among Kanaks, at 14%. Unlike other types of violence – psychological, verbal, physical – in long-lasting couples, they do not seem to decrease with age. Within families, 12% of Kanak women report physical and/ or sexual violence perpetrated by a relative other than their partner, a rate four times higher than for European women,[14] with a particularly tricky situation for younger women, who appear to be the most vulnerable, as inequal gender norms combine with social inequalities tied to age. Finally, 58% of women living with a partner and who have been physically or sexually assaulted by a relative have also been attacked, during the same year, by their partner. Such a context of repeated brutality, usually combined with verbal, psychological, and sometimes economic violence, reflects a constant coercive control, which Johnson (1995, 2008) calls patriarchal or intimate terrorism.

## What feminicides reveal

My analysis of 16 feminicides perpetrated by partners or ex-partners over 10 years (2009–2019)[15] also outlines the youthfulness of the victims and the over-representation of Kanak women among them. Their ages vary from 8 years – a little girl who was stabbed while trying to protect her mother, who ended up gravely wounded – to 71 years, with a median age of 28. However, the most affected group, with 7 women out of 16, includes women younger than 25.[16] Most victims as well as perpetrators (13 of 16) are Kanaks or Kanak Métis and lived (or had lived until recently) as cohabiting couples. Seven women died from knife wounds, and five were strangled and/or died from blows to the head inflicted with fists, sticks, or steel toe – capped shoes, often with a fierceness exceeding the violence necessary to kill. Four were executed by firearm, two at point-blank range.

According to the perpetrators' statements in court, it appears that violence is most often the result of minimal transgressions of the conjugal norm of submission of women to men, triggering their fury. Marie, a 71-year-old woman who was shot with a rifle, had apparently criticized her partner using an overbearing tone; Andréa – who was stabbed 14 times and survived but whose daughter Edena, an 8-year-old, was stabbed six times while trying to protect her mother, died – had supposedly contradicted her partner; Jacynthe, a 24-year-old woman who was beaten to death, had allegedly humiliated her partner by refusing to let him drive her car; Simone, 25 years old, also beaten to death, had apparently thrown a cup of coffee at the perpetrator's face after he had hit her repeatedly; Clarisse, who was 19 years old, was stabbed twice by her boyfriend at a party where people were drinking heavily, after she had allegedly tried to prevent him drinking more alcohol with his other friends; Marie, a 60-year-old woman who was beaten up and stabbed to death, had asked her partner bluntly to leave her place; Shirley, 22 years old at the time, died of a shotgun wound because she had seemingly refused to go out and buy a packet of cigarettes for her boyfriend; and Maureen, 28 years old, was beaten to death, because she had supposedly smoked the last cigarette in the packet. During the trials, several offenders justified their acts by explaining that their partner had 'upset' them and pushed them beyond their limit:

- 'I had enough. When I get angry, these things happen' (murderer of Marie, killed with a shotgun).
- 'When I get mad, I can't control myself' (murderer of Lindsay, killed with a firearm).
- 'It is possible to hit a woman, but it is not good. In our community [the Kanaks] it is . . . it is kind of normal. It happens when we do not have any solution' (murderer of Simone, beaten to death).[17]

Numerous other statements by men accused of committing severe violence against their partner – failed feminicide attempts where the woman survived despite her wounds, cases tried in criminal courts, or cases requalified before a lower court despite the severity of the lesions and notwithstanding the perpetrator's past sentences for similar facts – also participate in legitimizing the use of force. Following are some recent examples:

- 'I was upset. She shouldn't have gone downtown [his partner had brought the children downtown to watch the illuminations, although he did not want her to come]. It is because of women that there is violence. All men beat their woman'.

- 'A woman should be at home; it is in the law. When we give rights to women and children, we allow them to do just whatever they like, like not coming home on time. So of course, I get angry, but there are reasons'.
- 'Beaten women are trending. Men rule, here. Lately, we have been punished for beating up women. If she is hurt, she is responsible, I don't care'.
- 'I have been beating her for years. I don't know how many times. The last time, she insulted me, it is only natural'.[18]

Among the 16 identified cases of feminicide, 2 perpetrators put forward jealousy as their main motive – the murderer of Pascale, 38 years old at the time she was stabbed to death, as well as Lindsay's assassin, who killed her with a rifle when she was 25 – while 5 others explained their act by their rejection of divorce or separation. Indeed, two of the victims had just split with their partner – Lyse, 55, who was beaten and strangled, and Marie Line, 34, slaughtered with a knife – and three had shared their intention to ask for a divorce from their husband. Lydia, 40, was shot by her husband, a Kanak, who fired at her twice with a shotgun at point-blank range while she begged for her life. He explained to the court expert psychiatrist that she had upset him and was therefore as responsible for the death as he was. Hoang, 51, was stabbed in cold blood by her husband; during pre-trial investigations, he declared:

> Here [being himself a Caledonian of Vietnamese origin, he had brought Hoang to New Caledonia from Vietnam after marrying her], she saw that women had rights, and so she said that she was going to split, to divorce. I want to show to other women who come from Vietnam to take advantage of men how it works.

Finally, Olivia's husband, who killed her when she was 41, stabbing her four times, explains to the court:

> We had a customary wedding, we have to stick to the custom. Customary wedding is sacred, I was not resentful to my wife, we must not divorce, that's all. Divorce? It means betraying my family, it means shame falling upon me.[19]

I will come back later to the roots of these sacralized conceptions of the Kanak customary wedding whose tragic consequences we see here.

## The range of political responses

At the very moment when the first results of the general feminine population survey were released, the issue of violence against women appeared for the first and only time in an election campaign, in the context of the 2004 provincial elections. The government resulting from these elections, which included several women – including the president, Marie-Noelle Thémereau, a non-independentist European Caledonian; and the vice-president, Déwé Gorodé, an early Kanak independentist feminist – created a new public policy sector focusing on women's position in society. The government launched several public awareness campaigns, but they were too limited and lacked any consistent reflection on the best ways of questioning entrenched social norms legitimizing men's use of violence.[20] Public attention focused more on helping the victims: at the police station, in Nouméa, a dedicated service was created as well as another service the 'Day Centre for Treatment of Violence Against Women', called *Le Relais*. However, after the death of the elected deputy in charge of the centre, Eliane Ixéco, a Kanak feminist who also had been head of the association Women and Conjugal Violence, the approach developed by the service shifted quickly from a feminist to a familialist stance, a conservative ideology that gives priority to the family even at the cost of maintaining the male-dominated status quo.

*Le Relais* was given a new name and became the 'Centre for Treatment of Victims *and* Perpetrators of Conjugal Violence'. Women were offered 'couple's support' under the supervision of the association 'Mediation in New Caledonia'. Soon after, criminal mediations were developed in addition to conjugal mediations. And yet, despite the implementation of restorative justice in numerous court cases, a 2004 report in New Zealand explicitly advises strongly against resorting to such measures in cases of conjugal or family violence or sexual violence (Proietti-Scifoni & Daly, 2011). Even though directives from the French Ministry of Justice also recommended an 'absolutely residual, if not exceptional'[21] use of mediation as an alternative to prosecution in the case of conjugal violence, that is, a resort in exceptional circumstances, criminal mediation at *Le Relais* – renamed the 'Treatment Centre for Intra-family Violence' – was systematically offered to first-time offenders in the context of conjugal violence.

This approach is advantageous for perpetrators, as they avoid being prosecuted, and for the judiciary institution, since it alleviates the load on the court system. However, its advantage for victims appears to be highly problematic. During mediation sessions, they are made to face their attacker without any assurance about the risk of re-victimization, including through verbal and psychological violence (Parent & Digneffe, 1996). They often are made to feel guilty: they believe their comments triggered conflict and caused the resulting blows. Violence is thus presented as the outcome of a discrete, symmetric interaction, as stated by the European psychologist of *Le Relais*: 'Sometimes individuals introduce themselves as victims and become aware of the fact that they display violent behaviours. There is mixed violence here, both partners exchange violent behaviours' (*LNC*, 19 May 2008). While, as I have mentioned, the postcolonial turn of the 1990s and 2000s was in favour of Caledonian women, it is obvious that the following years were much less conducive, with a strong resurgence of masculinist and familialist ideologies.

A true backlash pitted Kanak women, once again, against the guardians of masculine domination, upholding customs and native identity. In 2005, the members of the Customary Senate, an all-male institution created to deal with issues related to Kanak identity and Kanak customary status, were due to be reappointed in line with 'customary norms'. Two Kanak feminist representatives, Déwé Gorodé and Eliane Ixéco, pushed to impose a democratic process of election instead, which would allow women to run for these positions. They failed. Patriarchy was reaffirmed as an intangible principle: 'Kanak society is a patriarchal society. Its social system founded on a transmission of rights, powers and responsibilities based on men' (my translation, charter of the Kanak People, 2014). Attempts by jurists (all men) to formalize customary Kanak civil law, which were backed by the Customary Senate, were carried out at the expense of women falling under customary status.

The process of dissolving conjugal ties – a dissolution often initiated by women because of the violence they have suffered – was made more cumbersome, and circumventing it via a recourse to common law was made impossible. The rupture of a union – in order to distinguish itself from the Western concept, customary law no longer uses the term divorce – requires the consent not only of both spouses but also of both clans 'because [a customary union] does not involve two individuals marrying, but two clans'.[22] When a woman wishes to divorce, if her family agrees but her husband or her husband's family opposes the dissolution of marital ties or does not show up to sign the documents, she needs to let a substantial, specified amount of time pass before she can appeal to a civil court with customary assessors, in the hope of being granted the rupture of conjugal ties and the ability to start a new life.[23] However, these very assessors often oppose any rupture of matrimonial alliance (Capo, 2017, p. 174). Upholders of customary law even looked to extend its reach to the compensation of victims. It was only after a politico-juridical battle led by the association *SOS violences sexuelles* that Kanak women under customary status were able to regain compensation on an equal footing with all the other Caledonian women (Salomon, 2018). Other juridical measures – such as protection orders, which allow family courts to grant emergency measures to shelter female victims of partner violence and their children, or eviction orders to force the violent partner out of the marital home – were made unenforceable, again because of customary status. Therefore, when a woman is of customary status, she is the one who must leave the home.

## Nativist familialism

Following a symposium on violence against women in 2010, the Northern Province decided to commission a survey to guide the development of dedicated policies. It was led by a sociologist, Jone Passa, who is close to the nativist political movement. His report acknowledges that Kanak women bear a much heavier burden than other Caledonian women in terms of violence. But among explanatory factors, neither inequal gender norms nor such obvious social factors as poverty or spatial isolation are mentioned. The survey only stresses the processes of social dissolution, which it refers to the effects of colonization and which would translate into suffered and/or inflicted violence, understood as social dysfunctions affecting men as well as women. Among the contemporary transformations that would explain the deregulation of violence, the author cites 'a weakening of authority figures and of kinship ties' (meaning the contestation of the authority of the elders over the younger ones, within the family or in the community, and of men over women), 'a renegotiation of social roles' (meaning the questioning of traditional norms by women and youth), 'a softening of the rules of alliance', and 'tolerance of forbidden relationships' (meaning the free choice of one's partner) (Passa, 2013). The report rightly stresses the need for societal support rather than a purely individual support for victims. However, it does not question the principles of masculinity and seniority as the roots of unequal Kanak social norms, nor does it question patriarchy. On the contrary, it promotes the restoration of traditional social positions, the normalization of situations by revitalizing 'meaning and legitimacy', to fit the people back into a society still essentially seen as rural, even though by then almost half of the Kanak population was urban. Besides, in the presentation of his work, the author does not hesitate to shame women who aspire to break away from an unhappy customary union:

> In Kanak society, rupture is never an option. The woman is aware that one day or another, she or her children will have to pay. . . . Before being a victim, the woman is Kanak, daughter of [a patrilineage], and all its attributes.
>
> (*LNC*, 10.07.2012)

This type of wording about the loss of identity references usually frames the city as a problematic category. Yet, within the islands and even more so in small Kanak villages called *tribus* (tribes), intimidations against women who disclose violence within their couple or their family and, in doing so, who contest family and conjugal norms, are still so prevalent that the women are often forced to leave. Nouméa thus appears as a practical way out, given the absence of structures to protect female victims of violence in the Loyauté Islands and their scarcity – only one emergency shelter with two beds – in the Province Nord (Northern Province). Two associations, one dedicated to helping victims in Lifou and in the Loyauté Islands, and the other devoted to supporting women in Mont Dore, a municipality in greater Nouméa, tried to create such institutions to offset the limited available places (120) in the three existing shelters in Nouméa. In the first case, the attempt failed altogether, while in the other case, the shelter, which is managed by volunteers, can only be accessed during weekends, while provincial refuges are expected to take over after the weekend.

Institutional responses in the Province Nord and in the islands, which are held by independentists, appear to be a compromise with nativist views: of course, public authorities have created services aimed at providing victims with generic juridical support, and these are widely used by victims of gender violence. Nevertheless, rather than opening specialized shelters with sufficient hosting capacities, they developed a host family system that emulates the existing model for at-risk children and teens. This system not only aims at protecting the victims during the crisis by putting them in a safe place, but it also aims at avoiding what Passa (2013, p. 20) calls the 'dissolution of ties' by deterring women from seeking shelter in Nouméa. The Province Nord thus set up a network of host families, who are chosen from Kanaks of high social ranking and whose identity is kept secret, to house women in danger on a temporary basis, in a different municipality, when emergency shelters are full. The Loyauté Islands province preferred to turn to the churches to provide one shelter on each island: at pastors' homes in Lifou and Ouvéa, and in a Catholic presbytery in Maré. However, cases of violence registered by the juridical system show that neither religious consecration nor high ranking within Kanak social hierarchies can be held as an assurance. In addition, there is no evidence to support the idea that female victims forced to leave the home because of severe violence would not prefer being sheltered in a structure with other women, where they could seek support from competent professionals and work on a mid or long-term project to gain their autonomy, rather than being housed in a host family or at a religious place. The host family system is only viewed as a temporary respite, limited to five days; with no prospects or support to reflect on their future, women are most likely to go back to their partner and to withdraw their legal complaint when the crisis is over.

## Religious and nativist conservatisms

The idea of host families for Kanak victims of gender violence in the Kanak Northern Province and in the islands appears as a supplementary form of familial-ism, a pervasive social ideology in the territory. Despite the contemporary waning of religious practice, New Caledonia is still influenced by the legacy of the mis-sionaries who showed a constant hostility towards the dissolution of unions. Dur-ing the 19th century, the settlement of missions had deeply reshaped structures of authority within chieftaincies, as well as pre-existing gender relations and the family. This was the case, for instance, in the Loyauté Islands, where the Lon-don Missionary Society, on the Protestant side, and the Marists, on the Catholic side, played a major role even before the imposition of French rule and sover-eignty over the territory: in Maré, as early as 1885 English missionaries Jones and Creagh and chief Naisseline established 'Scriptural Laws' which punished non-believers and adultery; in Ouvéa, in 1860 father Bernard and chief Bazit put in place a similar code, which prohibited divorce; finally, in Lifou, in 1863 mis-sionary McFarlane, who was part of the London Missionary Society, and chief Boula promulgated a series of laws inspired by the Decalogue (Rognon, 1991, pp. 100–101). Among these imposed transformations, those touching on sexual life and unions were substantial, considering that they banned juvenile sexuality, polygyny, cohabitation, adultery, and divorce, framed as pre-existing behaviours incompatible with Christian union. At the end of the *indigénat* regime[24] in 1946, the defence of marriage and the 'protection of indigenous family' – and, at the same time, the call to act with determination 'against the destroyers of the fam-ily'[25] – were still part of the prescriptions upheld by missionaries and Melanesian associations, created at their initiative to channel natives' aspiration to freedom (Salomon, 2017b). However, nothing could stop the liberalization of values and behaviours after the end of the illiberal *indigénat* regime. In 1960, after several synods dedicated to the 'stability of unions and families', the evangelical Protes-tant church worried that divorce was becoming trivial and was concerned about the 'circumstances in which indigenous civil unions are being celebrated as well as the procedure followed in case of divorce', in particular the lack of concern given to the consent of the family.[26]

Head-on criticism of missionary influence by a number of young radical Kanaks[27] in the 1970s to 1980s, the emergence of a Kanak feminism claiming absolute equality of rights, and, during the two following decades, the expansion of a far-reaching feminine associative movement denouncing violence against girls and women somehow muted familialist ideologies for some time. But religious and traditionalist conservatism hit back with a move to institutionalize custom with the constitution of the Customary Senate and the rise of a nativist political force, particularly strong in the islands. The most striking example of this evolution is the project of a customary civil code, written in 2006 in chief Boula's district in Lifou, which re-enacted the code of laws promulgated over a hundred years before by McFarlane and proposed, among other repressive measures, to send back to their husbands women who had fled to seek shelter from conjugal violence and those who were categorized as adulterous, and to forbid entirely the dissolution of unions (Nicolas, 2012, pp. 725–756). Without going as far, when the Customary Senate worked towards defining and drafting a document laying out the shared foundation of Kanak values, it chose to base it on 'the maxim recognized by everybody: Kanak society is based on custom and religion'[28] (Demmer & Salomon, 2013, p. 73). The following year, a reflection on 'the dissolution of marriage and the separation of couples' stipulated:

> We only proceed once to the custom of marriage, and the given word is sacred. Only death can put an end to the union, that is, in other words, to the alliance thus created. If the alliance remains and must be honoured with/by children when they exist, the separation of bodies or the dissolution is attested today by customary act or before a court with customary assessors as long as the procedure has been exhausted.[29]

Customary union thus truly becomes a sacrament, as it is in the Catholic dogma, where indissolubility is a pillar of unions, to the extent that the only remaining possibility is the separation between the spouses' bodies. Besides, in the charter of the Kanak country, the term 'dissolution' no longer appears, as it is too close to the concept of divorce. The document only mentions the 'separation occurring in a couple tied by custom [which] does not involve the questioning of the concluded alliance' (Sénat Coutumier, 2014, p. 22).

However, such conservative concepts attached to both religious and nativist familialism are not likely to hinder the continuous transformation of practices. Of course, in the Loyauté Islands, there is still a strong discrepancy between the number of divorced or separated Kanak men and women[30] living in the region: there are twice as many divorced or separated Kanak men as divorced/separated Kanak women. This is a sign of the tendency of divorced or separated women to leave, as they choose or are forced to move to Nouméa. However, we do not find the same gap in the Province Nord, where Kanaks make up 70% of the population but where the weight of religion is much weaker. On a national level, the proportion of women 'separated or divorced' now increases at the same rate for Kanaks –

among whom a vast majority fall under customary status – as it does for other Caledonian women.[31]

## Conclusion

This chapter, which begins with the renewal of the feminist movement and the mobilizations against violence towards women in New Caledonia following the 'Me Too' movement, shows the way in which violence is considered and defined, in terms of gender violence or intra-family violence, and how it induces different political responses. It also stresses that the achievements are always susceptible to backtracking.

The fragile advances in taking care of victims in a context of a dynamic of women's emancipation and a relative feminist openness in the early 2000s have in fact come up against both a familialism deeply rooted in New Caledonia and the deleterious effects of institutionalization, linked to the increase in frameworks specifically dedicated to women's issues and the appointment of women to positions of responsibility.

This 'institutional feminism' found in New Caledonia produces, as found in Fiji, a discourse and a policy marked by hybridity (George, 2017). While using the concepts of gender and equality and advocating a number of measures in accordance with international guidelines, it ensures avoiding alienation of the most conservative fringes of society, no deviation from the patriarchal norm, defended in particular by supporters of a backward-looking custom. Here, it is important to remember Déwé Gorodé's words in one of her last published interviews, as her voice is still one of the few to have publicly contradicted the backward-looking, nativist activism of the Customary Senate, in the independentist political world and during the period studied:

> Society attributes roles to each sex. Today, women suffer from it, in the Kanak custom as in other spheres in Caledonia. It is against these inegalitarian effects of these gender stereotypes and these conservatisms that we work. What society has done, society can undo.[32]

## Acknowledgements

My thanks to Benoît Trépied for sharing with me a number of archival documents and to Olivier Fagnot for providing me with the 2009 and 2014 census data on divorce. I also thank Christine Hamelin, Christine Demmer, and Loïs Bastide for their review and their comments, and Caroline Carter for the suggestions she made to improve the English translation.

## Notes

1 Translated by Loïs Bastide.
2 Vœu No. 32/CP, 30 April 2020.
3 Between 2017 and 2018 legal procedures concerning conjugal violence increased by 5%, and they rose by another 15% between 2018 and 2019; in 2019, there were 3.8

acts of conjugal violence processed in courts for 1,000 inhabitants versus 1.6 in metropolitan France (State prosecutor, interview in *Les Nouvelles Calédoniennes – LNC* – 08.14.2020).

4  *LNC*, 03.02.2019.

5  www.congres.nc/wp-content/uploads/2019/08/190822-DPG-Thierry-SANTA.pdf

6  This obscure advisory body was created in 2017 on the initiative of loyalist representatives, while independentists had abstained.

7  A few months later, following the 'Grenelle des violences conjugales', a series of round-table talks organized during fall 2019 by the French State in metropolitan France and in France's overseas territories in order to set a road map to act against conjugal violence, the Caledonian loyalist government followed suit. Its president announced 'the inscription of violence against women as a major cause' of its mandate, with, again, the creation of a new institutional structure: a 'high council for the elimination of violence'. A year later, the only observable measure was the handing over of three 'grave danger' phones by the judiciary to victims, allowing them to instantly reach a special service in charge of alerting police forces, if needed.

8  In French scholarship, a 'settlement colony' (*colonie de peuplement*) involves a large-scale settlement of people from the metropolis taking over the land, as in New Caledonia, Australia, or New Zealand, contrary to many colonial territories where the presence of European settlers remained marginal.

9  Since 2019 census categories have allowed self-identification as belonging to more than one single ethnic community, such as métis (bi-racial).

10  These customary assessors are officially in charge of identifying and explaining the relevant 'customary law' to the presiding professional judges (all of whom come from metropolitan France).

11  In 2000, 25 years after abortion was legalized in France, it was legalized in New Caledonia, and in 2002, with the implementation of French law on equality between men and women in politics (*parité*), Caledonian women obtained greater access to elective mandates. Their education level and their employment rate have also progressed substantially.

12  Most from a partner or an ex-partner.

13  On the concept of the brutalization of social relations in the colonial context of New Caledonia, see Merle (2017). Regarding gender relations in this context, see Hamelin, Salomon et al. (2004).

14  However, they are three times more susceptible to these acts than women in metropolitan France.

15  These feminicides were documented under the 'short news' and 'justice' items of the *Les Nouvelles Calédoniennes* daily newspaper and of the *Nouvelle-Calédonie La 1ere* broadcasting network. During this ten-year period, five women, at least four of whom had also suffered violence, had stabbed their partner to death.

16  The young age of these victims is very distinctive of feminicides in New Caledonia when compared to the rest of France's overseas territories or with metropolitan France. Indeed, according to the national study on violent deaths within couples, in France in 2018, most at-risk women were between 40 and 49 years, followed by women between 30 and 39 years.

17  These words were published in trial reports (*LNC*, 06.22.2013; 03.26.2014; 06.17.2015).

18  *LNC*, 02.16.2019; 08.26.2019; 09.30.2019; 0.02.2019.

19  *LNC*, 03.19.2014.

20  On this specific point, see Heise and Manji (2016).

21  Direction des grâces et affaires criminelles, November 2011, www.justice.gouv.fr/publication/guide_violences_conjugales.pdf

22  *Conseil Consultatif Coutumier du Territoire*, 15 and 16 June meetings, quoted in Guy Agniel (2008, p. 91). This council was later replaced by the Customary Senate in 1999.

23 However, according to the Customary Senate, a new customary union is impossible (*La Parole, Journal d'information du Sénat coutumier*, Socle Commun des Valeurs Kanak, No. 17, June 2013, p. 23).

24 The *indigénat* was created to govern the peoples classified as 'natives' in the colonies of the French empire. In New Caledonia it was introduced in 1887, implementing a policy of spatial and legal segregation, and it remained in force until the Kanaks obtained citizenship in 1946.

25 Recommendation from the delegates of the Catholic association UICALO (Union des indigènes calédoniens amis de la liberté dans l'ordre) in 1949, Archives of New Caledonia, ANC 97W300.

26 Letter from pastor Elia Tidjine, general secretary to the Vice-President of the Government Council, 6 September, ANC 39W63.

27 The issues of the paper *Le Réveil Kanak* published in 1972 and 1973 contain several incendiary articles directed at the missionaries and their associations. Their titles speak for themselves: 'The church in question'; 'Assisted, Morons, Fucked, Bind, Tied up = AICLF (*association des indigènes calédoniens et loyaltiens français*, a Protestant group)'; 'Why would I believe in God?'; 'Charlemagnian Prayer' (pastor Raymond Charlemagne, whom the article qualifies as a slave trader, was a Protestant missionary who had settled in New Caledonia in 1947).

28 *La Parole, Journal d'informations du Sénat coutumier*, No. 16, December 2012, p. 20.

29 *La Parole, Journal d'informations du Sénat coutumier*, No. 17, June 2013, p. 29.

30 Given the lack of recent statistical figures on the dissolution of customary unions and on divorces, I use the category 'separated or divorced' from the population censuses which apply to individuals resorting to customary and common law statuses. In 2009, 114 separated or divorced Kanak men versus 63 women lived in the Loyauté Islands (where over 90% of the population is Kanak), while the figures for 2014 were 157 versus 75, respectively.

31 Population censuses show that the proportion of separated or divorced people among Kanaks went up from 1.57% in 2009 to 1.73% in 2014, against 5.94% in 2009 and 6.22% in 2014 among non-Kanaks.

32 *VKP Infos*, No. 49, June to July 2016, p. 26.

# References

Agniel, G. (2008). Statut coutumier kanak et juridiction de droit commun en Nouvelle-Calédonie. *Aspects, 3*, 81–96.

Capo, M. (2017). Le recueil de droit coutumier Paicî-Camûkî. Autopsie d'un projet classé sans suite. In C. Demmer & B. Trépied (dir.), *La coutume kanak dans l'État. Perspectives coloniales et postcoloniales sur la Nouvelle-Calédonie* (pp. 161–189). Paris: L'Harmattan.

Demmer, C., & Salomon, C. (2013). Droit coutumier et indépendance kanak, *Vacarme, 64*, 63–78.

George, N. (2017). Policing "conjugal order": Gender, hybridity and vernacular security in Fiji. *International Feminist Journal of Politics, 19*(1), 55–70.

Gorohouna, S., & Ris, C. (2017). Vingt-cinq ans de politiques de réduction des inégalités: Quels impacts sur l'accès aux diplômes? *Mouvements, 91*(3), 89–98.

Heise, L., & Manji, K. (2016). *Social norms*. GSDRC Professional Development Reading Pack No. 31. Birmingham: University of Birmingham.

Johnson, M. P. (1995). Patriarchal terrorism and common couple violence: Two forms of violence against women. *Journal of Marriage and Family, 57*(2), 283–294.

Johnson, M. P. (2008). *A typology of domestic violence: Intimate terrorism, violent resistance, and situational couple violence*. Boston, MA: Northeastern University Press.

Lieber, M., & Roca i Escoda, M. (2015). Violences en famille: Quelles réponses institution-nelles? *Enfances Familles Générations, 22,* 1–13.

Merle, I. (2017). De la brutalisation des rapports sociaux en contexte colonial: L'exemple de la Nouvelle-Calédonie. In A. Sirota (dir.), *Violences entre générations. Transmission et transformation en Océanie et ailleurs* (pp. 55–75). Paris: Ed. Le Manuscrit.

Nicolas, H. (2012). *La fabrique des époux. Approche anthropologique et historique du mariage, de la conjugalité et du genre (Lifou, Nouvelle-Calédonie)* (Doctoral disserta-tion). Aix-Marseille University, Marseille, France.

Parent, C., & Digneffe, F. (1996). A feminist contribution to ethics in criminal justice inter-vention. In T. O'Reilly-Fleming (dir.), *Post-critical criminology* (pp. 201–215). Scarbor-ough, ON: Prentice Hall.

Passa, J. (2013). *Femmes et violence, quel chemin?* Research report, 44 p.

Proietti-Scifoni, G., & Daly, K. (2011). Gendered violence and restorative justice: The views of New Zealand opinion leaders. *Contemporary Justice Review, 14*(3), 269–290.

Ris, C. (2013). Les inégalités ethniques dans l'accès à l'emploi en Nouvelle-Calédonie. *Économie et Statistique, 464–466,* 59–71.

Rognon, F. (1991). *Conversion, syncrétisme et nationalisme. Analyse du changement reli-gieux chez les Mélanésiens de Nouvelle-Calédonie* (Doctoral dissertation). University Paris X, Paris, France.

Salomon, C. (2017a). Quatre décennies de féminisme kanak. *Mouvements, 91*(3), 55–66.

Salomon, C. (2017b). Égalité totale ou évolution encadrée et séparée. Retour sur les années 1946–1956. In C. Demmer & B. Trépied (dirs.), *La coutume kanak dans l'État. Perspec-tives coloniales et post-coloniales sur la Nouvelle-Calédonie* (pp. 49–95). Paris: L'Harmattan.

Salomon, C. (2018). Genre, justice et indemnisation des victimes de statut coutumier kanak. *Ethnologie Française, 1,* 69–80.

Salomon, C., & Hamelin, C. (2008). Challenging violence: Kanak women renegotiating gender relations in New Caledonia. *The Asia Pacific Journal of Anthropology, 9*(1), 29–46.

Salomon, C., Hamelin, C., Goldberg, P., Sitta, R., Cyr, D., Nakache, J.-P., & Goldberg, M. (2004). *Premiers résultats de l'enquête santé, conditions de vie et de sécurité des femmes calédoniennes,* Research report, Inserm, 36 p.

Sénat Coutumier. (2014). *Charte du peuple kanak, Socle Commun des Valeurs et Principes Fondamentaux de la Civilisation Kanak.* http://www.senatcoutumier.nc/phocadownload/userupload/nos_publications/charte_socle_commun_2014.pdf

# 5 Naming violence

## Forms of economic violence in highland Papua New Guinea

*Richard Eves*

This chapter aims to contribute to a deeper and more nuanced understanding of family violence by focusing on one of the many kinds of violence suffered by women at the hands of their intimate male partners – economic violence or economic abuse. Although it is increasingly recognized, economic violence continues to receive less attention than other forms of violence (Adams, Sullivan, Bybee, & Greeson, 2008, p. 564; Jury, Thorburn, & Weatherall, 2017, p. 69; Usta, Makarem, & Habib, 2013, p. 357), and there remains a dearth of empirical insight into it (Postmus, Plummer, McMahon, Murshid, & Sung Kim, 2012, p. 412). Studies of violence are often restricted to physical violence, which is perhaps understandable given the trauma and injuries that result from this. While connections often exist between physical and economic violence, it is important to examine the latter in its own right, since it is another very serious harm that a great many women suffer. This chapter suggests, following the United Nations Secretary General, that: 'Naming forms and manifestations of violence against women is an important step towards recognizing and addressing them' (UN, 2006, p. 41).

Adams and colleagues define economic abuse[1] as behaviours 'that control a woman's ability to acquire, use, and maintain economic resources, thus threatening her economic security and potential for self-sufficiency' (Adams, 2011, p. 2; Adams et al., 2008, p. 564; Adams, Beeble, & Gregory, 2015, p. 363; see also Sedziafa, Tenkorang, Owusu, & Sano, 2017, p. 2633). In a study in Lebanon, Usta and colleagues say that economic abuse entails 'the withholding of earnings, restricted involvement in the labor force, and limited purchasing decisions' (2013, p. 356). Adding to these aspects, Fawole writes that economic violence includes 'acts such as refusing to contribute financially, denial of food and basic needs, preventing women from commencing or finishing education or from obtaining informal or formal employment, and controlling access to health care and agricultural resources' (2008, p. 169).

In their Scale of Economic Abuse, Adams and colleagues distinguish between two broad types of economic abuse – economic control and economic exploitation (2008; see also Adams, 2011; Adams et al., 2015). The former focuses on the types of behaviour that aim to control women's ability to obtain, use and make decisions about economic resources. The latter focuses on types of behaviour that involve the husband taking the wife's income and/or withholding or restricting the funds

DOI: 10.4324/9781003146667-6

they give to the family. While the Scale of Economic Abuse is wide ranging and satisfactorily encompasses many forms of economic violence, it is far more applicable to developed countries than developing countries. In developed countries, women have high levels of employment, much greater access to financial services, and more assets. Factors such as low workforce participation, high levels of financial exclusion, and lack of assets means that a wide range of the economic abuse related to employment, banking, and property that occurs in developed countries is simply not applicable to women in rural areas, where 85% of the Papua New Guinea (PNG) population resides.

## Research context

In seeking to increase knowledge about economic violence, this study takes the specific case of highlands PNG. Although the PNG Constitution states a commitment to equal human rights, and the country is a signatory to the Convention on the Elimination of All Forms of Discrimination against Women (CEDAW),[2] the picture for gender equality in PNG is bleak. The 2018 Gender Inequality Index (GII), which reflects gender-based inequalities in three dimensions – reproductive health, empowerment, and economic activity – ranks PNG 161 out of 162 (Yemen) countries (UNDP, 2019). Women in PNG are disadvantaged not only in relation to PNG men but also in relation to women in other countries. According to the UNDP, women have less education, with only 9.9% of women compared to 15.2% of men having at least some secondary education (UNDP, 2019). Women have zero representation in the national parliament, and violence against women is widespread and entrenched (Human Rights Watch, 2015, p. 15).

The research for this chapter was done in April 2016 in the PNG highlands provinces of Jiwaka (Anglimp-South Wahgi district) and Chimbu (Kundiawa-Gembogl district), where 91 interviews with women were completed (see Eves, with Kouro, Simiha, & Subalik, 2018). These comprised in-depth qualitative interviews, which sought to explore marital relationships, how the domestic economy is managed within the family/household, and what causes conflicts in relationships.[3] Fifty-three semi-structured interviews with key informants were also undertaken to gather contextual information, particularly the cultural, economic, and social factors affecting women's income-generating activities, as well as gender relations more broadly.

The great majority of women interviewed earned money through the informal economy – the selling of garden produce or cooked food at markets. A few earned income by selling livestock (pigs and chickens) and some in Jiwaka by selling coffee. A few women gained some income from elementary school teaching or filling roles in churches or as a women's local council representative. Overall, the women interviewed valued the opportunity to earn an income and spoke positively about its benefits. But income generation is not without negative impacts, including the extra burden of work it entails, the difficulty of finding someone to care for children, and the problems of accessing markets. A major challenge women confronted was economic violence, which saw their efforts to bring income into the family either eroded or erased altogether.

## Economic violence in Papua New Guinea

The research found that women are subject to several forms of economic violence. This chapter makes use of Adams and colleagues' two broad types of economic abuse – economic control and economic exploitation – since this captures the range of economic violence women in the PNG highlands experience. Sometimes, these two broad types are woven together, so that women are subjected to both economic control and economic exploitation. Sometimes, women are subjected to one broad category – economic control or economic exploitation – but not the other. So, in some cases, a woman has economic control over her earnings but is, nevertheless, subject to economic exploitation because her spouse refuses to contribute financially to the household. There is also considerable variability in the perpetration of violence. Some women are subject to economic violence and not physical violence. Some women are subject to physical violence and not economic violence. Although there is a close connection between economic and physical violence (see in the following text), men have other reasons for hitting their wives (infidelity, refusing sex, talking too much, and failure to satisfy a husband's expectations, such as not completing their work or not doing it to his satisfaction). Moreover, it should be noted that some women are not subject to violence in any form.

## Economic control

### *Control of spending and financial decision-making*

In the districts studied, financial decision-making takes place in two main ways: (1) 'household income management', where the husband and wife contribute their earnings to a common pool; or (2) 'independent income management', where the husband and wife manage their own earnings separately, but whether they both contribute to the household expenses or take responsibility for particular household expenses varies (Kabeer, 1997, p. 273; see Eves, with Kouro, Simiha, & Subalik, 2018). Sometimes, households use a combination of both, so that a husband and wife may pool some money, but each partner retains control over significant resources that they manage separately.[4]

Household income management is a feature of domestic relationships in Chimbu but less so in Jiwaka. In cases where money is pooled, husbands often seek to control wives' spending and monopolize financial decision-making, and several women interviewed indicated that their spouses made all the decisions about the use of pooled money. Indeed, in some cases, it appeared to be more akin to the husband seizing the wife's income.

Thus, economic control includes the alienation of women from making decisions about the use of money, including their own earnings. This lack of power and control over earnings is indicative of a lack of power and control over other aspects of women's lives (see also Jury et al., 2017, p. 71; Usta et al., 2013, p. 356). Some husbands demand that their wives seek permission for any expenditure of pooled income, though when it comes to their own expenditure they simply proceed without consultation or agreement. One woman in Jiwaka reported that, although the family's main source of income came from her sales of garden produce, she must ask her husband's permission to spend money to benefit her family. When her husband earns money, he does not consult with her about its use, though, in this case, she said he does spend it for the benefit of the household. Another woman reported similarly that she gives her earnings to her husband to deposit in a joint savings account, but to which only he has access. While they both make decisions about expenditure which is for the benefit of the household, if she wants to spend some of the money she must seek her husband's permission.

A respondent from Chimbu reported that her husband is the main decision-maker in the household and if she tries to participate, he tells her she must submit to him. He also tells her to listen to him so that their marriage will be strong, and though she used to argue with him, she no longer does so. He is also in control of income each fortnight and prepares a budget, telling her what to buy, and if she does not follow his orders, he slaps her. Despite this, she keeps the money she earns from her harvest separately and spends it as she wishes, which suggests that violence and power within relationships can sometimes be manifested in contra-dictory ways. Another respondent from Chimbu reported that her husband makes all the household decisions, which she accepts as the man's role. She believed that a husband should hold the household money and decide how it is spent. When, occasionally, she spends money without her husband's permission, he responds by getting angry. However, he has been known to spend all of their money on beer and cigarettes, and if she questions him about this, he responds with anger, though not physical violence.

In some cases, husbands take control of household income even when they do not themselves contribute to it. One respondent's violent husband, who has no income and only occasionally contributes labour towards earning income, takes control of the income she earns. She says that her husband looks after her well, spends their money on the family, and sometimes helps her with the garden and selling produce, but he also beats her if she is not fully submissive, does not do all the work he requires of her (both in the garden and in the home), or does not make a profit at market. The husband makes all the decisions, with his wife only occasionally con-tributing to them. If she earns money at the market, she must take it straight home and hand it over to her husband. Some income is held in a joint savings account to which both have independent access. She is expected to ask permission for any expenditure, whether this is to spend cash immediately after it is earned or entails withdrawing money from their joint bank account. However, both husband and wife do spend money without telling each other, which leads to conflict. If the wife fails to consult her husband about her own spending, he responds by beating her, though he does not usually consult her about spending for his own benefit.

### Preventing women from generating income

Some different examples of economic violence in the literature are concerned with men creating economic dependency in their wives by barring them from earning, restricting their employment, interrupting their work, or making it unnecessarily difficult for them to earn income (see Adams et al., 2008, p. 568; Sedziafa et al., 2017, p. 2624; Usta et al., 2013, p. 357). For example, Jury and colleagues describe how, in New Zealand, the 'stripping of economic power represented, for many women, a simple and inescapable method of securing dependence upon their abuser' (Jury et al., 2017, p. 72). In such cases, husbands withheld money for household essentials, and this comprised a source of humiliation and shame for victims (Jury et al., 2017, p. 73).

The research in the PNG highlands did provide some examples of men seeking to control or prevent women's income generation, particularly if it prevented a wife from performing her gender-defined duties (such as doing domestic chores). However, another significant reason was that many men, being extremely jealous, wish to control their wives' movements for fear of extramarital liaisons on her part. Then again, many men welcome their wife earning money, since it allows them to opt out of contributing financially to the household. One example, a respondent from Jiwaka, told us that although she has control over her income and decides how it is spent, her husband endeavours to control her movements, not allowing her to walk with others and sometimes forbidding her from going to the market where she earns money. Other women are subject to controlling behaviours from their spouses who give them detailed daily instructions as to how they should use their time, disrupting their efforts at income generation.

One woman reported that if the time she spent at the market earning money left her with insufficient time to do all her domestic and child-raising tasks in what her husband regarded as a timely manner, he would become verbally aggressive towards her and 'argue with me for not preparing food for the kids early'. This appeared to be a common problem, with several women commenting on the risk of physical violence for women whose income generation requires them to go to market. If husbands consider them to be away from the home too much or if they return home late, the men become physically and emotionally violent, because they consider their wives to be neglecting their domestic duties. Putting women under pressure to fulfil gender norms has the effect of making income generation a risky enterprise with costs that include violence.

The behaviour of husbands in the PNG highlands is far more concerned with maintaining power and control over wives than with creating dependency in them. This is partly due to a rigid gender hierarchy in which men value their own status and welfare far more highly than women's. It is also due to marriage practices – in particular, to the exchange of bride price, which is often considered to give men absolute control over their wives and to justify domineering behaviour and physical and other forms of violence. Men use the expression 'full price, full body', meaning that since the full bride price requested was paid, the husband has complete control of the wife's body. Bride price, men say, entitles them to total control over their wives, 'from their feet to the hair on their head' or 'from head to toe' (see Eves, 2019). Though the forms of economic violence evident in the rural highlands of PNG are not so much about creating dependency as in the New Zealand case study, Jury and colleagues also argue that the men they studied were, at base, similarly motivated by the desire for power over women. Economic abuse, they say, 'appears to be exercised primarily to gain and exercise control and domination over women' (Jury et al., 2017, p. 70).

## Economic exploitation

### *Demanding/seizing money*

The most common form of economic exploitation women endure is demands for money. Husbands routinely pressure and bully their wives for their earnings or savings, so that they can use the money for their own discretionary spending on alcohol, marijuana, gambling, or other women.[5] Sometimes, the demands for money come in the guise of asking for 'loans' which are not repaid. While men usually harass their wives for money, they sometimes seize the money, or steal it from their wives. This harassment often includes physical violence or threats of it. Several women reported that when their husband was drunk he would subject them to aggressive bullying and physical violence, especially if he had spent all his money on alcohol and wanted money to buy more. A key informant described the common situation of men demanding money when drunk:

> They are mad, they go and beat their wives with a stick, demanding they give them money or any of the small earnings they made from marketing. Men expect their wives will give them money, so that they can go around, drink beer and play cards. The woman will think about the family and looking after the children. She will budget for the children but the man comes and puts pressure and demands that she give him the money.

In one case, a respondent reported that when her husband came home drunk, he would demand money and break things and steal her money if she refused to accede to his demands. One woman from Jiwaka reported that even though she is no longer married to him, her former spouse still comes to her regularly and demands money, threatening her with violence if she refuses. He also plundered several of her gardens which were ready for harvesting, taking the food for himself and his new wife. When she was still married to him, he would demand money from her after she had earned it at the market, beating her if she refused.

Husbands who contribute no income to the household still demand money from their partners. For example, one woman reported that her husband has no source of income but relies on her earnings for his discretionary spending. She receives little or no help from him when it comes to income generation, but he habitually takes half of the income she earns for his own personal spending on cards and cigarettes. This is an ongoing problem in the marriage, and when she criticizes his behaviour, he becomes angry and they have verbal arguments (though there is no physical violence). Some husbands expect full control of all the income their spouse generates, even when they have not contributed to earning it. This is especially common in the context of cash crops, such as coffee, that bring in a larger amount than is usually gained from market vending. Income from cash crops is often appropriated by husbands, even though their spouse was the major contributor of labour to its production. This applies especially to Jiwaka, where coffee is an important source of income. Key informants noted that despite women doing all of the labour to produce the coffee, many men seize the coffee when it is ready for sale, so that they can, as one remarked, 'see the money first'. One key informant described the resulting inequity in sharing coffee income:

> When you look closely at coffee, the husband does not pick the coffee. When it comes to picking coffee, it is the wife who picks coffee. She will pick it, bag it, and carry it ready to sell it. Men are happy to sell coffee but only a few men in the community have good thoughts about the money and divide it up well. If a man gets K100 (USD 30), he will only give K50 (USD 15) to the wife to look after the children. When the man gets K50, he will go off and drink cola or other things with other men. When the woman gets K50, she will buy cooking oil, rice or other things needed for the house. When the man returns home, he doesn't buy anything for the house with the K50 he had, but still expects to eat from the K50 he gave to his wife. A lot of men when they sell a bag of coffee and they get K100, they will keep K80 (USD 25) and give K20 (USD 6) to the wife or keep K70 (USD 22) and give K30 to the wife. Think about how much K30 (USD 9) or K20 will buy. K70 or K80 will go on beer and then he will return home to the house and kick plates and cups about, demanding more money. Where will the woman get it from? K30 or K20 is not a lot of money.

Men justify their seizure of coffee income by recourse to arguments about land and the fact that the coffee trees are planted on land that is owned by men (see also Eves & Titus, 2020). Women have more control over the income they earn from selling garden crops, but this is generally because men believe that selling vegetables brings in little money compared to coffee. Although income from vegetables is seen as belonging to women, this does not prevent some husbands from demanding money from their wives when they have depleted their own resources. Even though many men may consider that the income from vegetables belongs to women, they are, nevertheless, keen to know what their spouse has earned. One man suggested that a man will do a 'stocktake' when his wife returns from the market in an effort to ascertain whether there is money he can demand or seize.

### Men's refusal to contribute to the household

Economic violence is not just a question of women keeping control of the income they have earned themselves and preventing it from being seized by their spouse, for it is also a question of husbands contributing financial resources to the household. Numerous men consider household well-being to be secondary to their own personal priorities and wants. Regardless of the impact on their spouse and their children of their spending, men put themselves first, about which the women respondents complained bitterly. Indeed, a by-product of women's income generation is that it enables men to reduce their financial contributions to the household or to opt out completely – that is, they deny wives' access to their income or allow only limited access to it (see also Mayoux, 1999, p. 972). This is largely because many men view the money they earn solely as their own, to use in whatever way they wish. This was confirmed by key informants, who said that men refusing to give money to their wives is very common, regardless of whether their income comes from wage labour or from selling garden produce or other cash crops. The result is that the women of Chimbu and Jiwaka often bear full responsibility for the financial support of the household, even when their spouse does have an income. By default, women become the sole breadwinner of the household, something that sees them overburdened with work.

Men in paid employment also do not often share their income with their wives. According to one key informant:

> lots of working men don't use their money properly, they spend the money on beer. It's a big issue. A few men spend their money wisely but most of the men spend the money on alcohol. . . . Some men are ok they share their money but lots of the women who come here [to the community-based organization Voice for Change] the husbands don't share the money equally with them, especially the men like teachers, or those working in mining companies.

In some cases where men had an income, they considered that they should only contribute half, or less, to the household, though they, nevertheless, expected their spouse to contribute all of her income.

Some men refuse to tell their wives how much they earn, some do not tell the truth about their income, and some refuse to contribute any money to the family. For example, a woman from Chimbu reported that her spouse lied about his earnings and what he spent his money on. A woman from Jiwaka reported that she did not know how her husband spent his wages, which she tried complaining about, but eventually resigned herself to not knowing. Sometimes, he would give her money for the household but would tell her how she had to spend it.

One woman in Chimbu recounted how her husband earned money irregularly from work in a trade store and although he did occasionally contribute some money to the household, mostly he did not. While she controls the money she earns and spends it on household items to benefit her family, she is unable to save because she directs all of her income into the household. By contrast, her husband saves money because he does not direct all of his income into the household. That is, her earning money is taken advantage of by her husband, who directs his money into his own separate savings. Since he does not tell her what he is actually saving for, she resents this.

Some men do not contribute financially to the household because they do not earn an income, preferring to live off their spouse's earnings. One woman from Chimbu reported that her husband used to work as a security guard but no longer does so, preferring to live off her earnings and beating her if she does not give him money, which he spends on other women. He, nevertheless, makes all the household decisions. Another woman from Chimbu reported a similar situation. Although her husband had a source of income, he would not share his money with his wife and generally wasted his money on his own discretionary spending while expecting his wife to provide for his daily needs. Indeed, the reason some women started income-generating activities initially was due to their husband's failure to provide financially for the household.

Economic violence is often a feature of polygynous marriages and arises when a man takes a new wife.[6] Polygyny often results in the first wife being abandoned, or 'dropped' as one woman remarked, with the husband refusing to take any financial responsibility for the household or the children from the first marriage. All the costs entailed in looking after children, such as feeding, clothing, and meeting their health and education expenses, then falls to the first wife. Not only does this place enormous strain on her, particularly if she has several children, but also, in some cases, the children are unable to attend school because their mother cannot afford the expenses. A significant volume of the caseload of Voice for Change is concerned with managing the negative impacts of polygyny on women. According to one key informant, 70% of the women seeking assistance from the organization do so because their husbands do not share resources with their wives or take responsibility for their children. Sometimes, polygynous husbands will resort to physical violence, other forms of ill treatment, or neglect in an effort to drive the first wife away. This was the situation described by one woman in Jiwaka, who has since divorced, who recounted that following her marriage to a man who already had one wife, her husband would not give her any money or help her in the garden. Instead of supporting both wives, he favoured the first wife, giving her money. Both he and the first wife, nonetheless, considered the second wife's assets as their own and there have been conflicts over property.

Some husbands minimize or withdraw financial support to the household and others withhold labour, refusing to take up paid employment or to carry out subsistence labour, relying solely on their spouses' efforts. So, while some men contribute nothing or almost nothing to the household, their wives work hard to feed the family and to bring in income to meet household expenses. A recurring refrain from our respondents was the imbalance in workloads and the lack of support from their spouses, especially in the often heavy labour in the garden.

The husband of one woman, mentioned earlier, who contributes very little to the household either through employment or in the garden, usually spends his time with the other young men doing nothing. Meanwhile, she is responsible for all the work in the house and the garden, and even does the types of labour that men typically do, such as the strenuous work of cutting down large trees or digging drainage trenches. The husband of another woman from Jiwaka did not share his income with her or help with labour in the garden or selling at market or at home, but he expected her to perform domestic tasks for him, such as washing his clothes, and would become enraged if she did not do so. He also aggressively pressures her to give him the money she earns. The experience of these two women is common in Jiwaka and Chimbu. Not only are they solely responsible for the labour that ensures that the family has food to eat, but they are also responsible for the burden of unpaid work in the home (such as carrying water and firewood to the house, cooking, cleaning, and child care).

## The nexus between economic violence and physical violence

While physical violence and economic violence are distinct forms of violence, the nexus between the two is strong. It is important to recognize that economic violence is one part of a repertoire of violent behaviour which uses various forms of violence with the aim of achieving power and control in intimate relationships (Adams et al., 2008, p. 563; see also Postmus et al., 2012, p. 412; Postmus, Plummer, & Stylianou, 2016, p. 692). Thus, economic violence is also sometimes accompanied by threats of, or actual, physical harm by male spouses. Physical violence can be used to enforce economic violence and can comprise a coercive strategy to force wives to hand over income. As some of the aforementioned examples show, spousal conflicts over money and income generation often degenerate into physical violence, because women resist handing over their hard-earned income to their spouses. This is not to suggest that women are at fault, or that the responsibility for physical violence lies with them, but simply to point out that one of the triggers for physical violence can have economic violence at its heart.

This has led some scholars to argue that economic violence comprises a risk factor for physical violence (Usta et al., 2013, p. 357; see also Fawole, 2008, p. 167). Given that women are usually responsible for maintaining the household, it is not surprising that they are aggrieved about, and often contest, their husband's demands for money or his failure to contribute to the household. Several of our respondents reported that their husband became physically violent if they refused to give him money. Similarly, women's contestation of their spouse's failure to contribute to the household or his wasteful personal expenditure can produce a violent response. Some respondents reported that even a simple request to their spouse to contribute to the household was enough to provoke physical violence. For example, one woman from Chimbu told us her husband responded to her requests for money to support their children by beating her. Another woman from Chimbu reported that her husband beats her when he believes she is not doing enough work in the garden or tending the pigs properly, both of which are income-earning activities. The husband of another woman, mentioned earlier, beats her when she returns from the market if he deems that she has not earned enough money or is withholding some of the earnings. She reported that the only way to avoid being beaten on her return from market is to bring all the money home and show it to him. Her husband holds and controls the money she earns and decides how it is spent, and she must ask his permission for any expenditure. Occasionally, he has prevented her from going to the market and the produce that was readied for sale was wasted; he also responds violently if she questions his unnecessary expenditure. Economic violence can also lead to women being trapped in physically violent relationships. When husbands demand or seize income, prevent women from generating income, or refuse to contribute funds or labour to the household, women are less likely to be able to develop independent financial resources, making it difficult to leave dysfunctional and violent relationships.

## Conclusion

Economic violence, which is often overlooked, is one manifestation of violence in a spectrum of aggressive behaviours, which includes emotional, sexual, physical, and economic violence. Economic violence causes significant harm not only to women but also to any children or other dependents in the household. Life is quite precarious for the women interviewed in Jiwaka and Chimbu, who are dependent on selling commodities at market and whose profits are usually very small. Economic violence causes financial hardship for the family, making existence even more precarious than it is already. Economic violence can cause women to be pushed further into poverty; unable to accumulate savings or acquire other assets, women are unable to prepare themselves for economic and other shocks. Moreover, a shortage of assets means that no funds are available for expenses such as health and education; women must forego treatment for themselves or their children, because there are no funds for user fees, medicines, or transport to health facilities, and children's education is curtailed.

The data from highlands PNG show that economic violence is all too common and can take a variety of forms. The research was not specifically designed to examine women's experience of economic abuse, but focused more broadly on the relationship between women's economic empowerment and violence. Had the research been focused more exactly on economic violence, the data gathered might have revealed more varieties of economic violence than discussed here. Nevertheless, the data clearly show that many women in the provinces studied, and probably more widely in PNG, endure this form of violence. Much as the quotation at the start of this chapter puts it, '[p]roblem recognition is the first step toward finding a solution' (Postmus et al., 2012, p. 426). It is therefore important to name violence in all its forms.

## Notes

1  Sometimes also referred to as financial abuse or economic coercion.
2  PNG ratified the convention on 12 January 1995 and submitted its first report in 2011.
3  Family and household are used interchangeably since in PNG a family/household does not always centre on the nuclear family of husband, wife, and children, but includes other extended family members and dependants. So, in addition to their own children, 35 of the women who were respondents had from 1 to 5 such dependants, making a total of 60.
4  Decision-making is not always restricted to the husband and wife, but sometimes involves other members of the immediate family, such as children, or extended family members, including blood relatives and in-laws. In one case, the husband's brother was sometimes involved in decision-making, though it was unclear what type of decisions he participated in. In another case, the husband's parents had a role in making decisions about land. One woman who was separated from her husband made decisions with her two daughters. In some cases, the authority shifts from the husband to an eldest son. In one case, the eldest son occupied the position of head of household and told his mother to stay home and do the gardening and not go to town because it is expensive. She had some decision-making power over health, education, and resources, though this son also joined in making decisions about the spending of money.

5 It is important to recognize that this type of economic violence is the preserve not only of male intimate partners, but can come from other relatives, affines, and beyond. Many of the women interviewed commented that one of the negatives that accompanied income generation was that it was met with increased demands for money, particularly from family and in-laws but also more widely. One woman, for example, was so intimidated by the threats of violence from her husband's brothers that she gave in to their demands for money. Another woman was harassed, not only by her husband, but by his sisters who demanded money which was not repaid. Women also complained more generally that people demand goods on credit but do not repay the debt (see also Eves & Lusby, with Araia, Maeni, & Martin, 2018).

6 Polygyny, referred to as 'dubal marit' (double marriage) in *Tok Pisin*, was a pre-colonial practice among the peoples of Jiwaka and Chimbu, as well as other parts of the highlands. Despite many men aspiring to having polygynous unions in the past, this was actually the preserve of leaders with wealth who were seeking to increase their renown by the practice. Such men had sufficient land to marry a number of wives and could increase their wealth through the labour of these wives. Traditionally, domestic discord between co-wives was mitigated by maintaining absolute equity among the wives and ideally, men with polygynous households should have separate houses, pigpens, and gardens for each wife (see Eves, with Kouro, Simiha, & Subalik, 2018, pp. 20–22). Of the 91 women interviewed, 15 indicated that they were separated, divorced, or abandoned by their husbands. Fifteen of the women who were currently married had been married before, and five women indicated that they were currently in a polygynous marriage. Aside from the economic violence discussed in the text, polygynous marriages could also entail physical violence. For those women who had either been in, or were currently in, a polygynous marriage, nine said that there was physical violence, though this is not necessarily male violence. This included violence by the husband against the wife, violence from the husband and co-wife against another wife, violence from a co-wife or co-wives against another wife, and violence from female respondents towards husbands or co-wives.

# References

Adams, A. E. (2011). *Measuring the effects of domestic violence on women's financial well-being*. CFS Research Brief No. 5.6. Center for Financial Security. Madison, WI: University of Wisconsin-Madison.

Adams, A. E., Beeble, M. L., & Gregory, K. A. (2015). Evidence of the construct validity of the scale of economic abuse. *Violence and Victims, 30*, 363–364. doi:10.1891/0886-6708.VV-D-13-00133

Adams, A. E., Sullivan, C. M., Bybee, D., & Greeson, M. R. (2008). Development of the scale of economic abuse. *Violence Against Women, 14*, 563–587. doi:10.1177/1077801208315529

Eves, R. (2019). "Full price, full body": Norms, brideprice and intimate partner violence in Highlands Papua New Guinea. *Culture, Health and Sexuality, 21*, 1367–1380. doi:10.1080/13691058.2018.1564937

Eves, R., with Kouro, G., Simiha, S., & Subalik, I. (2018). *Do no harm research: Papua New Guinea*. Canberra, Australia: Department of Pacific Affairs. http://hdl.handle.net/1885/143397

Eves, R., & Lusby, S., with Araia, T., Maeni, M.-F., & Martin, R. (2018). *Do no harm research: Solomon Islands*. Canberra, Australia: Department of Pacific Affairs. http://hdl.handle.net/1885/143396

Eves, R., & Titus, A. (2020). *Women's economic empowerment among coffee small-holders in Papua New Guinea*. Canberra, Australia: Department of Pacific Affairs.

Fawole, O. I. (2008). Economic violence to women and girls: Is it receiving the necessary attention? *Trauma, Violence, and Abuse, 9*, 67–177. doi:10.1177/1524838008319255

Human Rights Watch. (2015). *Bashed up: Family violence in Papua New Guinea*. New York, NY: Human Rights Watch.

Jury, A., Thorburn, N., & Weatherall, R. (2017). "What's his is his and what's mine is his": Financial power and the economic abuse of women in Aotearoa. *Aoteroa New Zealand Social Work, 29*, 69–82. doi:10.11157/anzswj-vol29iss2id312

Kabeer, N. (1997). Women, wages and intra-household power relations in urban Bangladesh. *Development and Change, 28*, 261–302. doi:10.1111/1467-7660.00043

Mayoux, L. (1999). Questioning virtuous spirals: Micro-finance and women's empowerment in Africa. *Journal of International Development, 11*, 957–984.

Postmus, J. L., Plummer, S.-B., McMahon, S., Murshid, N. S., & Sung Kim, M. (2012). Understanding economic abuse in the lives of survivors. *Journal of Interpersonal Violence, 27*, 411–430. doi:10.1177/0886260511421669

Postmus, J. L., Plummer, S.-B., & Stylianou, A. M. (2016). Measuring economic abuse in the lives of survivors: Revising the scale of economic abuse. *Violence Against Women, 22*, 692–703. doi:10.1177/1077801215610012

Sedziafa, A. P., Tenkorang, E. Y., Owusu, A. Y., & Sano, Y. (2017). Women's experiences of intimate partner economic abuse in the Eastern Region of Ghana. *Journal of Family Issues, 38*, 2620–2641. doi:10.1177/0192513X16686137

United Nations. (2006). *Ending violence against women–From words to action: Study of the Secretary-General*. New York, NY: United Nations.

United Nations Development Programme. (2019). *Human development report 2019: Inequalities in human development in the 21st century*. Briefing note for countries on the 2019 Human Development Report, Papua New Guinea. New York, NY: United Nations Development Programme.

Usta, J., Makarem, N. N., & Habib, R. R. (2013). Economic abuse in Lebanon: Experiences and perceptions. *Violence Against Women, 19*, 356–375. doi:10.1177/1077801213486313

# 6 Culture-based counselling at the domestic violence shelter of the Sisters of the Anglican Church of Melanesia in the Solomon Islands

*Xandra Miguel-Lorenzo*

The 'Christian Care Centre', known as the 'CCC', is a shelter for abused women and children founded and staffed by Anglican religious Sisters[1] of the Church of Melanesia in the Solomon Islands. The 'Maeva House', a two-storey building and the main house in the compound, officially opened its doors in 2004 to survivors of gender-based violence called 'clients'. The compound includes an education centre and a house for 'young women'. The Sisters working at the shelter belong to The Sisters of the Church and The Sisters of Melanesia religious communities and represent with the Sisters' diverse Island origin representing the country's provinces. The Sisters have individual rooms in bungalows next the compound's gate, by an open kitchen, and on the second floor of the Maeva House. Thus, the Sisters easily attend to visitors' and clients' needs. The Sisters and clients are safe from the alleged perpetrators of abuse inside the compound, especially once the metal fence is locked at sunset. Merry (2006) argues that the women's rights movement is transnational, not a Global North to a Global South movement. The CCC is an illustration of Merry's vernacularization of transnational women's rights involving 'transplantations' of institutions and programmes, such as gender training programmes, domestic violence laws, shelters, counselling centres, or human rights' commissions, from one place to another; and the work of 'intermediaries' or Indigenous activists translating human and women's rights into local terms and frameworks of power and meaning (Merry, 2006, 2009). The Sisters act as translation agents among community leaders, non-governmental organization (NGO) workers, government representatives, or academics in the Solomon Islands. Sister Kathleen, for instance, represented the CCC in the 2006 UN Commission on the Status of Women's 50th session in New York. Merry notes on this matter that 'intermediaries' 'hold a double consciousness, combining both human rights conceptions and local ways of thinking about grievances' (Merry, 2006, p. 229). Solomons' picture is more complex. Responses to gender-based violence entail bearing in mind the Solomon Islands cultures, known as '*kastom*' in Solomon Islands Pidgin (SIP); the State's legal criminal justice system; the Churches' canons; and the women's international rights and related policies. Merry further argues that human rights promote ideas of individual autonomy, equality, choice, and secularism, and seek to transform existing relations of power, displacing alternative visions of social justice towards a homogenization of local communities. In this chapter, I argue

DOI: 10.4324/9781003146667-7

that the CCC, a religious response to domestic violence, enables women to remain relational human beings in the taking of individual women's rights.

Firstly, to 'remain relational' at the CCC means that the Sisters and clients reproduce Solomon Islands kin relations underpinning a moral system of personal protection against intimate, domestic, and interpersonal violence – which is customary. The clients are 'under' the Sisters' care and protection, as Solomon Islands people see themselves as being 'under' the protection of the 'head of the family'. Sister Daisy once referred to a client as 'the person who belongs to me' [SIP *person blong mi*]. Unlike in Solomon Islands family settings, women staying at the shelter make decisions to deal with their problems with autonomy, according to their multi-layered normative regimes and rights. The 'head' of the client's family does not make decisions for her and the Sisters are not meant to influence the client's decisions. Secondly, the Sisters protect their clients from violence by filling the gap created by the women's relatives who fail to protect them against gendered violence, ameliorating the impact that urbanization has in family relations. Christianity allows people with different Solomon Islands cultures to belong to a multicultural Christian family. The Sisters act, I argue, as a 'foster Christian family' for the clients. In Honiara, Solomon Islands' capital city, the clients' relatives often lack the authority to stop domestic abuse, or they fear retaliation from the abuser. And women often lack relatives to protect them from domestic abuse in their post-marital residence. Honiara is considered a space where culture has 'broken down' because Honiara is a multicultural space where one Solomon Island *kastom* does not dominate over another Solomon Island *kastom*. People for the most part avoid applying their particular *kastom* to stop domestic and sexual violence. An exception to this is Malaita Islands groups who exchange a high bride price for women in marriage (Pollard, 2000). Gendered or sexual violence devalues women, and therefore, it also devalues the bride price paid for the women at marriage and received by the women's relatives (who use it to pay for their own brides). In Honiara, violence against women is usually visible to others in the streets, but people feel they cannot intervene to stop the abuse. It is not that gendered violence goes unseen in the city (Miguel-Lorenzo, 2020). Thirdly, promoting and taking care of the client's social relations, the Sisters as community religious leaders, alongside priests and religious Brothers, offer pastoral counselling to couples and families affected by domestic abuse, listening and giving advice. In addition, the Sisters have created a domestic violence 'culture-based counselling' and advocacy method to help women amend their broken intimate relationship or family relations.

In this chapter, I situate the Sisters' shelter and counselling method in relation to the Solomon Islands' country profile regarding domestic abuse and the Solomon Islands' policies and laws. I examine how understandings of *kastom*, Christianity, and blood underpin Indigenous ideas of acceptable and unacceptable intimate violence. While the concept of 'domestic violence' is foreign to the Solomon Islands, interpersonal violence is not. The Sisters use Solomon Islands shared understandings of kinship relatedness to inform their culture-based counselling method and the running of the shelter. The Sisters aim at restoring the clients' family relations from a neutral position, and because of this, I conclude that the CCC remains the most effective response to domestic abuse in the Solomon Islands.

## Gender violence in the Solomon Islands

The Solomon Islands comprises six major islands and more than 900 smaller islands and atolls, grouped into 10 administrative provinces, which encompass Melanesian and Polynesian cultures, matrilineal and patrilineal societies with different systems of land tenure, inheritance, and marriage. The country's population is 515,870, and Honiara's population is 64,609, according to the 2009 Solomon Islands Population and Housing Census (Solomon Islands Government, 2009). In Honiara, 45% of married couples are composed of spouses from different islands (2013 People's survey in Moore, 2015, p. 436). In the 1980s, domestic and sexual violence was identified as an urban problem resulting from alcohol consumption, Western influence, unemployment, crime, lack of education, urban migration, and the break down in traditional values (Schoeffel Meleisea, 1986, pp. 39–40, in Douglas, 2003, p. 6; UNICEF Pacific & Solomon Islands Government, 1993, pp. 48, 51, 65, 1998, pp. 36, 45; Jourdan, 2008, pp. 14, 24–26; Deroeck, 1988, p. 7, in UNICEF Pacific & Solomon Islands Government, 1993, p. 90). In 1992, the first Pacific Regional Meeting on Violence Against Women took place at the Fiji Women Crisis Centre, including Solomon Islands delegates, challenging the normalization of domestic violence as a family affair in the Pacific (Afu Billy in the video 'Mere Blo Iume. Stori Blo Oketa' by Regional Assistance Mission to Solomon Islands Public Affairs Unit, 2012). The Solomons inherited English Common Law from the British protectorate, and Solomon Islands churches, NGOs, and the government have advocated for domestic violence legislation since at least 1993 (UNICEF Pacific & Solomon Islands Government, 1993, p. 65).[2]

The Solomon Islands are a state party of the United Nations Committee on the Elimination of Discrimination Against Women (CEDAW) since 2002 and condemn violence against women and girls, regardless of customs, traditions, or religious considerations. Amnesty International (2004) documented violence against women and children, as breaches of human and women's rights, during the country's civil unrest known as the 'The Tensions' (1998–2003). Against cultural responses to domestic abuse, Amnesty International outlined a policy agenda with a focus on domestic violence legal remedies. Accordingly, milestones have been achieved: the publication of the Solomon Islands Family Health and Safety Study (2009) stating that 64% of ever-partnered women had experienced physical and/ or sexual violence; the formulation of the National Policy on Violence against Women (2009); the outlaw of marital rape by the Solomon Islands High Court (2012); and the Family Protection Act (2014), implemented in 2016, including the penal code reform, criminalized domestic violence with custodial sentences. The Family Protection Act gave further powers to the police to issue domestic violence Protection Safety Notes (PSNs), in addition to court restraining orders. After the UN Security Council Resolution 1325 was passed in the Solomon Islands in October 2000, women have been included in post-conflict reconciliation processes.

Comprising the legal remedies to domestic violence, a forensic clinic for gender-based violence called 'Seif Ples' ('Safe place') opened in Honiara in 2015, complementing the work of Indigenous organizations: the 'Family Support Centre' and the 'Christian Care Centre' – operating since 1998 in the country. Seif Ples offers counselling, information, and advocacy services; a temporary shelter; a 24-hour advice line; and referrals to the hospital, police, the public solicitor's office (offering legal aid), the CCC, and medical aid, with a round-the-clock nurse available to facilitate collection of forensic evidence for legal prosecution. Legal remedies which entail reporting to the police domestic or sexual violence with evidence, collected at Seif Ples or the hospital, have not eliminated community responses to domestic abuse from families and community leaders (chiefs and religious leaders). The Sisters' 'culture-based counselling' remains a relevant response to domestic violence in the Solomon Islands (Ride & Soaki, 2019).

## *Kastom* and violence against women

Urbanization has an impact on family structures. On the one hand, '[i]nfluential family members who could mediate conflict and control violence are often absent and family support is often minimal in urban areas' (Pollard, 1988, in UNICEF Pacific & Solomon Islands Government, 1993, p. 90, ibid., p. 64). On the other hand, intimate violence is normalized and underpinned by Christian ideas. One Television series, 'Domestic Violence' (aired in 2009), interviewed people in the streets of Honiara about the causes of domestic abuse. The interviewees explained that the 'head of the family', normally a husband, coordinates the family members' actions as a production unit and protects the family from outside violence. The 'head' can also use violence against his partner or wife if she fails to listen to him or to act as he tells her. When a woman acts with autonomy from her husband, the couple does not 'communicate together' and their marriage can 'break down'. If the woman does something which is 'not right', such as not preparing her husband's meal, a husband has the right to hit her. As a man explained:

> In Melanesia we have *kastom* and the man is the family leader. When a woman does not follow the men's thinking or mind and the disagreement is longstanding, the man hits the woman.

It seemed that Christian ideas on marital relations coincided with customary ideas on wives' subordination to their husbands. A woman said, 'God likes it when a woman and a man communicate together their [family] planning'. Another woman explained that the man hits the woman to 'kill off' his anger resulting from the woman's misbehaviour. And a young man said that a man could hit a woman if she was 'too bossy' and overrode the man. A different man explained that according to *kastom*, the woman does not override the man, and this was reflected in God's creation, because the man was created first and the woman after. However, he added, the man will try first to clarify the conflict by 'straightening' (SIP *stretem*) the situation with the mother and the children, but if she is headstrong (SIP *bikhed*), if she 'does not follow' the husband's instructions and acts before her husband instructs her or independently from the husband, her husband will hit her.

Other reasons to hit a woman given by the interviewees were: if the woman made the man feel jealous by acting immorally, for example, if she walked without purpose (SIP *wokabaot*) in Honiara, attended a night club, and/or drank alcohol. Only one Polynesian-looking woman interviewed said that 'the Church' (SIP *Lotu*) established that it was not okay for men to hit women, regardless of whether men were 'in their right because violence hurt women' (SIP *mere save cry*). She asked women to apologize to their partners for their wrongdoings while 'standing in their right' of not being hit if the man was not within his right to hit them. She encouraged women to hit the man back 'to make him see right' – positing a gender-equal model to use violence to correct another person's behaviour. Solomon Islanders often regard their societies as violent (Regional Assistance Mission to Solomon Islands Public Affairs Unit, 2012), despite the country being known as 'The Happy Islands'. Yet 'domestic violence' is often considered as a foreign concept, an issue to which I now turn.

## Domestic violence as a foreign concept

In 2009, the Solomon Islands gender-based violence referral network (SAFENET) gave domestic violence awareness talks in Honiara's settlements and its outskirts, which I attended. In one of those talks, representatives from the CCC, the Family Support Centre, the Ministry of Health and Medical Services, the Royal Solomon Islands Police, and the Regional Assistance Mission to Solomon Islands (RAMSI) acted as 'translators' of women's rights (Merry, 2006). They sat in a semicircle facing the villagers who had gathered under a 'rain tree', in front of their Catholic church. Men were sitting to the right and women to the left. Between the speakers and the audience stood a table. The talk was serious. The CCC staff stated that 'domestic violence' and 'rape' belonged to the realm of knowledge of the '*white man*', as newly introduced concepts in the Solomon Islands. While representatives from the CCC identified different types of gendered violence (the causes being physical, sexual, financial, social, or emotional), domestic violence was linked to 'grievous bodily harm', that is, violence resulting in a wound and making a person bleed.[3] This type of violence, the representatives said, was not acceptable according to *kastom* and the law, giving women's justification to act autonomously from their partners and seek refuge at the CCC.

Similarly, a Sister of the Sisters of Melanesia, talking to the Pentecostal Sunday Harvest Church on a praying visit to the CCC on a Saturday evening, noted that marital arguments (SIP *rava-rava*) were 'normal' until the man beats the woman and makes her bleed or cuts off her hand with an axe. This was 'domestic violence', she said, and it 'made women come to the CCC'. Blood therefore serves as evidence that the intention of the abuser was to cause harm to the woman, not to correct the woman's behaviour. Nonetheless, women also seek refuge at the CCC because of coercive control, threats, intimidation, and/or gaslighting from their intimate partner, brothers, parents, or other male or female relatives. Women sometimes reported their cases to the police, especially if they had evidence of injury or had required hospitalization. The Sisters, however, avoided involving the police without the woman's consent, fearing that the woman's problem would worsen. Involving the police can result in a restraining order or prison for the abuser, a forced separation of the victim and the abuser, potentially leaving the woman without the man's economic support and protection from strangers' physical and sexual violence. I next show the Sisters' reluctance to involve the police, in favour of the Sisters' culture-based counselling with an ethnographic case.

## No police

One early morning, the Family Support Centre called the CCC office to refer an abused woman to the shelter, and I managed the case in my role of research-volunteer. I had met the woman before. She had showed me digital photos of her face disfigured with bruises, blood, and swollen parts caused by domestic abuse. She lacked family support in Honiara. Knowing that the woman had already waited an entire day to go to the CCC, I rushed to organize her transport to the shelter before her husband returned from work. The shelter's coordinator had not come to the office yet, so I could not ask her to pick the woman up with the shelter vehicle. The phone network was down, and the office's radio station did not work. When I told a fellow Solomon Islands female volunteer that I had asked Laura[4], an expat RAMSI police officer, for a lift to the shelter, some tension ensued.

The Solomon Islands volunteer complained that she did not know where the shelter's vehicle was and Family Support Centre could have paid for a taxi to transport the woman to the shelter. She said 'it was not our [the Christian Care Centre] responsibility' to transport the woman to the shelter. In hindsight, I think she was expressing doubt over our right to call Laura, a RAMSI police officer, to give us a lift. The Sisters said they had received funding from Australian donors to buy a vehicle with dark tinted glass to protect the identity of the abused women and to transport women to the shelter safely. She complained that not all victims of abuse qualify to go to the shelter; this is decided after an initial 'counselling' at the office to assess if the woman has 'the right to leave' her husband, even if temporarily, and to stay at the shelter.

The woman arrived at the office at the time that another young woman with a baby asked for shelter. Her partner had abused her physically, emotionally, and financially, and he had rejected her. The woman's brother had housed her for a while, but this had created tension between the siblings. When Laura arrived at the shelter's office, the former shelter coordinator told me that 'the Church wanted the fewer people involved in the cases the better' and that in order to involve the police, I needed 'the permission of the Christian Care Centre Board'. This is the managing body of the shelter, which is chaired by high-ranking members of the clergy or the Church, including the archbishop, and has the ultimate authority about the shelter operation policies.

Not knowing what to do at this stage, we eventually left in Laura's truck to go to the shelter. Laura dropped us at the shelter and left. A Sister welcomed the clients and took them to their rooms, where they are provided with toiletries and the shelter rules are explained to them. I ate a rice meal at the Sisters' open kitchen and helped Sister Daisy to clean pots with sand by the beach. A member of the CCC board drove in her pickup truck to the shelter almost immediately after Laura. This was *Mami* Judith Siota, the main representative of the Church's Women Desk and an important member of the Mothers' Union, an international Anglican women's group. Meeting us at the beach, she laughed when she saw me washing pots with Sister Daisy, perhaps she felt relieved as I was that the police involvement had ended. I had called Laura because I had prioritized the clients' safety and I had not yet understood that I did not need to rush transporting women to the CCC because within the Sisters' household in Honiara and beyond women are safe, or out of boundaries for alleged perpetrators.

In the past, the Sisters had once helped a woman pursue a court order against her husband. The litigation, however, brought negative attention to the Sisters' shelter, stirring up public questioning about whether the Sisters wanted 'to break up marriages' and causing concerns about the impact of the shelter on family relations. Furthermore, the legal prosecution did not deter the man in question from allegedly abusing the woman. This prompted the Sisters to reconsider their work with the police and the criminal justice system and to develop their advocacy counselling method. This method does not incorporate claims of compensation payments, which are within the *kastom* conflict resolution realm, including family members and possibly chiefs.

## Culture-based counselling

The Sisters' counselling method is cultural, Christian, and community-based. It firstly entails that when women arrive at the shelter office or 'go directly' (SIP *kamap*) to the shelter, the Sisters or the volunteers assess the couple's '*kastom* relations': whether the woman is married or not, and if so, what kind of marriage, if Christian, customary, or de facto; whether or not a bride price was paid for her at marriage, and if so, how much; who 'owns' the children or if the children are integrated into the father's or the mother's lineages; and whether the woman has 'the right to run away' according to the cause of the marital conflict, the severity of the injury, and if blood was shed. The shelter staff also assess if the couple are practising Christians. The Sisters believe that marital problems result from not worshipping God. When a woman goes to the shelter, the Sisters seek her husband and report to him that his wife is at the shelter because 'she had enough beatings', and that she 'is tired' and 'has suffered enough' (SIP *naf nao*), or that 'the children are sad because of the domestic violence'.

If the Sisters 'take' women to the shelter without letting their husbands know and without their ad hoc permission, the husbands could judge that according to *kastom*, the Sisters do not have 'the right' to act like this, and the marital conflict could escalate. It is important, I was told that 'the husband knows where his wife is and that she is coming back home'. Different than in the West, the area and location where the shelter is located is publicly known. If a husband had left or rejected his wife, however, his permission was unnecessary. The Sisters thus position themselves as the 'caretakers' of the women staying at the shelter, and as advocates of women's rights to live free from intimate violence, stepping into the woman's male relatives' traditional protective role. The Sisters do not act as 'heads of the family' – they do not tell women what to do, but act as a protecting 'Christian family'. The Sisters offer a safe house and a family counselling service that helps women make a decision about staying or leaving an abusive relationship.

## The women's house

The Sisters' culture-based counselling secondly entails that the clients have a respite from the abuse at the shelter. When women first go to the shelter, it is considered a time during which the couple's problems will '*cool down*' (SIP *koldaon*) before women can return home with their partners. The shelter's leading founder, Sister Lilian, envisioned the shelter as a space 'for women to be free and in peace' and 'for the safety of women and children' (Feinberg, 2000). The shelter is considered to belong to the abused women and children (SIP *blong women*). And the shelter stands for the Sisters' hospitability (Munn, 1983, p. 288). The Sisters provide food for the clients and even the Sisters cook for the clients at the Maeva House. Other times the clients eat with the Sisters at their open kitchen.[5] For one of the clients the CCC was 'like a family place where she could run away to because she did not have '*wantoks*',' this is family or people from her own Island offering help as an informal welfare system. The shelter was another woman's 'second home from home' and because of this, she said she 'felt free' there. Because the shelter was 'her house' (SIP *haus blong mi*), she helped the shelter family too, emphasizing reciprocity: 'with your family you feel free to contribute with money, food or ideas', 'I feel like an outsider when I cannot contribute in these ways'. The Sisters referred to the shelter as the 'Christian Care Centre family', a place where no one was 'treated differently'.

The clients' repeated stays at the CCC could be interpreted as if the situation which brought the women to the shelter in the first place had not changed. The Sisters, however, had vernacularized the 'cycle of violence' (Walker, 1979). The cycle of abuse entails that after a period of positive interaction between a couple, known as the honeymoon period, abuse occurs again. The sequence repeats in cycles. Normally, it is considered that a woman who endures several cycles of abuse has difficulties, practical and psychological, in leaving the abusive relationship. For the Sisters and the clients, returning to the shelter indicates that the woman is in the process of leaving the abusive relationship; reconciliation is not possible. Repeat stays at the shelter give women the socially accepted right to separate from the abuser and to return to their family of origin. For some clients, protection orders made their husbands understand that the violence had to stop, not the relationship; or, conversely, it increased the separation from the abuser. Some clients claimed child maintenance to hold their husbands accountable for their parental responsibilities.

This progressive way of disentangling women from an abusive relationship has been reported elsewhere. Critelli has shown that Pakistani women stayed at a shelter repeatedly before they finally left their abusive partners (2012, p. 452). Other studies have shown that women attempt to leave abusive relationships an estimated four to six times (Gondolf, 1988; Okun, 1986; Walker, 1979, in Oths & Robertson, 2007, p. 250). Loseke has argued that, in the West, we define 'wife abuse' as 'a pattern of physical abuse, or as a continuing series of abuse and degrading acts' (1992, p. 18), not as a one-off event or 'accidental violence' (1992, p. 16). The series of abuse is characterized by 'increasing severity and frequency' (1992, p. 19) and by 'extreme violence' (1992, p. 16). Loseke further explains that although no act of violence is thought of as acceptable, in practice, the definition of 'wife abuse' is founded on an 'escalating and unstoppable victimisation' (1992, p. 19).

## Restoring social relations

The Sisters considered the clients 'broken people', because their social relations are broken. In order to 'fix' the woman's 'social relations', the Sisters either try to reconcile the couple or to reunite the women with their family of origin.[6] Thus, the Sister's culture-based counselling method, thirdly, entails counsel and reconciliation. The Sisters primarily try to reconcile the couple by 'straightening' (SIP *stretem*) the relationship problem. This means understanding the root cause of the conflict, mediating between the parties, and praying. A volunteer explained that 'the standard of the shelter is that you need to cure the victims but also the perpetrators' and so 'we provide counselling to all the parties, also to men involved in something that causes children or mothers to become victims of abuse'. This is why children might be also present in counselling sessions. The Sisters' conflict resolution is based on Solomon Islands Indigenous counselling techniques in which all parties involved are present and the problem is mediated by a person of authority or a religious person (Watson-Gegeo & Gegeo, 1990; White, 1990).

The shelter coordinator, that is, the Sister with the highest authority at the shelter, first, approaches the man or husband and invites him to come to the shelter office in Honiara, where they talk. At the same time, the shelter coordinator talks with the woman or wife at the shelter. When the abused woman feels better, the Sister arranges a meeting with the family at the shelter's office in Honiara to reconcile the couple. If the reconciliation does not work, the Sister would say that the woman 'does not agree with the terms of the reconciliation' (SIP *mami no agri*) because 'she is still frightened of the husband because he beats her'. The Sisters' counselling aims at 'changing the minds of the couple'.

The Sisters use a table to mediate the couple's counselling, that is, a table is placed between the Sisters and the couple. A similar use of a table is found in East Timor, where the procedure in which a domestic violence case is formalized through a resolution process is referred to as 'to put on the table' (see United Nations Development Programme, Timor-Leste, 2017, p. 159). The Sisters called it the 'round table talk', entailing all voices being heard. The Sisters 'changed the couple's attitude' about violence by providing information about different approaches to domestic violence (law, church, *kastom*) that challenged the idea of gender violence being acceptable in the realm of *kastom*.

> The law does not have any justice, but the Church will forgive you. I am afraid whether you like it or not, it does not matter that she is your woman, in relation to women's rights, you are not allowed to abuse her (SIP *busim*). This is what human rights say, all right? *Kastom* says that you have the right, but the Church says that you should look after your wife as a person that God has given to you to love. If you do not, you are not very true to your faith. *Kastom* says that your wife is something you paid for. But human rights say that it is the right of women that you do not abuse them (Sister Doreen interview).

This allows for a different understanding of intimate violence. It reifies the relation between *kastom* and violence against women, and its juxtaposition to women's rights as the women's individual right to live free from violence. It offers an interpretation of Christianity, which does not justify the use of violence against women by husbands and it places scarce trust in the legal criminal system.

The Sisters told me that the shelter is understood not as a domestic violence housing service imported from the West to the Solomons, but a Solomon Islands adaption of the women's customary right to seek refuge in their family's households when they 'run away' from domestic abuse. Thus, the CCC enables a form of marital separation which is customary and allows women to remarry (Dureau, 1994, p. 260). When the Sisters do not succeed in reconciling the partners, they help the women go 'back home' to their islands to be reunited with their family of origin. The CCC is not state-funded (2009–2010), and to cover the women's travel fare the Sisters advocate for funding on the women's behalf to the clients' relatives, the welfare department, or parliament members who represent the clients' home constituencies in Honiara.[7] Also, the Sisters employ their personal connections and relations to help the clients. During the entire counselling process, the Sisters attempt to heal the clients, also considered spiritually 'sick people', by praying for the women to restore their relation with God, or by asking the couple to attend church to pray for God's marital blessings.

## The Sisters' neutrality

The Sisters' authority as conflict mediators is highly respected because they are considered God's agents and capable of causing misfortune or curse if disrespected. The Sisters are 'holy' and *tabu*, out of boundaries. God, the supreme authority of all Christians, works through them, and so their agency is God's agency. The Sisters 'follow' (SIP *falom*) the Sisterhoods' Constitutions and Rules, under the authority of their Sisterhoods' leaders. Because the Sisters do not follow *kastom*, they are considered as *kastom*-neutral or objective as a chief (Burt & Kwa'ioloa, 1997, p. 272). Nonetheless, the Sisters' diverse *kastoms* are celebrated, incorporated into religious rituals, and employed strategically. The Sisters pool an array of *kastom* knowledge that helps the Sisters understand the clients' situations culturally, and support them accordingly at the shelter.

In taking on a peace-making role vis-à-vis men, the Sisters, who protect women, act out a kind of 'masculine femininity'.[8] Sister Doreen is said to be 'aggressive', a manly characteristic, when she stands up to abusive husbands. She 'puts herself in front of the men' and she is 'strong enough to talk to them' and explain why their wives are at the shelter. Sister Doreen used the term 'ambushment', a war-like term, to refer to running away from angry husbands. During the civil unrest (1998–2003), Sister Doreen claimed to have protected women by standing up to the militants, in her role of peace-maker. On one occasion, I witnessed how, outside the Sisters' household in Honiara, a man chased and threw stones at his partner. Sister Doreen got between them and stood in front of the woman, protecting her with her own body and in doing so smashing her toe on a stone herself, ending up bleeding, like Sister Lilian had done before (Feinberg, 2000).

The Sisters, far from saying that they help women from a masculine position, say that they go about it like women. They do not talk over men but instead talk 'gently' and 'softly' to them. The Sisters are never 'rough' with the men, who could get angry (inside their hearts and minds) and make things worse. On the contrary, the Sisters smile and laugh to make the situation less tense. It is important to make the husband feel well, the Sisters told me, for instance, by sharing betel nuts, used to welcome strangers and signal peaceful relations.

## Conclusions

In this chapter, I have argued that the Sisters at the CCC act as the women's foster family and protect them from violence at the shelter, and they lead counselling with victims and perpetrators of abuse with the goal of changing the perpetrators' minds, stopping domestic violence, reconciling couples, and/or creating evidence that attempts of reconciliation were made, so that women are free to return to their families of origin if the domestic violence does not stop. The women remain relational human beings (existing within a network of kin relations) and under the protection of an important family, the Church of Melanesia. The Sisters can take on this kin role because they are 'neutral' when it comes to *kastom*. The Sisters have no interest in gaining compensation from the damage caused to the clients, as kin could have arguably. In addition to this, the Sisters' counsel has a positive outcome in changing men's minds and abusive behaviours, because the Sisters are highly respected and tabu.

During my research at the CCC, reporting domestic violence to the police was infrequent and women's relatives' interventions to protect women were ineffective. In the last decade, the Solomon Islands have developed legal structures to criminalize domestic violence. The National Policy on Elimination Violence against Women and Girls 2016–2020[9] and the Women, Peace, and Security National Action Plan 2016–2020 (EVAWG) emphasized the role of the police, court officials, and local courts in stopping domestic abuse (Ride & Soaki, 2019, pp. 8–9). The Family Protection Act (FPA) (2014) criminalizes domestic violence (including physical, emotional, or economic violence) from any person in a family or living in a family setting (ibid., p. 9), and seeks to 'penalise perpetrators' (ibid.).

The CCC remains nonetheless a key service provider under the FPA (ibid.). Family Support Services and Seif Ples have a key role in encouraging women to use the newly introduced FPA Protection Safety Notes (PSNs)[10] issued by the police (ibid., p. 35) that turn family violence into a serious crime (ibid., p. 108). The FPA counselling provision remains under the Family Support Centre and the CCC. The Family Support Centre counsels women alone and the CCC counsels families. Paradoxically, under the FPA the police lead reconciliations among couples (ibid., p. 5), encouraging women to go back home with the perpetrators but not challenging the perpetrators' behaviour. Women have reported that police reconciliations favoured men (ibid., p. 5), whereas the counsellors at the CCC did not take sides (ibid.) and could change the perpetrators' behaviour (ibid., p. 25).

Nowadays, shelter at the CCC and domestic violence PSNs are used for cases of physical violence (ibid., p. 11). The PSNs are seen as having the potential of '*breaking up families*' (ibid., p. 7), as the CCC was seen at its inception. And the CCC and the PSNs can equally help to reconcile the partners and stop the abuse (ibid.) or give a woman the right to leave an abusive relationship (ibid., p. 36). Relatives and brothers of abused women encourage women accessing a PSN to reinforce kin authority to stop marital violence and enforce compensation payments (ibid., p. 23). The CCC remains the most effective option for clients to be protected from domestic abuse risks in a family setting prioritizing, without other persons' interests at play, the clients' wishes and choices to deal with the abuse and stay safe. In a media release for Asia Pacific UN Women, Sister Doreen, from a recently opened Sisters' second shelter in the Province of Malaita, in 2019, explains that '[With] our cultural norms, there is something in the mind of men – and some women too – that inequality and violence is acceptable in our communities, but it's not'; and domestic violence is now 'against God's law' and 'a crime under the national Family Protection Act 2014' (Berrell, 2021).

## Notes

1  I refer to the Anglican religious sisters as 'Sisters' through the chapter firstly to differentiate a religious sister from a sister and secondly, because being a 'Sister' in the Solomon Islands endows a woman with a special title in society.

2  The research paper noted that the Solomon Islands' constitution granted equal rights to Solomon Islands women, yet assaults on women were treated as a family matter; the police did not record assaults as domestic violence, asking women to settle the matter within the family or through *kastom* (ibid., p. 65). Women normally withdrew charges before their cases were prosecuted (ibid., p. 65).

3  Similarly in other Melanesian societies, violence against women entailing the shedding of blood is considered unacceptable and justifies protective action and compensatory claims from the women's relatives (Ayers Counts, Brown, & Campbell, 1999, for PNG; Jolly, 1996, p. 178, for Vanuatu).

4  Anonymized name.

5  Kinship relations substantiated with food exchanges between clients and other residents similarly reported in a Christian shelter for abused women in PNG called Haus Ruth (Demian, 2017).

6 In Fiji, Shamina Ali has argued that not knowing what to do with women and children after they stay at a safe house has prevented the Fiji Women's Crisis Centre from opening a shelter (Fiji Women's Crisis Centre, 2012).
7 The appeal of support to politicians is borrowed from the British welfare system with its direct writing to local MPs.
8 Dominique Somda similarly identifies forms of masculine femininity in the south of Madagascar, where women's capacity to lead is associated with masculine attributes (Somda, 2013, p. 8).
9 A revised policy from its first implementation, 2010–2015.
10 The PSNs are valid for 21 days and set conditions for the alleged perpetrator of abuse, and they differ from the protection orders in which are issued by a judge in family courts (ibid., p. 24). The PSN rules might include not asking men to drink; not to use a knife or axe to threaten the woman; whip or treat badly the woman (Ibid:30).

# References

Amnesty International. (2004). *Solomon Islands: Women confronting violence* (Index no. ASA 43/001/2004). Retrieved from www.amnesty.org/en/documents/ASA43/001/2004/en/

Ayers Counts, D., Brown, J. K., & Campbell, J. C. (1999). *To have and to hit: Cultural perspectives on wife beating.* Oxford: Marston Book Services Limited.

Berrell, J. (2021, September 16). *It's against god's and the nation's laws – Sister Doreen calls for a stop to gender-based violence.* UN Women. Asia and the Pacific. Media release. Retrieved from October 4, 2021, from https://asiapacific.unwomen.org/en/news-and-events/stories/2021/09/sister-doreen-calls-for-a-stop-to-gender-based-violence

Burt, B., & Kwa'ioloa, M. (1997). *Living tradition: Changing life in Solomon Islands.* London: British Museum Press.

Critelli, F. M. (2012). Voices of resistance seeking shelter services in Pakistan. *Violence Against Women, 18*(4), 437–458.

Demian, M. (2017). Making women in the city: Notes from a Port Moresby boarding house. *Journal of Women in Culture and Society, 42*(2), 403–425.

Deroeck, D. (1988). *Alcohol and drug abuse in the Pacific: The impact on women.* Fourth Regional Women's Conference, Suva, Fiji, 19 to 23 September 1988. South Pacific Commission, Noumea, New Caledonia.

Douglas, B. (2003). Christianity, tradition, and everyday modernity: Towards an anatomy of women's grouping in Melanesia [Special issue: Women's Groups and Everyday Modernity in Melanesia, Oceania]. *Oceania, 74,* 6–23.

Dureau, C. (1994). *Mixed blessings: Christianity and history in women's lives on Simbo, Western Solomon Islands* (Doctoral dissertation). School of Behavioural Sciences, Macquarie University, Sydney, Australia.

Feinberg, R. (2000). *Sister Lilian: Autobiography of sister Lilian Takua Maeva of Anuta, Solomon Islands and the Church of Melanesia.* Unpublished interview. Retrieved October 4, 2021, from http://anglicanhistory.org/oceania/feinberg_lilian2000.html

Fiji Women's Crisis Centre. (2012, November 12). *6th regional meeting: Ethical standards and empowerment essential for women's safe-houses.* Nadi, Fiji. Media release. Retrieved October 4, 2021, from www.fijiwomen.com/research/research-archive/6th-regional-meeting-ethical-standards-and-empowerment-essential-for-womens-safe-houses/

Gondolf, E. W. (1988). The effect of batterer counselling on shelter outcome. *Journal of Interpersonal Violence, 3*(3), 275–289.

Jolly, M. (1996). Woman ikat raet lond human raet o no? Women's rights, human rights and domestic violence in Vanuatu. *Feminist Review, 52,* 169–190.

Jourdan, C. (2008). *Youth and mental health in Solomon Islands: A situational analysis. Tingting helti, tingting siki!* NZAID & Solomon Islands Development Trust. Commissioned by the FPSI Regional Health Programme. Suva, Fiji: Foundation of the Peoples of the South Pacific International.

Loseke, D. R. (1992). *The battered women and shelters: The social construction of wife abuse.* SUNY Series in Deviance and Social Control. Albany, NY: State University of New York Press.

Merry, S. E. (2006). *Human rights and gender violence: Translating international law into local justice.* Chicago, IL: Chicago University Press.

Merry, S. E. (2009). *Gender violence: A cultural perspective.* Chichester: Wiley-Blackwell.

Miguel-Lorenzo, X. (2020). CIDEM's femicide archive and the process of gendered legal change in Bolivia. *Journal of Legal Anthropology, 4*(1), 23–45.

Moore, C. (2015). Honiara arrival city and Pacific hybrid living space. *The Journal of Pacific History, 50*(4), 419–436.

Munn, N. D. (1983). Gawan kula: Spatiotemporal control and the symbolism of influence. In J. W. Leach & E. Leach (eds.), *The Kula: New perspectives on massim exchange* (pp. 277–308). Cambridge: Cambridge University Press.

Okun, L. (1986). *Woman abuse: Facts replacing myths.* New York: State University of New York Press.

Oths, K. S., & Robertson, T. (2007). Give me shelter: Temporal patterns of women fleeing domestic abuse. *Human Organization, 66*(3), 249–260.

Pollard, A. A. (1988). *Solomon Islands in Pacific women: Roles and status of women in Pacific societies* (pp. 40–58). Suva: Institute of Pacific Studies of the University of the South Pacific.

Pollard, A. A. (2000). *Givers of wisdom, labourers without gain: Essays on women in the Solomon Islands.* Suva: University of the South Pacific.

Regional Assistance Mission to Solomon Islands Public Affairs Unit. (2012). *Mere Blo Iume. Stori Blo Oketa.* Video.

Ride, A., & Soaki, P. (2019). *Women's experiences of family violence services in Solomon Islands.* Honiara: Australian Aid/Solomon Islands Government.

Schoeffel Meleisea, P. (1986). The rice pudding syndrome: Women's advancement and home economics training in the South Pacific. In J. Nesbit et al. (eds.), *Development in the Pacific: What women say* (pp. 36–44). Canberra: Australian Council for Overseas Aid.

Solomon Islands Government. (2009). *Solomon Islands population and housing census.*

Somda, D. (2013). *Une humble aura. Les grandes femmes au sud de Madagascar, FMSH-WP-2014–56, January, 56.* Working Papers Series.

UNICEF Pacific & Solomon Islands Government. (1993). *A situation analysis of children and women in the Solomon Islands.*

UNICEF Pacific & Solomon Islands Government. (1998). *A situation analysis of children and women in the Solomon Islands.*

United Nations Development Programme, Timor-Leste. (2017). Bikan ho Kanuru mak Tarutu – When plates and spoons make noise: Domestic violence and customary law in Timor-Leste. In S. Nine (ed.), *Women and the politics of gender in post-conflict Timor-Leste* (pp. 132–149). London: Routledge.

Walker, L. E. (1979). *The battered woman.* New York, NY: Harper and Row.

Watson-Gegeo, K. A., & Gegeo, D. W. (1990). Shaping the mind and straightening conflicts: The discourse of Kawara'ae family counselling. In K. A. Watson-Gegeo & G. M. White (eds.), *Disentangling conflict discourse in Pacific societies* (pp. 161–213). Palo Alto, CA: Stanford University Press.

White, G. (1990). Emotion talk and social inference: Disentangling in Santa Isabel, Solomon Islands. In K. A. Watson-Gegeo & G. M. White (eds.), *Disentangling: Conflict discourse in Pacific societies* (pp. 53–121). Palo Alto, CA: Stanford University Press.

# 7 Women-only households in Port Vila, Vanuatu

## Sites of social resistance

*Daniela Kraemer*

Belinda, Celine, and Lani are roommates. They rent the middle unit of a row house in Port Vila, the capital of the Pacific Island nation Vanuatu. The house is small for them and their combined number of three children. It has one bedroom, a living room, a kitchen, and an outdoor bathroom shared with their neighbours. Though the house is small, the significance of living in a women-only household is large; large with the freedoms, possibilities, and aspirations that a household without men brings.[1]

The Vanuatu government has ratified both the Convention on the Elimination of All Forms of Discrimination Against Women and the Convention on the Rights of the Child. In 2008, the Family Protection Act was also passed into law, criminalizing domestic violence. While most literature on violence in the region focuses on the 60% to 69% of women who experience violence from spouses (Vanuatu Women's Centre, 2011), according to a 2011 report by the Vanuatu Women's Centre on women's well-being, the prevalence of family violence, that is, violence perpetrated by fathers, brothers, male cousins, and uncles, is one of the highest in the world. Almost one in three women in Vanuatu experience sexual violence before the age of 15 years, many by male family members (Vanuatu Women's Centre, 2011).

Tired of waiting for behaviour change or social change, some women in Port Vila are forming female-only households. What do these friends all have in common? Experience of sexual violence, violent arguments, and beatings administered by male family members who disagree with their desire to make their own life choices.

This chapter examines this emerging trend of women-only households. I begin by introducing the reader to a generalized account of women in Port Vila. I then present some of the factors for gender-based family violence, specifically a reinterpretation of *kastom*, the introduction of a Western gender equality discourse, and women's increasing economic success.[2] Finally, I examine Belinda, Celine, and Lani's women-only household. I argue that this form of living enables them, and women like them, to mediate patriarchy and society in their own terms – financially, sexually, and in terms of deciding where they go and how they spend their time. As has been noted elsewhere, an analysis of gender violence 'demands' a focus on both women's and men's experience of violence, in particular, men's confrontation

DOI: 10.4324/9781003146667-8

with modernity and women's efforts to gain agency and safety in a time of significant economic, cultural, and social change (cf. for PNG, Zimmer-Tamakoshi, 2012, p. 73; also Hukula, 2012).

## Port Vila: a gendered place

Vanuatu is an archipelago of 83 volcanic islands spread across 800 kilometres in the South West Pacific. The majority of ni-Vanuatu, as residents are called, live in hamlets or small towns spread across the archipelago. Vanuatu's capital city, Port Vila, referred to as 'Vila', is the largest urban area and is growing at an unprecedented rate. The population was 8,000 in 1970, and it was 44,039 at the time of the last census in 2009 (Vanuatu National Statistics Office).

Vila's growth began shortly before 1980, the year the archipelago, known then as the New Hebrides, gained independence from Britain and France, who had jointly ruled the area for 74 years. During the colonial administration, ni-Vanuatu could only be in Vila if they had a work permit. It was a policy that operated through explicit ideas of race, and the town developed as a 'white' space (Rodman, 1987, p. 1). But Vila also developed as a male space. Men worked in town on coconut plantations, in construction, and loading and unloading cargo on ships, while women remained on the islands. Women began migrating to town after independence, when restrictions on settling in town were lifted and when men began staying in town for longer periods. Women joined their husbands and came to town to work in the service industry, which was booming with increased economic development (Haberkorn, 1989, p. 14). Spaces and places in town have been gendered from the beginning. Men more freely frequent nightclubs and bars in the central business district, and walk through their community streets. The expectation of women, on the other hand, is to remain at home. A phrase, 'you have the legs of a chicken' (*yu yu gat leg blo faol*) is used to describe a woman walking around 'too much' from yard to yard. While it is said jokingly, it is weighted with social norms and judgement and reflects restrictions on female freedom of movement in town. If they are not at work, school, or church, women should be home. It is believed that women are safe at home; safe from sexual violence by other townsmen, black magic, and particularly safe from temptations like premarital or extramarital sex, drinking alcohol, and using drugs. Men do not face these kinds of restrictions. I observed men moving freely day and night without impunity. While some women do 'sneak out', their fathers or mothers find them and drag them home. Such spatial gender segregation and social restrictions on female mobility reproduce and legitimize status differences between genders (Spain, 1993) and a different experience of town and urban living for men and women. Women like Celine, Belinda, and Lani push against these differences, and as I explore later, much of the family-based gender violence stems from men trying to maintain control.

Nestled in Vila Bay, Port Vila comprises a central business district surrounded by residential communities, including the Freswota community, where I carry out my research. The demographic makeup of Freswota is varied in terms of island affiliation (in contrast to other communities where people from one island congregate) and in terms of economic stability. Some households are middle class; they work as teachers, government administrators, and in construction, or are small business owners. They also supplement their income through owning busses, baking and selling bread, running corner stores, and renting out housing. They expect their children to graduate from school in year 13 (grade 13) and land well-paying jobs. It is expensive to live in Vila, and these families have found ways to thrive. Other families have not found as much success. Many in this category are unemployed. However, they create their own productive work, sometimes paid, in the community, organizing community governance and community events (Kraemer, 2013). A third category of residents is renters. Some are new migrants looking to begin their life in town, others are long-time urban residents who have only ever been able to afford to rent. This category of residents moves around depending on their circumstances. Violence in the home occurs in all of these categories.

As migration to town continues, communities are becoming overcrowded. Relatives from the islands move in with families in town, and it is common to find more than ten people living in one house. When houses have only one or two bedrooms, home life becomes difficult. Many young men are 'sent' out of the house during the day to reduce crowding (Kraemer, 2017). Some young men also prefer to sleep in abandoned sheds or unfinished rental houses than in the overcrowded home.

Women in Freswota say they don't feel safe at home, and they exclaim that overcrowding is one of the reasons. Lesara, a woman in her mid-30s, exclaimed: 'You might trust the uncle, the grandfather or the brothers now living in your home, you might think that your child is safe in the home with them, but they are not. The girls easily become victims'. Stefanie, a woman in her late 20s, explained: 'There is no respect. When the man wants to make trouble with the girl he just does'. It is not uncommon for men to rape, beat, and whip their female relatives – daughters, nieces, cousins, sisters-in laws – in their homes. Simone, now in her forties, said one of the worst experiences of her life was when her grandfather whipped her after he learned she had snuck out to attend a dance. 'I was already home sleeping, he found out and whipped me right over the blankets. My grandmother tried to defend me, but he started whipping her too. We ran away and slept in the graveyard'.

One of Vanuatu's most famous *kastom* legends, and the story that frames Vanuatu's Land diving or Nanggol ritual, is about a woman trying to escape gender-based violence. According to the legend, a woman ran from her husband during a beating. She climbed to the top of a tree, but her husband climbed after her. The woman threw herself from the tree, a suicide to finally end the abuse. The husband jumped to follow her. In some versions, he jumped out of grief; in others, he was trying to catch her to continue the beating. What the husband didn't realize was that she had tied vines to her ankles. She survived the jump, but her husband did not. Every year, the people of South Pentecost Island remember this incident by re-enacting the story. Men wrap tree vines around their ankles and jump off wooden towers 20 to 30 metres high. We don't know the origin date of the legend, but the story reveals notions about ni-Vanuatu gender relationships and gender-based violence relevant today: men beat women, and women are innovative in their response. Women-only households, the focus of this chapter, are one way women innovate to escape from violence and assert what independence means to them.

## Identifying factors of gender-based family violence in town

Sandy wouldn't come out of her bedroom when I visited the family that day. Her sister explained why. The night before she had snuck out to see her boyfriend and had been caught. Enraged, her father whipped her with a plastic telephone cable. Her limbs and back were full of welts and her body was swollen from her head down to her toes. I asked Sandy's sister why their father had beaten her, her answer: 'it is *kastom* that's all' (*hemia from kastom nomo*). I heard this explanation articulated often, and each time with the same uncritical gaze. Why do men and women evoke *kastom* as the explanation for gender-based violence and gender-based family violence? And how has violence against women become so normalized?

Little has been written on family violence in Melanesia, but there is extensive writing on gender violence in the region. These works focus on the relationship between gender violence and tradition (Counts, 1990; Douglas, 2003), modernity and development (Jolly, 1996; Spark, 2011; Taylor, 2010, 2008), transforming masculinities (Eves, 2006; Jolly, 2000; Taylor, 2008; Zimmer-Tamakoshi, 2012), and increased eroticism of female bodies (Rosi & Zimmer-Tamakoshi, 1993). Writers explore gender violence, not through any biological reductionist theory, a viewpoint which has been 'debunked' (McPherson, 2012, p. 47), but through an examination of 'ideological, socio-economic and spiritual ethos that permits and perpetuates the violence' (McPherson, 2012, p. 50). Here, I follow the same perspective by outlining three socio-cultural factors for the violence: a reinterpretation of *kastom*, the introduction of a Western gender equality discourse, and women's increasing economic success. My discussion draws on writings on the relationship between changing masculinities and gender violence (see Taylor, 2008; Eves, 2006; Jolly, 2000; Zimmer-Tamakoshi, 2012).

### *A reinterpretation of* kastom

Today, men and women use *kastom* to justify violence against women. Sandy's father beat Sandy because of *kastom*. But what does *kastom* instruct? The normative view is that women should remain home and not venture to other places, especially not at night, and especially not to meet men. Premarital sexual activities, as well as children born out of wedlock, reduce the bride-wealth a family can ask of a groom's family. Likely, Sandy was also beaten to discourage a 'teenage pregnancy' which could lead to Sandy dropping out of school and a loss in her future capacity to contribute to her parents' retirement – an expectation of middle-class families in town. Either way, Sandy was beaten because she disobeyed a *kastom* belief that men have the right to control women, their reproductive capacity, and their bodies.

But this is a reinterpretation of *kastom* (Jolly, 1996; see also Hobsbawm, 2012). Jolly writes that men's belief in the right to control women developed out of decades of men's misinterpretation of Bible passages, using them to proclaim women's secondary status and to justify men's right to physically discipline them (1996, p. 179). The phrase 'a woman must submit' (*woman mas sabmit*) is spoken often in Vila. Men explain that the instruction is from the Bible; Eve was born out of Adam's ribs and so the woman is 'always secondary to the man'. When women do not submit, violence is used to make them. Arthur, age 27, explained: 'Women these days think they are equal, but they are not, they are underneath the man. So, we have to make them respect the man using the fist. You punch women to teach this lesson'. This is not just in marriages, but between male and female family members, as I observed with Sandy and her father, and as I saw one day when a brother punched his sister in the face. He yelled about her disobedience, told her to listen to her family, and explained that if she didn't return home she would be disowned. I later learned that the sister was living with her boyfriend and had no intention of returning. She was a woman in her 20s, had a child, and worked full time. The men in her family saw her assertion of agency as subordination of *kastom* and were trying to get her to submit.

### Introduction of a Western gender equality discourse

Why are so many men violent towards women? Manu, aged 25, gave me his opinion:

> Women are starting to change, now they think they're equal. Men don't want to listen to this. So, we have to talk to the women and tell them to follow *kastom*. Tell them they are not allowed to follow the thinking of education.

The education Manu is referring to is a Western gender equality discourse introduced by development agencies and non-governmental organizations (NGOs). In Vila, people take to the streets often to advocate for women's rights, and 'End Domestic Violence' posters adorn walls and buildings. But as Taylor writes, many men see the women's rights discourse as undermining Vanuatu's 'natural' *kastom* patriarchal gender order, and interpret it as a form of 'violence against men' (Taylor, 2008, p. 167). In neighbouring Papua New Guinea, men are also acting out of 'status insecurities' amidst women's new agency (Zimmer-Tamakoshi, 2012, p. 73). In Vanuatu, particularly in urban areas, men struggle with their disempowerment. They interpret their sisters, daughters, and nieces, leaving the house freely, enjoying themselves, choosing their own marriage partners, deciding how to spend the money they earn, as women 'exerting their rights', and they respond with physical and sexual violence legitimized through discourses of *kastom* in order to stop them.

When asked why there is so much gender-based family violence, a common answer given in Port Vila is 'women are too strong minded' (*oli strong hed tumas*), meaning that they are enacting their own will, a will that goes against *kastom* or the wishes of a family. Anita, a woman in her forties who works in a pharmacy, said: 'My father hit me often, because I was too strong minded'. Even educated women say this about themselves with little critique, demonstrating how women are as much enculturated as men into this way of thinking (McPherson, 2012, p. 68). Most women expect to be beaten in their lifetime for failing to fulfil obligations of what it means to be a 'good woman', which is defined by acts of domestic and reproductive labour (McPherson, 2012, p. 69). In a life skills programme run by the Vanuatu Cultural Centre, I observed young people's responses when the coach brought up gender equality. She asked whether young men wash dishes or do laundry. The boys nodded yes. 'That's gender!' she said. 'It doesn't mean one is better than the other'. She continued '*kastom* puts man high up and boys today are afraid of women taking over, but that's not true'. The girls in the room were stone-faced, the boys all laughed. Part of the difficulty of introducing the notion of women's equality into a patriarchal system is how it sets up a dichotomous tension where men become equated with tradition and women with oppression, modernity, and women's liberation (Jolly, 1996, p. 183; see also Taylor, 2008). The way to challenge this 'insidious dichotomy', Jolly writes, is for women to insist that human rights are not inconsistent with *kastom* but appropriate and indigenize notions of the 'human' to suit their local contexts (1996, p. 183).

### Female economic success

Men in the community are outraged by gender equality and how the discourse is transforming their sense of masculine identity. Many men feel threatened by the earning capacity of women, and how this places them in a position of financial dependence on their daughters, sisters, and wives. Port Vila has a booming service and hospitality industry, and more women are working than have ever before. If men are unemployed, they become dependent on the income (and generosity) of the women in their lives. I observed young men frequently asking their mothers, sisters, female cousins, and girlfriends for money. Moreover, I observed families evaluating their children's contributions to the household income, rewarding daughters and nieces for the money they bring in, while sending their unemployed sons and nephews out of the home during the day, every day, so as not to use valued resources, such as food and electricity (Kraemer, 2017). Men feel aggrieved by the change in social positions of the genders. As Benson, age 26, said: 'The power of the woman is coming up and this is not right'. Young men often spoke longingly about a time when they weren't the ones taking care of babies, doing laundry and other domestic labour – a real gender role reversal in their points of view. While they don't mind the work or spending the money they are given for this labour, there is a growing narrative around transforming gender roles and a sense of their own emasculation in these new 'modern' times (Kraemer, 2013). Men see women as gaining power and thereby reducing their own sense of masculine efficacy. But while they have no choice but to live with this social transformation, many do not recognize women's increased power as legitimate – they experience this gender equality discourse as foreign and not applicable to them locally. As I am arguing in this chapter, much of the gender-based family violence in Freswota is the result of men propping up a manhood threatened by this increased female power seen as imported into the culture (cf. for PNG Zimmer-Tamakoshi, 2012, p. 73).

### Defining violence and family violence

These are some of the socio-cultural factors leading to gender-based family violence in Port Vila. But what does violence actually mean to people in Port Vila? And how is family violence defined? What levels of violence are acceptable, even normalized? (cf. Counts, 1990, p. 3). How are cultural concepts of gender preventing women and men from seeing alternatives to the violence they live with every day?

Violence is defined as behaviour intended to hurt, damage, or kill. McPherson defines violence for neighbouring Papua New Guinea as

> always about relations of power, more specifically, 'power over' in the sense of both structural violence, where violence is based on inequality – economic, political, social, religious – and cultural violence where individuals are enculturated to a system of beliefs that hold violence to be legitimate and normal.
>
> (2012, p. 49)

When I asked young men in Vila why they hit women, they say that hitting is their first response, because it is what they learned. As Jaksil, age 26, remarked:

> men do know it is wrong to hit women. They see the fear in the woman's eyes. But men only know to respond with the fist, sure women's rights associations tell us to talk instead. Many will nod yes, but then they hit and punch because it has been practiced for two or three generations like this already.

The gender-based family violence I am describing in this chapter is violence perpetrated by fathers, grandfathers, uncles, brothers, and male cousins to the women in their kin groups and households. It is a type of violence that specifically occurs within a relationship characterized by intimacy, dependence, and/or trust. Women are also violent in homes, but this is mainly towards their spouses and partners, and mostly in response to their partners engaging in extramarital affairs. The violence takes the form of beatings, whippings, and sexual violence. Other acts like poisoning and psychological violence also take place but are beyond the scope of this chapter. The violence I am describing takes place neither solely in the home nor in private. Gender-based family violence is very much part of public discourse, and people openly discuss what they see happening in people's homes, on the street at night, in abandoned sheds, and in the back bushes of the community. The frequency of gender-based family violence and the limited prosecution of perpetrators have created conditions wherein gender-based family violence has become 'normal' (cf. Hukula, 2012, p. 197).

There is a line between what is acceptable gender-based family violence (punching, hitting, and beating) and what is not, and it lies in the gruesomeness of the act, as in the rape of very young girls and when blood is drawn. The more blood spilled during an act of violence, the greater the critique of the offence. When a young woman and her child were gang raped and bludgeoned to death in a shed during my last fieldwork, the community was aghast. Photos of the blood-stained walls circulated, and a public meeting was called. In contrast, during reconciliation meetings between community chiefs and families, the violence that does not leave a physical mark elicits little discipline, perhaps just a fine and an apology. Writing about Papua New Guinea, Zimmer-Tamakoshi says that in the past, a woman who was raped would be avenged by her husband or brother, but today, rapists must be caught and tried, and the system is 'often too lenient or indifferent' (2012, p. 92 for PNG; Servy, 2017, for Vanuatu). Women do not call the police often either. Police officers, mostly men, offer little protection, recourse, or even sympathy. For example, when police came across a woman in Freswota being raped by two men in the bushes, the police arrested the men but said to the woman 'no one put a gun to your head to make you have sex with these men'.

Taylor astutely points out that a problem with the term 'violence against women' is that it implicitly elides the fact that it is violence being carried out by men (2008, p. 129). Due to the frequency and normalcy of gender-based family violence in the community, few men and women imagine alternatives to using violence everyday (McPherson, 2012, p. 50). One of the exceptions is the women I will now turn to who are innovating a different way of living in women-only households.

## Life before and after moving into a women-only household

In her ethnographic work with wayward women in Papua New Guinea, Wardlow (2006) argues that the women she works with engage in embodied 'negative agency', a phrase she uses to describe women's refusal to use their bodies for the normative purpose of genealogical reproduction and the social circulation of wealth or debt. The women Wardlow works with intentionally disrupt the social categories by which women are expected to live. Wardlow writes that society tells women they should be fenced in and that they should not engage in sexually provocative language, so they hop on busses and run away, and publicly swear and use sexy talk instead (2006). Wardlow argues that these are acts of agency in which the women transgressively depart from 'traditional femininity' (2006, p. 164). Ni-Vanuatu women living in women-only households are similarly transgressively departing from contemporary *kastom* definitions of what it means to be a ni-Vanuatu female. By living in women-only households, they disrupt patriarchal relationships; innovate an escape from gender violence; resist the unequal gender social system; and reimagine what independence means to them (for PNG, see Rosi & Zimmer-Tamakoshi, 1993; Spark, 2011).

Belinda, Lani, and Celine are three women living like this. The following are the life histories that brought them together.[3]

*   *Belinda, age 26. Finished school in year 13. Works in an office in town. She is unmarried and has one child.*

I was born on a small island. I grew up with my grandparents and cousins. Our parents were all in Vila working. When I started high school, I went and lived with them. Right away they talked about marriage. I didn't want to get married; I was still in school! They chose four men, but I blocked it every time. Eventually I forced a boy in the community to have sex with me so I wouldn't have to follow my parents' choices. This led to big fights. My father whipped me with dried coconut leaves. He wanted me to agree but I wouldn't. Finally, they sent me away to my aunty and uncle. Sometimes, my father would come and whip me again, but I still wouldn't agree. Arranged marriage isn't what I was thinking for my life. I wanted to make my own decisions. Yes, now, if I'm short of food I can't get help from them. If I had followed what they wanted, then they would help. But this is a better life for me, now I live as an independent woman.

- *Celine, age 24. Finished school in year 12. Works in an office in town. She is unmarried.*

I was born in Vila. My mother left my father when I was one, and I lived with my grandmother. When I was 12, I went to live with my mother and stepfather and his three children. It was a small house with only one room. At night, we would divide the room by hanging a cloth. Every night we could hear my stepfather wanting to have sex with my mother and my mother refusing. One day when my mother was out, my stepfather forced me. I was 13. He wanted sex and found another way.

- *Lani, age 33. Finished school in year 13 plus 1-year teacher's college. Works as a teacher in town. She is separated from her husband and has two children.*

I was born in Port Vila and grew up happy in my home with my parents and brothers. I married when I was 24. It was good until my husband wanted to be with another woman. He beat me trying to make me leave. Then, he started beating our two children. Life in town is expensive, so I went back to my parents. They live in a house on land they own. My two brothers, their wives, and their kids also live there. This was the dynamic I went into. The house was small and crowded. I would get frustrated. I am the oldest and the only one who worked. I paid for everything, food, light bill, water bill. My parents are retired, and my brothers don't work. My brothers' wives don't work either. It was difficult. I was feeding my children, my parents, and then the other families that live in the house too. One of my brothers asked for extra money often. I would get cross at him for asking. Sometimes, I would come home from work and see that he had beaten my children. He was upset, because I didn't give him money. This is not right. For a long time, I had to surrender, I had to live in this small house, I had to live in this dynamic.

This is how they describe their life now living in a women-only household:

- *Belinda*

Life is good now. I don't have to follow anyone, I can go here, I can go there. I own my own time and I own my own will. I can really enjoy myself.

I feel freer. I come home and no one is going to discipline me. My parents wanted me to follow their choices but in my mind that wasn't right for me. Yes, sometimes we face hard times, but well life is up to me now and that's a better life.

- *Celine*

   Before, it wasn't safe. In Vanuatu, men think that they can force the woman. But that's not right. Rape has become common in Vanuatu. If you live with your biological family (*stret famili*), you might be safe, but if you live with extended family or stepfathers, then homes aren't safe, because brothers, uncles, and stepfathers do what they want. Now, living here, when I sleep, I worry less.

- *Lani*

   When I think about that time, it was a hard time in my life. If a man doesn't have paid work, then he stays home. But if a woman doesn't have paid work, she is still working washing, looking after children, and cooking. It's not fair. What a man can do and what a woman can do is the same. It's just what we learn that is different. When they tell you that you can't climb the tree, it is the work of boys, or no you can't wear trousers, because it's the dress of boys. Before this thinking was okay, but now we have adopted Western policies that give rights to women. And so men are cross and they hit women because of this. Living here with my friends and my children is better. If I work, then I have money and I can pay for my children and myself. There is no man to say do this or pay for this. Now I can do what I want. Girls must have an education and get a job and know their rights and stand up in this country.

## Women-only households: sites of social resistance

These are the contexts that brought these three women together in a one-bedroom row house with a black corrugated iron roof in the Freswota community. At first, it was just Belinda and Celine renting together, but they invited Lani to help split the expenses. They share cooking, childminding, and laundry. They laugh, tell stories, and are pleased to be together. What these three ethnographic profiles suggest is that living in women-only households is enabling women to be 'independent' (*gat indepense*), defined by them as engaging with patriarchy and society in their own terms, specifically with regards to finances, their bodies, and being able to decide where they go and how they spend their time.

As Belinda's words reveal, making decisions about her life herself is important (cf. Spark 170 for a discussion on 'personal freedoms'). She knows her rights and believes in female self-determination, particularly in terms of whom she marries, whom she has sex with, and where and with whom she spends her time. Belinda makes clear that her improved circumstances pivot on her mediating her own time. Belinda uses the word 'enjoy' when describing life now. She goes to clubs, meets friends at night, and works in the house when she chooses. Belinda's actions reveal a successful pushback at gender proscriptions and a creation of a living situation where she 'feels more free' (*filim mo fri*).

Living in a women-only household is also experienced as safer. Women in Freswota say that they don't feel safe in homes with men, because men believe they are in charge of women's bodies and 'take' women whenever they desire. Young women living in households with stepfathers seem particularly vulnerable to sexual violence. The women-only household gives women a safe space in which they can reduce this risk and be in charge of their own bodies. Moreover, women I spent time with say that their families should not direct whom they marry and with whom they reproduce. As Belinda's words reveal, she weaponized her body by having sex with a young man as a way to take charge of her body and sexuality herself and to take this control out of the hands of her parents. Like the women Wardlow works with, discussed earlier, Belinda used her own body as a tool to control her life herself.

Another point to highlight from the aforementioned testimonies is the sense of independence that comes with economic self-sufficiency. For Lani, earning her own money allows her to escape relationships of dependence on family, and the power dynamic and control that this financial dependence creates. As many women explained: 'In Vanuatu women depend on men, so if the man beats the woman and the woman wants to leave, where will she go? She doesn't have money. How is she going to live?' Economic self-sufficiency grants these three women the ability to live a life of greater personal freedom as they choose to spend the money they earn. They can make purchases for the home and family, go out, or save money for the future without criticism or having to field requests. As Lani's words illustrate, relatives can ask for money, but living in her own house and not being dependent on family enables her to share on her own terms. Lani continues to give money to her parents, but this is money she wants to share, rather than is obligated to give.

It is important, however, not to 'romanticize' the women-only living situations for all women (Spark, 2011, p. 169). Many female 'disruptors' find themselves outside their kin groups and other available support networks. Belinda's words reveal that her choices have caused family estrangement and she no longer has family she can rely on. This can leave women vulnerable. Indeed, Belinda, Lani, and Celine's house has been broken into, they are referred to as lesbians throughout the community, and Lani stopped attending church because of gossip.

In Port Vila, the women-only house is the physical space from which women are prompting individual and social change. In this sense, the women-only house can be analysed as a site of social resistance. In terms of individual change, the women-only household enables women to build the kind of everyday life they want for themselves and their children. Being educated and employed full time is the social capital engendering this. As MacIntyre writes: 'education is seen by many women as a route to economic independence and thus the only means they have of avoiding the constraints that men place on their lives' (2000, p. 167; see also Spark, 2011). It is common in Freswota to hear girls say that they want to marry later in life, and they want to choose their own partners. Girls in school say that they want to finish their studies first, and all say that they want to find work so that they can have more personal freedoms (see the discussion in Rosi & Zimmer-Tamakoshi, 1993, on elite women's resistance to marriage and the social system). Not all women in Freswota have the social capital to realize their dreams, and there is a growing divide between women who have been educated and are able to seek this type of living, and women who are not.

While there have always been Melanesian women like Lani, Celine, and Belinda, who have found ways to push back at social restrictions to make their own decisions and enact their own desires, what is different here is that women-only households, like other women-only groupings in Melanesia, are something quite 'radical' (Douglas, 2003, p. 15). It is in women-only households that women are finding solidarity with like-minded peers to critique and subordinate patriarchal dominance. This might not be their explicit intention and they are not enacting any kind of revenge on the men in their networks, rather these women know about their rights and are aware of how other women in the world live more freely. They have innovated a solution for themselves where their interests are above *kastom* and patriarchy.

But living in a women-only household can also be described as 'political' (Douglas, 2003, p. 15), and the women-only household as a symbol of women advancing the status of women in Vanuatu. Violence against women is often highest at times when women begin assuming non-traditional roles (Krug et al. cited in Spark, 2011, p. 166). In Vila, rapid urbanization, international development, tourism, and education are all contributing to shifts in cultural and social norms. Today, many women are unwilling to 'embody the culturally sanctioned versions of womanhood' prescribed by their families (Spark, 2011, p. 165). Living in a women-only household can thus be analysed as a practice of resistance that challenges power dynamics within Vanuatu households and drives forward broader social change. The women-only house is a site in which women are negotiating and contesting their place in the world.

## Conclusion

Women in Freswota talk about aspiring to live a 'man free life'. This is a sentiment similar to what Spark has reported for Papua New Guinea, where educated women say that partnerships with their countrymen are 'more troublesome than they are worth' (2011, p. 164). Women-only households are a growing phenomenon in Port Vila. Young women, particularly women who are still in school, talk openly about aspiring to living conditions that will engender this kind of increased independence.

Women are tired of the violence inflicted upon them by men and by the systemic gender inequality they experience from living in a patriarchal social system. Many women learn about women's rights from the efforts of local and international NGOs in Port Vila. However, few women have the education and employment opportunities to uphold them. Belinda, Lani, and Celine are three women who have managed to create a more independent life for themselves, and as their testimony illustrates, they are much more satisfied and fulfilled for it.

## Notes

1  This chapter is based on ethnographic fieldwork in Freswota, one of Port Vila's residential communities and the place where I have been carrying out fieldwork since 2007. During the 2020 COVID-19 pandemic Geraud Bato, one of my long-time research participants, and his partner, Julienne Metan, collected supplemental data for this paper. I am grateful to them for their help.
2  *Kastom* is the Bislama term for culture and tradition. Bislama is one of Vanuatu's national languages.
3  Each paragraph is an assemblage of a selection of quotes taken from an interview with the research participant. I chose this methodology for the purpose of brevity.

## References

Counts, D. (1990). Introduction [Special issue: Domestic violence in Oceania]. *Pacific Studies, 13*(3), 1–5.

Douglas, B. (2003). Christianity: Tradition and everyday modernity: Towards an anatomy of women's groupings in Melanesia. *Oceania, 74*, 6–23.

Eves, R. (2006). *Exploring the role of men and masculinities in Papua New Guinea in the 21st century.* Sydney: Caritas Australia.

Haberkorn, G. (1989). *Port Vila: Transit station or final stop? Recent developments in Ni-Vanuatu population mobility.* Canberra: National Centre for Development Studies, Research School of Pacific Studies, Australian National University.

Hobsbawm, E. (2012). Introduction. In E. Hobsbawm & T. Ranger (eds.), *Inventing traditions* (pp. 1–14). Cambridge: Cambridge University Press.

Hukula, F. (2012). Conversations with convicted rapists. In M. Jolly & C. Stewart (eds.), *Engendering violence in Papua New Guinea.* Canberra: ANU Press.

Jolly, M. (1996). "Woman Ikat Raet Long Human Raet O No?" Women's rights, human rights and domestic violence in Vanuatu. *Feminist Review, 52*, 169–190.

Jolly, M. (2000). "Woman Ikat Raet Long Human Raet O No?" Women's rights, human rights and domestic violence in Vanuatu. In A. M. Hilsdon, M. Macintyre, V. Mackie, & M. Stiven (eds.), *Human rights and gender politics: Asia-Pacific perspectives* (pp. 124–146). London: Routledge.

Kraemer, D. (2013). *Planting roots, making place: An ethnography of young men in Port Vila, Vanuatu* (Doctoral dissertation). Department of Social Anthropology, London School of Economics, London, United Kingdom.

Kraemer, D. (2017). Family relationship in town are brokbrok: Food sharing and "contribution" in Port Vila, Vanuatu. In L. Lindstrom & C. Jourdan (eds.) [Special issue: Urban Melanesia]. *Journal de la Société des Océanistes, 144–145*, 105–116.

Kraemer, D. (2020). Planting roots, making place: Urban autocthony in Port Vila, Vanuatu. *Oceania, 90*(1), 40–54.

Macintyre, M. (2000). "Hear us, women of Papua New Guinea!": Melanesian women and human rights. In A. M. Hilsdon, M. Macintyre, V. Mackie, & M. Stivens (eds.), *Human rights and gender politics: Perspectives on the Asia-Pacific region* (pp. 147–171). London: Routledge.

McPherson, N. (2012). Black and blue: Shades of violence in West New Britain, PNG. In M. Jolly & C. Stewart (eds.), *Engendering violence in Papua New Guinea* (pp. 47–72). Canberra: ANU Press.

Rodman, M. (1987). *Masters of tradition: Consequences of customary land tenure in Longana, Vanuatu.* Vancouver, BC: University of British Columbia Press.

Rosi, P., & Zimmer-Tamakoshi, L. (1993). Love and marriage among the educated elite in Port Moresby. In R. A. Marksbury (Series ed.), *ASAO monograph series: The business of marriage: Transformations in Oceanic matrimony* (pp. 175–204). Pittsburgh, PA: University of Pittsburgh Press.

Servy, A. (2017). "Forcing is not violating": Sexual violence against women in a disadvantaged neighbourhood of Port-Vila. In L. Lindstrom & C. Jourdan (eds.) [Special issue: Urban Melanesia]. *Journal de la Société des Océanistes, 144–145,* 171–184.

Spain, D. (1993). Gendered spaces and women's status. *Sociological Theory, 11*(2), 137–151.

Spark, C. (2011). Gender trouble in town: Educated women eluding male domination, gender violence and marriage in PNG. *Asia Pacific Journal of Anthropology, 12*(2), 164–179.

Taylor, J. P. (2008). The social life of rights: "Gender antagonism", modernity and *Raet* in Vanuatu. *Australian Journal of Anthropology, 19*(2), 165–178.

Taylor, J. P. (2010). Changing Pacific masculinities: The "problem" of men. *Australian Journal of Anthropology, 19*(2), 125–135.

Vanuatu National Statistics Office. (2009). *Vanuatu national census of population and housing.* Port-Vila: Vanuatu National Statistics Office.

Vanuatu Women's Centre in partnership with the Vanuatu National Statistics Office. (2011). *Vanuatu national survey on women's lives and family relationships.* Port-Vila: Vanuatu Women's Centre.

Wardlow, H. (2006). *Wayward women: Sexuality and agency in a New Guinea society.* Berkeley, CA: University of California Press.

Zimmer-Tamakoshi, L. (2012). "Troubled masculinities" and increased violence in Melanesia. In M. Jolly & C. Stewart (eds.), *Engendering violence in Papua New Guinea.* Canberra: ANU Press.

# 8 From structural violence to family violence

## Insights into perpetrators' experiences in French Polynesia today

*Marie Salaün, Mirose Paia, and*
*Jacques Vernaudon*

The current criminal code in French Polynesia is that of metropolitan France, as is most of the code of criminal procedure. The magistrates of the various jurisdictions are almost exclusively from metropolitan France. In contrast, almost all prison officers are of Polynesian origin. The local incarceration rate is twice as high as that in metropolitan France: around 200 per 100,000. Among the grounds for conviction, only domestic violence (including sexual violence) is specifically high in French Polynesia, as is theft without violence against persons. In ratio, sexual and family violence is three to four times higher than in the rest of the French Republic (Bastide, 2020). Rape and indecent assaults on minors are greatly over-represented, accounting for 20% of detainees in Tatutu at the time of the survey at the beginning of 2019.

According to a survey conducted in 2016 (Mai), most offenders are men (97%) of French Polynesian origin (97%). A total of 94% of them left school before completing secondary education. Two thirds of them had no or only partial undeclared employment before their incarceration. Their families live in a very precarious situation, with average resources of less than 50,000 Pacific Francs per month for a household composed of an average of five people, that is, 10,000 Pacific Francs per person per month (USD $100). A total of 90% of them declare that they are bilingual (French plus one of the seven Polynesian languages).

The empirical material on which this chapter is based comes from a survey carried out in early 2019 as part of a research project funded by the French penitentiary services (Salaün, Vernaudon, & Paia, 2020). The research project was focused on the relevance of specific penal care for the Indigenous *mā'ohi*[1] populations in French Polynesia. It was in line with the need for individualized monitoring of people placed under judicial authority, and the need for better knowledge of the conditions of desistance in order to prevent recidivism.

The research project's initial aim was 'to document the specific characteristics of the groups being monitored in closed environments, in particular their cultural and linguistic background, their family ties and their inclusion in the local socio-economic fabric'. We focused our research on the meaning the respondents attached to their prison sentence. One of the ways we chose to gain insight into that broader issue of meaning was a 'linguistic' approach, as the researchers were able to conduct

DOI: 10.4324/9781003146667-9

in-depth interviews in French and Tahitian. Our intention was to study more precisely the Tahitian (or local French) lexicon used to express their interpretation of the crime or offence, their sentence, their guilt, and their efforts (or not) to amend it. The point was thus to explore the hypothesis of a possible hiatus between a legal-rational interpretation of the prison's vocation and the inmates' specific moral economies (Thompson, 1971; Scott, 1976; Fassin, 2016), a hiatus that could lead to misunderstandings between the institution and the inmates' lived experience.

In this chapter, we focus on a striking aspect revealed by the empirical investigation: namely, the pervasiveness of multifaceted violence at the heart of prisoners' experience, both as perpetrators and as victims. We argue that interpersonal violence requires an analysis in terms of structural violence, because violence as a process goes beyond individuals and their immediate social circles, to include contemporary French Polynesian society as a whole. After presenting a few portraits depicting the diversity of individual situations, we then return to a core feature of the offenders' narratives: interpersonal violence. Finally, we identify the way in which cycles of violent exchanges bring about specific moral economies, built on a sense of justice and injustice, good and evil, which is strongly out of step with the legal categories through which violence is comprehended, assessed, and punished by institutions.

## Back and forth: from interpersonal to structural violence

Initially, 'violence' was not the target of our research project. Its centrality arose incidentally over the course of the interviews.

We needed to characterize it before analysing it. Our literature review confirmed Michel Naepels' significant remark about an anthropologically informed 'field of violence studies': 'No sooner was that field of research put forward than it seemed to be disintegrating, as the very definition of the concept is so delicate' (2006, p. 487).

The vagueness of the concept can prove to be crippling when extremely diverse types of expressions of violence are interwoven or causally linked. In this regard, we would like to take a step aside from some of our colleagues who are concerned about 'rediscovering the deep cultural roots of island behavior' (Huetz de Lemps, 2008). This is notably the case when one brings together 'a warlike background' of the Pacific islanders, and the 'uprooting' of unemployed urban youth who gather in 'predominantly ethnic' groups and confront each other in 'a sort of ritualization of conflicts' inherited from their ancestors. Unless assuming a kind of Polynesian atavism, whereby traditional forms of violence which used to be directed against the usual old enemies have now resurfaced under the guise of domestic violence, nothing predisposes us to incriminate 'culture' as the matrix of the multifaceted violence observed today. Like Michel Naepels, we believe that 'the notion of violence is less an operative category for analysis than the index of a field of experiences which remains to be specified' (2006, p. 489). It is precisely this 'field of experiences' that the prisoners' life stories allow us to approach.

In our quest for a performative approach to 'violence', some definitions of the concept drew our attention: that of violence as an 'assault on the body, personhood, dignity, sense of worth or value' (Scheper-Hughes & Bourgois, 2004, p. 1) and that of Paul Farmer, who uses the expression 'structural violence' as a synonym for 'unequal social structures' (2003, p. 230) and defines it as 'the social machinery of oppression' which relies on 'the erasure of historical memory and other forms of desocialization as enabling conditions of structures that are both "sinful" and ostensibly "nobody's fault"' (Farmer, 2004, p. 307).

Broadly equivalent to 'sinful' social structures characterized by poverty and steep grades of social inequality, including racism and gender inequality, in Johan Galtung's seminal definition (1969), the notion of 'structural violence' seems all the more fruitful as it leads us to understand violence differently than through the prism of individual 'psychology' or 'cultural alterity'. The structural perspective helps us avoid two pitfalls: psychologization, when violence is referred to as expressing individual deviance, and culturalism, when one's behaviour is referred to as being determined by the culture to which he or she belongs. The theory of structural violence has the merit of imposing a shift in our view of violence carried out by individuals: 'a violent act is to be placed in a process of violence of which it is only a significant moment' (Bouju & De Bruijn, 2008). This process goes beyond individuals but also their immediate social circles and involves the whole of society. Beyond the extraordinary nature of the acts of which the detainees were victims or perpetrators, we must take into account local context as well as the time- and space-related social relationships which allow for what is ordinary social violence. Individual violence echoes another kind of violence, that of society. The key to this chain of violence in individual trajectories is undoubtedly to be found in a collective past.

For the two past centuries, colonial and post-colonial experiences have been disruptive and devastating without being acknowledged as such by those who provoked them. As stated by Paul Farmer:

> Erasing history is perhaps the most common explanatory sleight-of-hand relied upon by the architects of structural violence. Erasure or distortion of history is part of the process of desocialization necessary for the emergence of hegemonic accounts of what happened and why.
>
> (2004, p. 308)

Apart from a recent and modest official recognition of the environmental and health impacts of the French nuclear tests in the second half of the 20th century, a denial of the long-lasting traumatic effect on the Polynesian peoples who were subjugated still prevails. But the prejudice is vivid, albeit mostly unspoken.

That is for the big picture. In detail, the materiality of the consequences of French colonization and ongoing rule has to be addressed. The question is not only that of a dramatic cultural loss but also that of a permanent struggle to live decently when resources are lacking. The rapid social change that occurred in the 1960s and the development of the nuclear testing economy, as well as the crisis experienced by the territory ever since this economy collapsed in the mid-1990s, have generated a context of widespread social insecurity for some groups. The resulting specific conditions of vulnerability include and go beyond individual situations of violence, which are the only ones subject to criminal sanctions.

The first register of social inequality that establishes a specific area of vulnerability for the majority of the detainees interviewed is that of poverty and economic precariousness, in a society that is unable to provide for its members' basic needs. A majority of the detainees interviewed left school well before the end of compulsory schooling, some as early as the age of 11, to help parents who were struggling to provide for their family, notably due to lack of access to land and a stable housing situation (Salaün & Le Plain, 2018). Finding a place to live in Tahiti, particularly for families from the archipelagos, can be very challenging and leads to insecurity, over-crowding of plots of land, stress within extended families, and forced mobility.

Our data established the prevalence of violence in everyday life, given that it occurs at home, in the street, at school, at work, etc. This violence is physical, but it is symbolic and social as well. The narratives, which include many descriptions of humiliations experienced in ordinary relations with institutions, reflect a lack of benevolence from society as a whole and the indifference of the wealthiest towards the realities facing the underprivileged fraction of the Polynesian population. In the words of Jacky Bouju and Mirjam De Bruijn, who worked for their part in African contexts, their life stories describe 'a cycle of violent exchanges that takes place within a framework for the continuity of a social relationship whose violence is entirely contained in the statutory inequality of the actors involved' (2008, p. 4).

## Four portraits

To illustrate the multidimensional nature of violence, this section presents some biographical features of four inmates: two murderers, one incestuous father, and one drug dealer. They were drawn up from information gathered during biographical interviews carried out in detention. These interviews aimed to explore different dimensions of the convicts' lives: their childhood, their adolescence, their educational and professional background, their judicial career, their relationship to the judicial institution, their relationship to the legal norm, their daily life in prison, and their vision of future.

The four portraits presented in the following are not intended to provide an exhaustive panorama of the properties of detainees incarcerated in French Polynesia today, but they are nonetheless representative of certain types of criminal paths marked by local characteristics that this chapter intends to explore.

### *Paul*[2]

Paul, aged 40, was sentenced in 2013 to 30 years of imprisonment, with a 22-year period of unconditional detention, for the rape and murder of his daughter, after premeditation was retained at the criminal court, which he always denied at the time of the trial and did not mention at any time during the two interviews.

Born in 1980 in Papeete, he is the eldest of three boys and two girls. Immediately after his birth, his father, from the Austral Islands, and his mother, from the Tuamotu Islands, returned to Marokau, in the Tuamotus, where they were working. He stayed there until the age of 8, when his mother decided to come to Tahiti to 'educate' her children, who until then had not attended school. Paul thus discovered school at the age of 8 when he enrolled in year 3.

Paul's father was working as a pearl diver in the Tuamotu Islands, and Paul only saw him very occasionally, as his father only came back for a month every one and a half to two years. His father was physically violent with his children. Paul says: 'it was hell when he beat us up'. Paul grew up in a popular neighbourhood close to the city, where he was exposed to violence. He started fighting at the age of 11. He dropped out of school in year nine. At 16, because he 'always screwed everything up', his father took him to the Tuamotus to moonlight as a pearl diver. There, aged 17, he met his wife, who was then 21. They had four children, who, under existing rules on pearl farms, could not stay with their parents. The children were brought up in Tahiti by his in-laws, with whom he did not get along. Paul only saw his children for one month each year, and thus relived what he himself had to go through with a father who was away due to professional distance. He suffered from not being recognized as a father, as his wife's parents had somehow taken over from the biological parents. He complained about being just considered then as a 'moneybags': 'This is what it boils down to here in Polynesia. When you work, you get money, the in-laws like it. But if you don't work, there's no more family, they don't know you anymore'. He blames his criminal act on being frustrated by his inability to exert paternal authority, at a time when he was weakened by the loss of his own mother, the source of his emotional balance.

### Thierry

Thierry, aged 42, was sentenced in 2016 to 12 years of imprisonment for rape of his daughter, aged 10 when the assaults started, over a period of almost 3 years. Born in Tahiti in 1978, he was the only boy and the youngest of seven siblings. He grew up in a poor neighbourhood near the city. His parents worked in a nearby hotel, his mother as a maid and his father as a caretaker. Thierry was first exposed to street violence in his neighbourhood, famous for its brawls and paka (cannabis) trafficking. His father, who was 'no good at boxing', got beaten up regularly by his brothers-in-law. When Thierry was 13, his family had to leave their home in Tahiti because of land rights issues, and they moved to Moorea. His parents lost their jobs and Thierry joined the Young Apprenticeship Centre in Moorea. But he ended up leaving school at 15 to help his father, who had a series of odd jobs. In order to take on the role of 'protecting [his] family', a role for which his father seemed to be failing in his mother's eyes, Thierry learned to box without telling his parents, and he took part in competitions. He may even have become a real substitute for his father, as he admits during the trial that he slept in his mother's bed until the age of 14, 'going so far as to stroke her belly and breasts and enjoyed smelling her armpits'. He managed to become financially independent, and worked in turn as a dancer, a lobster fisherman, a sculptor, for a tarring company, selling archaeological finds, etc. He also became an artist. He met his wife at the age of 21, and they had three daughters. They stayed in Moorea, where they lived in great promiscuity on the same cramped plot of land where they had been joined by uncles, aunts, and a grandmother. Denounced by one of his sisters for incest, he was incarcerated in Nuutania in 2014 during the investigation. He was transferred to Tatutu in 2017 and was at once integrated into the west wing of the detention centre, in the Respect module, because there was 'nothing' in his offender file, 'no break-ins, no nothing. Typing it all up, it was clean'.

Described by experts as a 'manipulative man with an oversized ego' at the time of the trial, he considers himself a 'nice man', and he likes to emphasize his duties as gangway rep and religious observance facilitator, whose reputation as a boxer helps to calm down young people who 'are really terrible, terrible' – in short, as a model prisoner. He compares himself to prisoners with light sentences (between 8 months and a year): 'They're the ones who're always moaning and yelling. . . . Us, the heavy sentences (*sic*), we've never done that. We never moan about stuff' (whenever he reviews the facts surrounding his sentence, he hardly ever mentions his daughter, the victim, but he admits to having failed in his duty as protector of the family: 'When I did that, I even broke my parents' trust, and my sisters', my family's, yea even my wife's trust, didn't I?').

### *Franck*

Franck was sentenced to life imprisonment for having sequestered and strangled his ex-girlfriend, after stabbing her and slitting her throat.

He was born in 1964 and was incarcerated in 2007. He was detained in Nuutania once already for robbery that he says that he did not commit but for which he claims to have taken the blame instead of his boss's son, while he was working as a nightclub bouncer. He maintains he was brought up by an 'exemplary' metropolitan father and Tahitian mother. He is himself the father of five children, the youngest being currently incarcerated in the same building as him for criminal damage, theft, and violence. He works full time in the laundry room, is gangway rep, and is considered a trusted prisoner. A female warder told us: 'It's a good thing we have inmates like him', acknowledging that the reason he is respected by the other detainees 'is also because he's a bit scary'. He considers himself to have nothing to lose, something his fellow inmates are very much aware of, and they know he can become 'very, very dangerous'. He is the one who advocates on behalf of those he calls 'veterans' against the young prisoners who bully them, pointing out that the prison governors expect him to 'act as a nanny' for the 'young wankers'.

He experienced a heart attack a few years ago and owes his life to the obstinacy of a Nuutania warder who did everything he could to ensure Franck could be taken care of as soon as possible under optimum conditions. Officers who know him well say that he was radically transformed by the whole episode and has gone from being an unwieldy prisoner to a model one. He was not enrolled in the Respect programme due to the nature of his life sentence. He considers himself to have seen it all, and as he thinks there is very little chance of him ever getting out of jail, he is very critical of both prisons and the criminal justice system. He believes the trial was entirely biased in favour of the prosecution and that he was a victim of unfair justice, as evidenced by what was arguably, according to him, the world record for fastest deliberation; the jurors retired for only 17 minutes before pronouncing the sentence. He nevertheless acknowledges the facts, explaining that he 'screwed up' and that he knows that 'there is no need to make excuses'. He calls the prison a 'dump', a 'housing estate for social rejects'.

He argues that prisoners are unfairly treated twice over: their rights are less respected in Tahiti than in the metropolis, and they are treated 'like dogs' in traditional detention as opposed to being treated like 'metropolitans' in the Respect module.

He does not trust either the psychologist or his appointed probation counsellor to improve his condition, pointing out that 'there is no point in explaining your life to someone who doesn't understand anything'.

He 'serves his sentence' and mentions that he 'never got down on one knee' because he knows why he is there, why he drinks his coffee alone in his cell in the morning, why he goes to bed alone at night.

However, he believes that you can always try and 'install Jacuzzis' inside cells, but as long as detainees are not given any work, it will be impossible for them not to get involved in trafficking and violence in prison, and not to start re-offending once they are out.

### Hiro

Hiro is pushing 30. He was unexpectedly abandoned by his parents when they left the family home, each going their separate way when he was 12, and taken in by his grandmother, who lived on a meagre retirement pension in a poor neighbourhood of Tahiti. At first merely as an observer of street-level drug trafficking, he was in time noticed by the drug dealers, eventually taking over from them when his bosses were put behind bars. Poverty and the resulting shame seemed to have had a serious impact on him, shame of not being able to be 'like everyone else' and not knowing the codes, for feeling humiliated in public; at school, for always wearing the same clothes and having the same school stuff; when enlisting in the Navy, for being 'told off' for not wearing any shoes; in court, for being called a 'merchant of death' by the judge during his trial. Being responsible as a teenager for his three little sisters' survival, for whom he had to become a substitute father by providing for his family, also left a mark. He says defence of his family has always taken precedence over everything until now.

He was convicted several times of drug offences. A sometime 'kikiri banker'[3] and cockfight organizer, he dealt first and foremost in paka and ice (methamphetamine). He was a *boss*, and he kept that status in jail. He was first detained at the age of 21 but was allowed to wear an electronic bracelet while awaiting trial, thanks to the lawyer whose services he could afford. He organized drug traffick-ing inside the Nuutania prison with the help of his girlfriend who was then also detained, in spite of them having a very young child.

A top sportsman and former boxing champion, he never touched the stuff he dealt. The warders describe him as embodying a new kind of criminality among *icemen*. They sometimes criticize in the strongest terms his opportunism and lack of empathy – he does not have the excuse of drug addiction but is perfectly aware of the damage caused by ice – and his role in the destruction of Polynesian soci-ety, on whose values he is perceived as trampling. He occupies a lead position in prison. He was enrolled straightaway into the Respect module, where he has been using time spent in prison studying for degrees. He has many professional plans for his post-detention future.

Besides the differences in the grounds for their incarceration, the four men por-trayed have actually much in common. They bear witness to the most striking fea-ture of these life stories: the recurrence of violence in the narratives, encountered both as offenders and as victims. The omnipresence of this violence, and its protean and extensive scope, provoke questioning.

## A moral economy cast in the mould of violence

Having insisted on the structural dimension of interpersonal violence, a question remains: How can we apprehend the embodiment of the past? How can we relate the dramatic events of colonial history and the crimes committed by the men and women we interviewed?

As stated by Didier Fassin in his comments on Paul Farmer's article published in *Current Anthropology* in 2004: 'Embodiment of history can be understood in the theoretical framework of a performative social order' (in Farmer, 2004, p. 319). He reminds us of the two distinct ways the inscription of the past in present experi-ences can be framed:

> First, it refers to the social condition of individuals or groups and the sort of inter-actions it underlies. . . . Secondly, it refers to the historical experience, whether singular or collective, and the narratives through which it can be reached.
>
> (ibid.)

What does characterize the 'performative social order' in French Polynesia today? In the public sphere, it translates into policies of redistribution of wealth kept to a mini-mum, and into naturalization and concealment of inequalities, which are partially compensated but also fuelled by forms of community solidarity on a micro-scale, halfway between charity within religious groups and political clientelism. In the domestic sphere, when the exercise of authority involves corporal punishment as an educational technique and a mode of socialization (Bouju & De Bruijn, 2008, p. 4), the victims can in turn become the executioners, all the more so because the impos-sibility of turning against the 'system' diverts aggression towards close relatives.

A major impact of the drastic social changes which occurred in French Polynesia is that the environment in which the men and women we met grew up and lived is anomic in the broadest sense, marked as it is by a normative system which 'has lost all or part of its legitimacy, rigour and effectiveness' (Bouju & De Bruijn, 2008, op. cit.). The accounts we have heard from them testify to a system of values that is not only very different from that recognized by the criminal law imported from France, which eventually led them to jail, and very different from the Christian morality to which a very large majority of Polynesians nevertheless claim to adhere. It is also very different from what ancient descriptions of traditional Polynesian norms and values might have been telling us (Henry, 1952; Levy, 1973).

Instead of mobilizing a mere 'conflict of values' which would account for the specificities of criminal careers in French Polynesia, we favour the assumption of specific moral economies, defined as the 'production, distribution, circulation, and use of emotions and values and of norms and obligations' (Fassin, 2009, p. 1251; see also Scott, 1976; Thompson, 1971).

In a context of limited resources, the construction of masculinity seems to rely on the capacity to resist structural economic violence and respond to it, which can lead one to exercise some kind of violence oneself. A man's place, a husband's or a father's, is measured in terms of his social usefulness, itself linked to his ability to provide for his 'little family' (as opposed to *fēti'i*, the extended family). The responsibility to provide for this 'little family' becomes a moral imperative with which men struggle, especially given the limited resources at their disposal. In the absence of control over one's own destiny, one may come to seek control over one's relatives.

What is at stake here is honour, that is, the ability to keep one's place as a man in a group whose limits do not coincide with those of the global society the law seeks to protect (Bourdieu, 1972). What seems specific is a dichotomy between the harm caused to the 'collective of reference', in this case the family as a group, which is a matter of honour, and the (ultimately less serious) harm that can be caused to an individual, even if he is a member of that family, which is a matter of morality and responsibility in the criminal sense, as 'the obligation to answer for one's harmful or criminal actions before the law' (Ricœur, 1995, p. 41).

Understanding this moral economy requires endorsing the approach to legality defended by the Legal Consciousness Studies movement, as

> a form of social relations and representations that is given the force of law on a daily basis through *interpretative schemes*, which people invoke to construct the meaning of their actions and those of others, and *human and material resources*, which, in the form of capacities and resources that can be mobilised, make action possible.
>
> (Ewick & Silbey, 1998, pp. 31–32)

Admittedly, the interviews we conducted show that the emic categories of legality are out of step with the categories of law. This discrepancy refers to a normative discordance between a social order that is legitimate from the point of view of those who participate in it but is illegitimate from the point of view of other segments of society and, above all, is illegal under criminal law. One cannot otherwise understand the difficulty, noted on numerous occasions during the interviews, in identifying victims precisely as victims, in the sense of criminal law, or in overcoming defence mechanisms in order to psychically work through the acts committed. One cannot otherwise understand the difficulty in making sense of criminal sanction, when the most important thing is the 'forgiveness' granted by those who are believed to have been harmed and who may or may not be those identified as victims by the justice system.

One cannot otherwise understand what Hiro, the ice boss, explains about his indifference to the harm he was causing by selling drugs to individuals he was only linked to by trafficking, as long as it allowed him to protect and support his relatives and friends in need . . . until the day he realized that it was his 'little family' (wife and child) he was harming by being incarcerated. His narrative echoes what Philippe Bourgois (1995) says about Puerto Rican crack dealers in East Harlem in the 1980s, referring to 'a personal quest for dignity' when the legal means to succeed are lacking. On the whole, his trajectory reflects a rational use of the resources at his disposal, and he describes his career in business as he would describe his rise within a respectable company. His deviant behaviour sounds like an instrumental response to a set of conditions both objective (job insecurity, lived experience, and available opportunities in his neighbourhood) as well as subjective (feeling abandoned, responsible for providing for his family, etc.). He concluded his first interview by saying that judges, 'who've never starved', cannot put themselves in his shoes. He is rational (meaning that his resources match his objectives) but with a brand of rationality that puts moral judgement on hold, or rather rationality justified by a moral economy that considers resourcefulness and solidarity with relatives as positive values, to the possible detriment of his drug trafficking victims, whom he does not recognize as victims. As drug dealers operating in other socially disadvantaged contexts have also described, he displays a clientelistic type of sociability; he exists socially because he has 'friends', who very likely still 'owe' him even while in jail. By joining and creating clientelistic networks, he participates in forms of local solidarity, which can be regarded as a palliative to a 'performative social order' he does not control. However, he has never made any political statement denouncing poor neighbourhood deprivation

One cannot otherwise understand a mother's testimony about her daughter whose throat was slit by her father, Paul. Facing the cameras after the trial, she explained that her husband was both 'a good father' when it came to feeding his family and 'not a good father' when he killed his daughter. The murdering father clarified that his act was triggered by his feeling of dishonour when his daughter insulted him by questioning his role as a father. Paul's conception of the paternal role is probably inspired by that of his own father, of whom he says:

He is a simple person. For him, it's tradition: work, home. And that's all. My dad, he would go get money, take it to my mom, then my mom go get the food and bring it home for us. It was just that.

For this role, he considered assuming it by guaranteeing an income to his family thanks to his work in the Tuamotus. But he says he was dispossessed of his paternity by his in-laws who looked after his children in Tahiti:

> Maternal grandparents have taken the place of real parents. My children . . . I lived, eh, in the Tuamotus, I was all alone, for years. I would come back to see them for a month. The remaining eleven months is only for maternal parents. I could tell you, I was just a dough bag.

Nor can we otherwise understand Franck, sentenced to life imprisonment for the murder of his girlfriend, justifying how he reacted in anger to her lack of respect when she interrupted him on a night fishing trip, which is, according to him, a serious breach of Tahitian custom. Franck presents himself as a man of principles, ready to stop at nothing when his family is under attack. That is not to say that the motives for his life sentence don't leave a doubt as to the rather literal interpretation one should have of his project to 'tear out' an ex-friend's eyes. He explains:

> Never trust an inmate . . . NEVER, EVER. Even me, I got ripped off. Not me, my old man. Well, the guy who did that would rather not come back to jail. I'm waiting for him. But he will come back, he will come back. . . . He ripped off my old man, 80,000 francs (USD $750). It was in Nuutania. It was in 2014. He was out on leave. I asked him if he could pass on a message. Go see my father to tell him to bring me a pair of sneakers when he comes visit me. Don't know what he told him. He asked for much more than what my message would mention. It's okay. I thought he was a friend, but then. . . . When he's back in prison, for him I'm ready to get life again. (silence). There are people you don't play with. . . . I know he's coming back, as he is in Ice. . . . It is not impossible that he is in the lot. . . . Him, it's simple, I will tear his eyes out. Everyone knows. My fellow inmates tell me: 'you're right'. No, no . . . my old man, no one touches him. My family, no way. The guy stole from the wrong person, period. There are things. . . . Steal from me, okay. But when my family is involved, no longer okay. Especially when talking about my old man. There are things. . . . I'm sorry. I dream more often of this guy than of mermaids and stuff. I have not forgotten him yet, and won't forget. I have a memory like an elephant. I never forget. This is a priority. A promise I made to myself. Everyone knows. Don't worry. Those who get out tell him: 'he's waiting for you'.

We cannot understand the logic of Thierry, an incestuous father who pointed out he was an honourable, God-fearing breadwinner, protector, a hard worker and a good prison mate, etc., who was unlucky enough to make a stupid 'mistake', whose main victim was not his daughter but his family, whose trust he betrayed and whom he disappointed. He explains:

> Because like I said [before] to the family, 'I'll be there for you if you have a problem, all that.' And these things, I broke. Yeah. I broke eh. All my words

were empty words. When I did that, I even broke my parents' trust, my sisters, my family, even my wife too, eh. It's not a sin, it's my fault. It is a mistake, a mistake on my part, my own mistake. I even told my mom: 'the kindness that I had, the love that I had, I helped a lot of people, and now I did something that is stupid, eh. I fell into it, and there you go. You see, I am pushed away from you because of me'.

If Thierry admits to having failed in his role of protector of his family, his daughter, the first and most direct victim, remains out of the picture in his testimony.

## Conclusion

It is tempting to interpret the perpetrators' narratives in terms of a conflict between honour and norms. In the literature, the causes of deviance are overwhelmingly presented as resulting from a disjunction between honour, comprehended though its link to violence, and legal normativity. Far from appeasing social relations, honour disrupts public order and plunges society into chaos. Some authors, though, take a different path, considering honour to be an essential moral principle that regulates social interactions and secures social recognition. Julie Alev Dilmaç (2014) suggests drawing a distinction between what she calls a 'civic honor' – including all the civilities but also the legal elements (such as respect for the Other, that of the dignity of the person) which would aim to organize public space and therefore to maintain social order – and its opposite, an honour described as uncivilized, violent, destructive, and vile, which would define principles of an alterity automatically qualified as deviant. This duality of the understanding of honour gives rise to a 'We' and a 'Them' based on the differing conceptions of honour and framing the contours of otherness.

As interesting as this suggestion may seem, we also need to keep in mind Michael Herzfeld's (1980, p. 340) exhortation to always put the study of moral taxonomies into a specific context: categories such as honour or morality only make sense in localized linguistic and social worlds.

This is true for 'Polynesian culture', but it is also true for the French legal culture at work in the procedures that brought those we met behind bars. While it does not amount to opening the door for radical relativism, it does amount to taking into account a set of values and practices characterized by mistrust in public institutions, resulting from an intimate experience of the fact that global society and its institutions are powerless to improve the situation of certain categories of the population. Considered as a mechanism of self-defence, this specific ethos refers to what Edward C. Banfield (1958) has termed 'amoral familialism' in order to describe the tendency to limit moral sense to family, relatives, and friends, conceived as a network distinct from the rest of society. Just as there is God's law and human law, there is the law of the Republic and the law of the reference group. To understand what makes the individuation of an individual's life, we need to understand the way these legalities are articulated at the individual level.

Facing the analytical challenge of understanding how and to what extent interpersonal violence represents an embodiment of structural violence in the specific postcolonial context of French Polynesia, we might fruitfully consider Johan Galtung's concept of 'cultural violence' (1990). He suggested a triangular representation of violence, where interpersonal violence is an event, structural violence is a process, and cultural violence is invariant. The violence that he describes as 'cultural' is associated with moral space boundaries that determine whether structural or interpersonal violence is bad, correct, or acceptable. It can shift the value of an action from bad to good or from bad to acceptable. It can also cause the act not to be perceived, or not to be perceived as violent although it definitely is when perceived from another angle (Bouju & Bruijn, 2008).

Perhaps we could use this as a way of understanding otherwise totally opaque comments, such as the one made by Thierry, sentenced to 12 years in prison for raping his daughter, about the meaning of prison sentences: 'Prison gives us food for thought, doesn't it! Prison, it gives us food for thought: is the harm you've caused . . . good? Do you get it?'

## Notes

1 Native.
2 First names have all been changed.
3 Illegal games of chance.

## References

Banfield, E. C. (1958). *The moral basis of a backward society*. Glencoe, IL: The Free Press.
Bastide, L. (2020). *Les violences familiales en Polynésie française. Entrer, vivre et sortir de la violence*. INJEP Notes & rapports/Rapport d'étude.
Bouju, J., & De Bruijn, M. (2008). Violences structurelles et violences systémiques: La violence ordinaire des rapports sociaux en Afrique. *Bulletin de l'APAD* [online], pp. 27–28. http://journals.openedition.org/apad/3673
Bourdieu, P. (1972). *Esquisse d'une théorie de la pratique*. Geneva: Droz.
Bourgois, P. (1995). *In search of respect: Selling crack in el barrio*. Cambridge: Cambridge University Press.
Dilmaç, J. A. (2014). L'honneur: principe de prévention de la déviance? *Déviance et Société*, *38*(3), 339–360.
Ewick, P., & Silbey, S. (1998). *The commonplace of law: Stories of everyday life*. Chicago, IL: University of Chicago Press.
Farmer, P. (2003). *Pathologies of power: Health, human rights, and the new war on the poor*. Berkeley, CA: University of California Press.
Farmer, P. (2004). An anthropology of structural violence. *Current Anthropology*, *45*(3), 305–325.
Fassin, D. (2009). Moral economies revisited. *Annales. Histoire, Sciences Sociales*, *6*, 1237–1266.
Fassin, D. (2016). *Prison worlds: Ethnography of the carceral condition*, trans. R. Gomme. Cambridge: Polity Press.

Galtung, J. (1969). Violence, peace, and peace research. *Journal of Peace Research, 6*(3), 167–191.

Galtung, J. (1990). Cultural violence. *Journal of Peace Research, 27*(3), 291–305.

Henry, T. (1952). *Tahiti aux temps anciens*. Paris: Publication de la Société des Océanistes.

Herzfeld, M. (1980). Problems in the comparative analysis of moral systems. *Man, 15*(2), 339–351.

Huetz de Lemps, C. (2008). Quelques réflexions sur les sociétés insulaires du Pacifique. *EchoGéo*, p. 5. Retrieved from http://echogeo.revues.org/index3753.html

Levy, R. (1973). *Tahitians: Mind and experience in the Society Islands*. Chicago, IL: University of Chicago Press.

Mai, I. (2016). *Evaluation des besoins sociaux des personnes détenues au Centre pénitentiaire de Nuutania*. Rapport d'enquête sociale réalisée par Ina Mai, Assistante sociale au SPIP.

Naepels, M. (2006). Quatre questions sur la violence. *L'Homme, 177–178*, 487–495.

Ricœur, P. (1995). Le concept de responsabilité: essai d'analyse sémantique. In P. Ricœur (ed.), *Le Juste I* (pp. 41–70). Paris: Esprit.

Salaün, M., & Le Plain, E. (2018). *L'école ambiguë: histoires de familles à Tahiti*. Paris: L'Harmattan.

Salaün, M., Vernaudon, J., & Paia, M. (2020). *Amo i te utu'a. Porter sa peine. Enquête sur la condition carcérale à Tahiti*. Unpublished Research Report, Direction de l'administration pénitentiaire, Mission des services pénitentiaires de l'outre-mer.

Scheper-Hughes, N., & Bourgois, P. (2004). *Violence in war and peace: An anthology*. Chichester: Blackwell.

Scott, J. C. (1976). *The moral economy of the peasant: Rebellion and subsistence in Southeast Asia*. Princeton, NJ: Princeton University Press.

Thompson, E. P. (1971). The moral economy of the English crowd in the 18th century. *Past & Present, 50*, 76–136.

# 9 'This is not *Vaelens!*'

## Naming and reacting to physical abuse in a Vanuatu school

*Alice Servy*

In Vanuatu, as in other Oceanic countries, physical abuse[1] of children is wide-spread. According to the 2013 national Demographic and Health Survey, 72% of children aged to 2 to 14 had experienced 'physical punishment' (by being slapped, hit, or whipped) at the hands of a parent (their biological mother or father, or a guardian) over the previous month[2] (Ministry of Health, Vanuatu National Statistics Office, & Secretariat of the Pacific Community, 2014, p. 245). Also, among the students aged 16 to 17 who responded to the 2008 child protection survey, 27% reported that they had been 'physically hurt' by a teacher over the past month (Kanas, Norton, Tarileo, & Wernham, 2009, p. 2).

Physical abuse of children is, however, prohibited in Vanuatu. The 30 December 2001 Education Act includes a ban on the physical punishment of students. The Family Protection Act of 2008 cited 'domestic violence' (*domestik vaelens* in the Bislama language) as a criminal offence. Additionally, the United Nations (UN) Convention on the Rights of the Child, which Vanuatu ratified in 1993, recognizes that children have the right to be protected 'from all forms of physical or mental violence, injury or abuse, neglect or negligent treatment, maltreatment or exploitation, including sexual abuse'[3] (United Nations Human Rights Office of the High Commissioner, 1989).

In several of her books, Sally Engle Merry (2009, pp. 4–5) shows that violence is a fundamentally social and cultural construct. Society defines the contexts and forms in which inflicting pain is acceptable and those in which it must be punished. Some forms of pain can therefore be considered as erotic, heroic, justified, legitimate, or reasonable, where others are viewed as abusive and violent. While approaching violence as a social and cultural construct is thus important, we also need to consider the dynamic character of this construct, particularly in a contemporary context of 'globalization' (Abélès, 2008).

Despite the relative geographical isolation of the archipelago, which has been independent since 1980, Vanuatu is characterized by an intense transnational circulation of money, people, and ideas.[4] The country's residents, in particular in the capital Port Vila, are confronted with multiple sources of knowledge (including school, the media, ancestral knowledge, non-governmental organizations [NGOs], the Christian religion) that impact their ways of conceiving and inflicting physical abuse.

DOI: 10.4324/9781003146667-10

Against this backdrop, in an effort to understand how representations of the use of physical force on children in Vanuatu are constructed, reproduced, and changed, and how these practices and their acceptability are perpetuated and transformed, I have focused on the role of school. School is a place of primary socialization, as is the family. In school, one learns to name acts and react to them – a relationship to physical abuse develops.

As part of a post-doc project funded by the French Gender Institute's junior researcher mobility grant in 2018, I conducted a two-month fieldwork in a school located in an underprivileged neighbourhood of Port Vila. Drawing on this research, this chapter examines the abusive interactions between school staff, students, and the students' parents in a bid to understand the ways in which these actors refer to physical abuse, the reasons for resorting to such abuse, the relations of power and authority they involve, as well as the way in which abusive interactions and their acceptability are transformed. Here, physical abuse is considered on a relational basis, as social interactions and not as encounters between abusers and 'intrinsic victims' – the people I talked to could be abusers, witnesses, and victims at the same time (Carra & Faggianelli, 2003).

Having shown that schools are particularly suitable places to investigate physical abuse in Port Vila, I contend that an act is referred to as *vaelens* on the basis not only of the physical pain inflicted but also of the relational framework and the perception of the abuser's intentionality. I then demonstrate that schools are venues for abusive interactions that contribute to organizing power relations, including within families,[5] as well as places where different conceptions of the legitimacy of the use of physical force are confronted and transformed through interactions.

## Studying physical abuse in a school based in an underprivileged neighbourhood of the Vanuatu capital

This chapter draws mainly on material collected at the Mango School in Port Vila,[6] an English-language Presbyterian school built in 2008 with support from an Australian non-profit. Initially private, it has now become public. Its staff presented it to me as the most affordable school in the capital.[7] The non-profit that opened the school also sponsors the education of the most destitute students. The neighbourhood in which the school is located is considered one of Port Vila's poorest. Most residents have low-skill, badly paid jobs, such as hotel employee or security guard; some sell ready-made dishes.

As of 2018, the Mango School catered to boys and girls from kindergarten to year 10, aged 4 to 16.[8] Most lived in the same underprivileged neighbourhood of Port Vila where I have been conducting ethnographic research since 2009.[9] In many cases, students and staff had kinship ties (meaning socially recognized ties of consanguinity or affinity), albeit to a lesser extent than in schools I visited outside the capital. The relations of authority institutionalized by the educational system (such as the students' respect for teachers) were thus intertwined with power relations based on classificatory kinship. For instance, in the neighbourhood where many Mango School attendees live is Ego, who must show respect to his fathers, mothers, and older sisters and brothers, avoid his uncles and aunts, but maintain joking relationships with his cross-cousins (Servy, 2017a, pp. 149–158).

According to the school's principal, there were 473 students enrolled in July 2018. The staff comprised 24 members (3 of whom were men): 16 teachers, a principal, 2 librarians, a security guard, 2 canteen employees, and 2 elders.[10]

During my research at the Mango School, I observed everyday interactions between staff and students, among staff and among students in 10 of the school's 12 classes. I conducted observations during classes, revising sessions, and second trimester exams. I also observed breaks and religious services. I accompanied students and staff for trips to the stadium and to the facilities of the NGO *Wan Smolbag*. I also spent hours in the school library and in the staff room.

On these occasions, I collected various types of materials: posters, exam questions, handbooks, regulations, a logbook, a notebook on behaviours, etc. I was entrusted with a class on two occasions to fill in for an absent teacher. I moderated a discussion on 'mockery' (*jikim*) with year 9 students and a drawing workshop on 'blows' (*kilim*) with year 4 students.

Only after two weeks of observations and informal interviews, did I begin conducting recorded semi-directive interviews in Bislama, Vanuatu's lingua franca. Among a total of 47 interviews, 36 were done with students aged 10 to 16 years. The teachers selected the students based on their place of residence, gender, and family situation. I also conducted interviews with 11 of the 24 school staff.

The Mango School turned out to be an excellent place to study physical abuse in Port Vila. First, I was able to talk to students and staff in settings where they felt at ease and safe (such as the library), and that were more conducive to sharing intimate thoughts than their homes were. My interviewees were able to tell me about experiences of physical abuse that took place not only at school but also outside school (in the street and at home). Second, I was able to observe interactions that would be classified as 'violent' under international law (but are not always considered as such by victims, perpetrators, or witnesses): mockeries, insults, beatings, non-consensual diffusion of intimate photographs, etc. These interactions, which occurred within the school, involved not only people with student–student, student–staff, or staff–staff relations but also (simultaneously or not) people with kinship ties. These abusive acts thus fall at the intersection between the spheres of education and family, and challenge the distinction between domestic and non-domestic violence.

## Naming physical abuse

Before I began to examine occurrences of physically abusive interactions in school and their acceptability, I started with the key task of analysing the terms used at the Mango School to refer to physical abuse. In the course of my previous research, I had noted that the concept of *vaelens* was rarely used by Port Vila residents (Servy, 2017a, p. 429). Unlike most scholars in sociology and in the educational sciences who have addressed abuse in French schools (Carra, 2008, p. 320), I knew I could not start from the concept of 'violence' when conducting interviews. From an anthropological standpoint, it is indeed essential to consider local representations of acts considered violent under international law, in order to grasp the cultural and social norms that construct them. I therefore started by observing and listening to interactions between individuals at schools for two weeks, to note the terms used to refer to abuse and the situations in which they were used. The following draws solely on my data on physical abuse.

The term whose use most struck me in the course of my research at the Mango School was *kilim*, from the English 'kill', which in Bislama means 'hit'. Students and staff make a distinction between *kilim smol* and *kilim nogud*. *Kilim smol* means 'hitting softly, without leaving marks on the body'. Conversely, *kilim nogud* means 'hitting hard, leaving marks'. The difference essentially lies in the physical consequences of the act. A teacher, for instance, explained to me that '*Kilim nogud* is different from *kilim smol nomo*: in the first case, there are marks, injuries (*kil*) on the body; in the second case, there are no injuries (*kil*)'. Jimmy, a year 7 student aged 13, told me: 'All the year 7 teachers hit (*kil*) us but they do not *kil* us *nogud*. *Kilim nogud* is when they whip us and then we have marks'.

The terms *faetem* and *faet*, from the English 'fight', are also sometimes used at the Mango School as synonyms of *kilim* ('hit'). My interviewees essentially used them in my presence to refer to brawls, fights between students. A distinction was made between *faet strong* (in which the students have an actual reason to quarrel and hit hard) and *faet pleplei* (pretend fighting). The school's Presbyterian Elder told me that 'the difference between *faet* and *pleplei* is that in the first case there are tears'. The naming of the act is therefore not based on the intention, but on consequences. However, the boundary between play and actual fight varies depending on age, gender, status, and previous experiences. A secondary school teacher, for instance, told me that 'there are fights in all classes, but I am a man, so to me *faet* means *serious faet*'. Another female teacher said:

> The students hit one another but those are small fights (*smol faet*). It's when there's a big fight (*bigfala faet*) with injuries that it becomes a problem. The children pretend fight. Those in primary school cry more because they are more sensitive. The quiet ones are the ones who cry. The most headstrong cry only when the teacher whips them because it hurts.

During the course of my research at the Mango School, I never heard students or staff use the Bislama word *vaelens*. However, in interviews, all the staff and half of the students told me that they were familiar with the term and gave me a definition. This was more often the case for the year 9 and 10 students than their younger peers in years 4 to 8. Nearly all the students who gave me a definition of *vaelens* remembered where they had heard about it, which supports the hypothesis, proposed in my Ph.D., that the term recently appeared in Port Vila. Following the adoption of the Family Protection Act in 2008, many informative materials on *domestik vaelens*, funded essentially by the Australian and New Zealand governments, were developed and disseminated in Vanuatu, particularly in urban areas (Servy, 2017a, pp. 421–431). The Mango School's students mostly learned about the existence of the word *vaelens* from the media (in TV shows, papers, radio broadcasts, and on posters or T-shirts), during visits by members of NGOs, such as Save the Children Australia and the Vanuatu Women's Centre at school, or through the police's crime prevention team, which also frequently visits schools. This information pertained almost exclusively to *vaelens* between spouses and between parents and children.

While the Convention on the Rights of the Child presented in the introduction that 'violence' can be physical, sexual, or psychological, very few of my interviewees at the Mango School used the word *vaelens* when discussing mockery, bullying, or sexual assault. A majority defined *vaelens* as 'hitting hard' (*kilim nogud*). Fourteen-year-old year 9 student Sabrina told me, for instance: 'It's not *vaelens* when the security guard whips us, because we have marks, but the skin isn't torn off'. A secondary school teacher explained to me that '*vaelens* is when you hit a woman and then she's got injuries, a broken hand, a black eye, blood'. When asked if she saw insults as *vaelens*, she replied she was not sure.

In addition to the strength of the blows, the kinship ties between the abuser and the abused also determine whether an act can be referred to as *vaelens* or not. For most of my interviewees (students and staff alike), situations of *vaelens* can only occur within the family, and more precisely between spouses or between parents and children. Physical abuse outside the family is generally not referred to as *vaelens*, but rather as *faet* or *kil*. Only a few students, among the older ones and those who have been exposed to Save the Children's awareness campaigns on child rights, describe teachers whipping them or twisting their ears to discipline them as *vaelens*. The physically abusive interactions that occur between students or between staff and students are, in most cases, not perceived as *vaelens* by the latter. This is likely due to the fact that most of the information they have access to deals with *vaelens* within nuclear families.

Also, for many of my interviewees, *vaelens* is not simply hitting hard, but hitting hard without an educational purpose. In this sense, the term contrasts with *tijim*, from the English 'teach'. When I asked a year 9 student aged 14 if he would say his (classificatory) older brother whipping him after he had borrowed things from him without permission is *vaelens*, he replied: 'I don't know, because it's my fault too, it's a teaching (*tijim*) from home; next time I won't do it'. Angela, a year 6 student aged 11, told me that when you hit a child for a 'good reason' (they haven't been listening, they fight or steal), 'it's OK because it's for the child to learn'. But when it's not for a 'good reason' (their mother has been drinking, and she is unhappy about some insignificant thing), then it is *vaelens*. She added that her own mother would only hit her for 'good reasons'.

Ultimately, the analysis of the main terms used at the Mango School to refer to physical abuse – *kilim smol, kilim nogud, faet strong*, and *faet pleplei* – evidences a distinction based on the transformation of the body, and more precisely on the marks on the flesh induced by blows. The concept of *vaelens*, which is used infrequently at the Mango School, also relates to the question of physical integrity, but not all forms of physical abuse that leave marks on the body are seen as *vaelens*. The students and staff I interviewed generally share a similar conception of *vaelens*. Most of them believe that an interaction can only be *vaelens* if it leaves deep marks on the body, has no educational purpose, and involves family members. In other words, the naming of an act as *vaelens* is the combined product of the perception of intentionality, the seriousness of the physical hurt inflicted, and the relational framework in which it happens. These ways of naming acts of physical abuse also give us a glimpse of the practices at work in these schools, and will lead us to more thoroughly examine the motives that trigger such abuse and the relations between those involved in these abusive interactions – in short, to understand who hits who at the Mango School, and for what reasons.

## The school: a place of abusive interactions

Over the course of my research at the Mango School, I observed numerous exchanges of taps and blows between children, although they occurred less frequently than mockery. The students, particularly boys, play fight (*faet pleplei*) or fight for real (*faet strong*). Mostly 9th- and 10th-year students described their exchanges of blows as a form of play. Tom, a year 9 student aged 15, told me, 'I fight to *pleplei* (play) but not to make the others cry'. Vicky, a year 10 student age 14, explained to me that in her class, there are 'boys who often hit the girls but to *pleplei*', although the girls in question do not always perceive these blows as a game.

The blows and brawls that do not fit into the *pleplei* category essentially involve younger students. James, a year 10 student aged 16, for instance, told me that he would fight seriously (*faet strong*) when he was between 11 and 14, but no longer does. Fights between students are often linked to mockery (*jik*), unauthorized borrowings of objects, or the refusal to share food.

Kinship norms regulate the occurrence of physical abuse between students. Indeed, power relations based on classificatory kinship have an impact on who hits whom. Jacquy, a year 7 student aged 12, told me she hit a girl on the head for having told one of her friends that he was showing off after answering a teacher's question correctly. The boy asked Jacquy to hit that girl for him because they are from the same family (to be specific, classificatory cousins). Sophie, a year 7 student aged 12, told me that other children were afraid to hit her, because her mother teaches at school. Physically abusive interactions between students are thus informed by power relations based not only on gender, age, and the school but also on kinship ties.

During my time at the Mango School, I observed instances of physical abuse not only between students but also between school staff and students. On several occasions, in particular, I witnessed teachers hitting children with a stick or a ruler; the vast majority of students told me that they had been hit or whipped by a staff member before. Staff hit children more or less hard and may leave marks on their bodies or not (*kilim nogud* or *smol*). A year 7 student told me that the previous year, one of his classmates got his hand broken after their teacher hit him with a ruler.

Most teachers told me that whipping, hitting, or pinching students is prohibited. However, in interviews, four out of nine explicitly that they would rap children on the knuckles or whip them to discipline them (*tijim*). When I asked a secondary school teacher how she punished children, she replied:

> We punish them by telling them to get out of the room. We can whip (*wip*) them if they have not done their exercise, but it's not allowed. . . . Back in the day, teachers would whip us, we were very scared when we hadn't done our homework. You can whip their hands, their legs if they walk around too much, put duct tape over their mouth if they talk too much, or you can give them an extra assignment. During the first trimester, the children were OK, but in the second semester, we whipped them more because they're headstrong. But we don't whip them hard (*nogud*).

The other teachers denied using corporal punishment or told me about acts performed by other staff members.

According to the students, teachers hit them when they have not done their homework, are late for class, skip class, are chatty, or do not listen. These occurrences of physical abuse are thus responses to challenges to the teacher's authority or to failure to comply with the status of the student under the supervision of the school. Teachers use physical force especially to punish boys. But due to gender-based power relations, some female teachers told me they are reluctant to punish boys when they consider them to be 'too big' – meaning those who have potentially already been circumcised and as a result are no longer seen by society as children but as young men (Servy, 2017a, pp. 231–239). In that case, some ask the security guard to punish the older students for them. The man's kinship ties with many children allows him to be physically abusive to them (as a classificatory father, for instance). Collective punishments may also involve physical abuse. Several year 9 students told me that at the end of the first trimester, one of their teachers left the classroom in tears. The security guard then proceeded to cane each student – boys and girls – twice. Like the physical abuse that occurs between students, abusive interactions between staff and students are embedded in power relations based on the school, gender, age, and kinship ties.

Almost all the students I talked to reported having been hit by family members, especially their classificatory parents, grandparents, or brothers and sisters, for punishment purposes. According to the Vanuatu Demography and Health survey of 2013, 51% of parents consider that to raise their children aged 2 to 14 years properly, corporal punishment is necessary (Ministry of Health, Vanuatu National Statistics Office, & Secretariat of the Pacific Community, 2014, p. 243). The accounts given by Mango School students reveal complex family configurations (strong family and social networks in the neighbourhood, over two generations living under the same roof, adopted or foster children) and recent socio-economic transformations (parents employed as seasonal workers abroad, for instance) that have also been observed in other parts of Oceania (see Bastide and Regnier's contribution to this volume). The beatings are more or less intense (*kilim nogud* or *smol*) and occur generally at home, but they also sometimes happen in school, which reflects the interpenetration of the educational and family spheres. In August

2018, for instance, a little girl from the Mango School was whipped by her mother in the playground while the teacher and I were there. Despite the authority conferred on her by the school setting, the teacher was unwilling to challenge parental authority, and let the child be punished violently.

It should be noted that, occasionally, outsiders (parents, members of rival gangs) come in to settle scores with staff or students (especially the older ones). Fights (*faetem strong*) have broken out in school and there have been suspicions of sorcery attacks targeting staff. This was actually one of the main reasons why the school hired a security guard in 2017. While my interviewees did not refer to these fights and acts of sorcery as *vaelens*, they did involve physical abuse.

The Mango School is thus a place where acts of physical abuse occur that may or may not fall under the category of *vaelens*. These interactions involved a variety of actors: students and staff, as well as family members and other outsiders. Physical abuse contributes to the organization of power relations in school. These relations are based not only on the school as an institution but also on gender, age, and kinship ties. The school thus participates in socialization to physical abuse and in the reproduction of power relations through the repeated exposure of students (and staff) to abusive practices. Yet it is also a melting pot where representations of physical abuse and of its acceptability are transformed, being a place where different actors (students, teachers, parents, and NGO members) interact and different normative frameworks (educational, familial, and legal) intersect.

## The relational construction of the acceptability of blows

As I have shown, in school and at home, physical force is frequently used on children. When they are hit for disciplinary purposes (*tijim*), the children rarely denounce family members or school staff, as in most cases they consider this abuse to be legitimate. Marie, a year 9 student aged 14, told me 'the teachers whip our hands or back when we haven't finished our homework or we've been skipping school, but we don't denounce them because it's our fault'. However, not all blows struck by school staff are considered acceptable by the students, and my interviewees occasionally complain to their parents. Sophie, a year 7 student aged 12, told me:

> When we were in year 5, the security guard whipped us with a hose because we were playing outside instead of being in class. I cried. I told my mother [who teaches at the school], but she told me it was OK because we'd disobeyed.

Parents often support the use of physical force to discipline (*tijim*) their children but will occasionally complain to the principal when they perceive the blows as too harsh (*kilim nogud*) or unjustified, as in the case of collective punishments. When the security guard whipped all the year 9 students on the back at the end of the first trimester, for instance, some parents threatened the principal with filing a police complaint. The case was settled in customary fashion, with a gift of mats and money, but the principal asked the security guard to only beat students from his native island. These children have kinship ties with the security guard, given the fairly small size of the island and the high number of marriages between these islanders (Servy, 2020). In this instance, the intersection between the four frameworks of school (in which staff seek to maintain their authority on students), family (in which parents refuse to have their children abused), customary law (in which conflicts are settled through compensation, see Servy, 2017b), and national law (which introduced a ban on corporal punishment on children in 2001) have combined to change who is authorized to hit whom, so to speak, at school, and led to a reinforcement of kinship-based power relations (i.e. the security guard being asked to only beat members of his family).

While the students rarely report being beaten by staff to their parents, they do use denunciation (in particular to the adults at school) as a strategy to stop physical abuse by other students. Lisa, a year 6 student aged 12, explained to me that a boy from her class had slapped her hand after she had asked him to be quiet. So that he would not do it again, she threatened to report him to the security guard. The students, particularly the girls, support and assist each other to deal with the blows of other children, even when those are not considered serious by teachers (*kilim smol*). Camélia, a year 10 student aged 16, told me that a boy from her class would hit her in the back on a daily basis. Her friends comforted her when she cried and the class captain asked the boy in question to stop. Another strategy to avoid physical abuse consists in making presents – such as money or pens – to secure protection. Through their use of denunciation and mutual assistance, the Mango School's students also contribute to the transformation of abusive interactions and their acceptability in school.

For Mango School staff, the main response to physical abuse between students is direct intervention. The teachers punish the students when they get into serious fights (*faetem strong*), by hitting them, giving them chores to do, or humiliating them. They may, for instance, remind them that their parents pay enrolment fees or ask them if they have received an education at home. Additionally, two staff members have attended a training session on managing fights between students. However, I observed that the teachers do not intervene when they consider the students to be playing (*faetem pleplei*) or not hitting hard (*kilim smol*), even in some cases when students complain to them. Unlike the primary school students, the older children fight only when the teacher is not present, which shows that they have internalized what is and what is not acceptable at school. Students gradually internalize school standards on the use of physical force, even if they seek to distort or transform them.

School staff seldom ask children questions about what is going on at home. Also, they generally do not intervene when parents beat their children in school or outside of the school; they actually tend to legitimize their use of physical force. A primary school teacher told me that a student's father came to her to say that if she ever had a problem with his son, all she had to do was to send him home so that he would whip him. She added that since then, the boy had behaved much better in class. As she was admonishing the assembled primary school students, a teacher said: 'Sometimes your mother will insult you, your father will beat you, you have to love them, tell them you're sorry, tell them thank you passionately'. Because they have received dedicated training or due to previous experiences, some staff members do, however, listen to children when they encounter family problems. A teacher who was raped at the age of 13 years told me that she attempted to help a year 4 student who had been sexually assaulted by her grandfather. Staff members also intervene when the parents' beatings have an impact on the children's attendance. During the first trimester, for instance, the principal wrote a letter to the father of a year 9 student to ask him to beat his daughter in a way that would not affect her performance at school. In Bislama, the principal told me: 'If he wants to hit (*kilim*) his child, he must not incapacitate her, he should not create what one calls domestic violence (*domestik vaelens*), he must discipline his child in a way that does not affect her schooling'. The girl never missed school again, but her father never answered the principal. In this example, the frameworks of law (with the principal's reliance on the 2008 Family Protection Act), family (compliance with paternal authority), and school (mandatory attendance) intersect, but this does not result in a prohibition of all kinds of physical abuse – merely those that interfere with the child's schooling.

Governmental and non-governmental organizations also come to the Mango School to attempt to transform representations of physical abuse and its acceptability. Several students and staff told me about visits by representatives of the Save the Children and *Wan Smolbag* NGOs and by the police's crime prevention team. As a primary school teacher explained to me:

> We used to whip (*wip*) children more. We taught by whipping (*tijim lo wip*). . . . Now, you can only whip children at home. The Save the Children people told us last year about the child protection act. They told us we aren't allowed to beat (*kilim*) children at school.

This ban conflicts with the conceptions of discipline and education of several Mango School staff members. Another teacher put it this way:

> Corporal punishment is prohibited. It's forbidden to have a physical contact with a child, even to touch their shoulder. Since child rights have arrived, whipping them is forbidden. But we have to whip our children so that they listen. . . . When they hurt, they listen, they learn better. . . . The security guard does whip the children, especially those from his island now. But it's the teacher's job. The teachers are the ones who have to whip, to find a way for the children to become good children.

The Mango School is a place where interactions take place between actors (students, staff, families, and NGO employees) who do not all share the same views on physical abuse and responses to it. Different conceptions of the legitimacy of the use of physical force on children intersect and sometimes clash. These interactions and tensions can arguably gradually lead students, their family, and staff members to transform their conceptions and practices pertaining to physical abuse.

## Conclusion

In this chapter, I have sought to understand how representations of physical abuse of children are constructed, reproduced, and change, and how these practices and their acceptability are perpetuated and transformed in Vanuatu. My research at the Mango School shows the importance to these processes of the interactions between various actors (mainly school staff, students, and their families) and of the interferences between the normative frameworks of school, family, and law.

In school, socialization to physical abuse mainly occurs through students' repeated exposure to abusive interactions (as perpetrator, victim, or witness) as well as through the learning (often on the spot) of ways of responding to these practices (denouncing, complaining, fleeing, enduring, accepting, legitimizing, and fighting back). Overall, school perpetuates the idea that physical force is a legitimate tool for punishment and teaching. Only acts that are considered not to have an educational purpose or to be too violent are sometimes seen as inacceptable by my interviewees, and referred to as *vaelens*, when they occur in a family setting.

Practices and conceptions relating to the use of physical force on children are not only internalized in school but also transformed. These transformations are owed to the interactions and tensions between normative frameworks and between the actors, who may think and act differently on the subject. Depending on my interviewees' age, gender, status (student, staff, or parent), and past experiences, their representations of physical abuse and of its acceptability vary. Some occasionally oppose violent interactions.

Ultimately, this chapter poses the question of what leads some people to intervene when the physical abuse of children in school occurs. The stakes likely vary depending on their place in these abusive interactions. Most probably, a victim will first and foremost look for protection from the blows, as in the case when the young girl denounced her classmate's abuse to the security guard. A first-hand or second-hand witness may also intervene because he or she considers the abuse morally intolerable, as when the teacher who was herself raped attempted to help a student who had been assaulted by her grandfather. It appears, however, that tensions pertaining to the legitimacy of the use of physical force on children do not always or solely revolve around questions of morality. In my research on physical abuse at the Mango School, I evidenced conflicts of authority (particularly between parents and teachers) and of sovereignty (between international, national, and customary law).

## Acknowledgements

The author wishes to thank Loïs Bastide and Marie Durand for their useful comments on the text. This chapter was translated from the French by Jean-Yves Bart, with support from the Maison Interuniversitaire des Sciences de l'Homme d'Alsace (MISHA) and the Excellence Initiative of the University of Strasbourg.

# Notes

1 I use the term 'physical abuse' in a pragmatic sense, to refer to blows, meaning quick movements by which a body hits another body.
2 The recourse to 'any physical punishment' of children is equally frequent in urban (70%) and rural (72%) environments and in the economically richest (66%) and poorest (74%) households. There are, however, strong discrepancies according to socio-economic level and place of residence concerning 'severe physical punishment', with 43% of children from the poorest households reported having suffered from a parent over the past month, compared with 28% of those from the richest households (Ministry of Health, Vanuatu National Statistics Office & Secretariat of the Pacific Community, 2014, pp. 245, 277).
3 This international legal Convention promotes a broader definition of 'violence', which includes acts that are not referred to as such by perpetrators and their relations, or even by the victims themselves.
4 Until December 2020, this island country was ranked by the UN as among the least advanced countries (United Nations News, 2020), and as such received significant external funding (unlike, for instance, overseas French territories). Vanuatu is also home to powerful non-governmental organizations that are not necessarily active in other independent countries in the region (Servy, 2017a).
5 To my interviewees, 'family' is not an easily defined group of individuals. It is not limited to the family as defined by demographers, consisting generally of a couple and their children, or to the household as defined by statisticians, based on housing. It does not correspond either to a clan or a lineage. Empirically, family in this neighbourhood can be defined as a very broad set of people with whom kinship terms are used (Servy, 2017a, pp. 149–158).
6 The name of the school and those of interviewees have been changed.
7 Enrolment fees from years 1 to 6 are 5,600 vatu (45€) per year at the Mango School, compared with 51,000 vatu (411€) per year at a nearby school. Since 1 January 2018, Vanuatu's minimum wage has been 200 vatu (1.60€) per hour (Vila Times, 2017).
8 Vanuatu's education system comprises kindergartens for children ages 3 to 5 years, primary schools (years 1 to 6) for children ages 6 to 11 years (normally), and secondary schools (from years 7 to 13 or 14) for children ages 11 years and older. Classes are taught in English or French.
9 Between 2009 and 2018, I spent 20 months doing ethnographic research in Port Vila. My previous studies dealt mostly with the prevention of sexually transmitted diseases (Servy, 2017a) and the prevention of sexual violence (Servy, 2017b).
10 In the Presbyterian system, an Elder is an individual that has been elected by the assembled members of a church to see to it that discipline and morals are abided with.

# References

Abélès, M. (2008). *Anthropologie de la globalisation*. Paris: Payot.
Carra, C. (2008). Violences à l'école élémentaire. Une expérience enfantine répandue participant à la définition du rapport aux pairs. *L'Année sociologique*, *58*(2), 319–337.
Carra, C., & Faggianelli, D. (2003). Violences à l'école: Tendances internationales de la recherche en sociologie. *Déviance et Société*, *27*(2), 205–225.
Kanas, B., Norton, A., Tarileo, B., & Wernham, M. (2009). *Protect me with love and care: A baseline report for creating a future free from violence, abuse and exploitation of girls and boys in Vanuatu*. Suva: UNICEF Pacific.
Merry, S. E. (2009). *Gender violence: A cultural perspective*. Chichester: Wiley-Blackwell.

Ministry of Health, Vanuatu National Statistics Office, & Secretariat of the Pacific Community. (2014). *Vanuatu demographic and health survey 2013, final report*. Nouméa, New Caledonia: Secretariat of the Pacific Community.

Servy, A. (2017a). *"AIDS IS HERE!" Prévenir les infections sexuellement transmissibles à Port-Vila, Vanuatu* (Doctoral dissertation). School of Advanced Studies in the Social Sciences (EHESS), Marseille, France.

Servy, A. (2017b). "Forcer n'est pas violer". Violences sexuelles faites aux femmes dans un quartier défavorisé de Port-Vila. *Journal de la Société des Océanistes, 144–145*, 171–184.

Servy, A. (2020). "We've paid your vagina to make children!" Bridewealth and women's marital and reproductive autonomy in Port-Vila, Vanuatu. *Oceania, 90*(3), 292–308.

United Nations Human Rights Office of the High Commissioner. (1989). *Convention on the rights of the child*. Retrieved from www.ohchr.org/EN/ProfessionalInterest/Pages/CRC.aspx

United Nations News. (2020, December 4). *Vanuatu graduates from list of least developed countries*. Retrieved from https://news.un.org/en/story/2020/12/1079252

Vila Times (Publisher). (2017, December 31). *Vanuatu government increased minimum wage to 200 vatu per hour*. Retrieved from www.vilatimes.com/2017/12/31/vanuatu-government-increased-minimum-wage-to-200-vatu-per-hour/

# 10 Quarrels, corporal punishment, and magical attacks

## What is 'family violence' in Kiriwina?[1]

*Louise Protar*

This chapter provides insights into domestic violence in Kiriwina, Papua New Guinea. Based on an ethnographic study of daily kinship practices, it aims to examine the definition of intrafamily violence and its emic perception, by answering the following questions:

- What interactions are considered violent?
- Who are the relatives involved in this violence?
- What areas of social life are concerned?
- What does violence between relatives reveal about kinship norms and obligations?

After describing the practical functioning of 'the family' in Kiriwina and specifying the places and objects of conflicts between relatives: (1) I will look at two types of intrafamily quarrels. (2) The corporal punishment inflicted on children by their caregivers will allow an examination of the place given to physical pain, to hierarchical relationships, and to intention in the emic and sociological definition of domestic violence. (3) A third part will be devoted to magical attacks between relatives. I will show that fear and accusations of witchcraft constitute both one of the modes of expression of conflictuality and a form of social control of the obligations between relatives. These three forms of interactions (quarrels, corporal punishment, and magical attacks) will test the relevance of the 'intrafamily violence' category for the Kiriwinian context.

## Family conflicts in Kiriwina: definitions

### Methodology: re-examining material through the prism of violence

The analysis provided in this chapter is based on empirical material collected during ethnographic fieldwork on the division of domestic and horticultural labour in Vanubesa,[2] a village on Kiriwina Island, Papua New Guinea.[3] These data were collected with the aim of examining the links between the division of labour, and

DOI: 10.4324/9781003146667-11

gender and kinship relationships. I revisit them today from the perspective of intrafamily violence.

The notion of intrafamily violence, which was developed in specific historical and political contexts, calls two types of violent interactions to mind: child abuse and intimate partner violence. In order to distance myself from these representations, and to determine what the emic conception of intrafamily violence could be in Kiriwina, I flagged the facts that corresponded to an analytical definition of intrafamily violence in my fieldwork material. I considered that violence is an interpersonal interaction, marked by physical aggression, that is to say something that interferes with bodily integrity, or another form of aggression (verbal, symbolic, etc.) inflicted with the aim of harming the person targeted, or at least of controlling them.[4] I have only kept the interactions between people belonging to the same family, whether they were close relatives or not, regardless of their status. Finally, I examined conversations and discourse relating to several events within the family that I was investigating at the time and seemed to give rise to negative emotions.

I thus noted various facts: arguments, slaps, beatings, fights, verbal aggressions, humiliations, bewitchments, etc. In order to determine which of these interactions can be considered to be family related, the boundaries of the family must be delineated.

### A family-based society

Is the category of intrafamily violence relevant in a society where, to put it bluntly, everyone is a relative and everything is family related?

Indeed, in Kiriwina, daily kinship relationships go well beyond the framework of the nuclear family.[5] During my fieldwork in Vanubesa, I found that almost all the villagers were connected by a kinship tie, which they call on differently depending on the circumstances. Thus, a fight that breaks out between football players during a game, following the referee's decision or because the outcome is disputed, is in fact a fight between 'brothers'.[6] Is the term 'domestic violence' appropriate in such a situation?

The density of kinship relationships in the village must be taken into account to characterize intrafamily violence in Kiriwina. A second trait that must be taken into consideration is the fact that kinship is the foundation of all social life. The *dala*, the matrilineal clan, is a powerful political institution because the land belongs to the clans. Each village has an owner clan who regulates access to village and horticultural land. In Vanubesa, several clans coexist with the owner clan, each occupying a neighbourhood. The place of residence of households is determined by kinship. This division of the village also appears in the division of parishes, in the population census, in the constitution of sports teams, etc. In addition, production takes place within the family. Kiriwinians are horticulturalists. In Vanubesa, each family cultivates at least two gardens, and the vegetables harvested are the primary food source, which is supplemented by fishing. Despite the large population, much land is available and, apart from periods of drought, these gardens provide ample food for the villagers. Resorting to the market economy is marginal. In the village, only ten civil servants or so receive a salary. Income-generating activities, such as selling fish or betel nuts, supplement horticultural work. Funeral ceremonies and celebrations are the largest expense for families, who can then seek the assistance of relatives who moved to the city. Whether it is productive and reproductive work, politics, religious practice, or sports activities, kinship relationships permeate social life.

### Interwoven family groups

Given the complexity and omnipresence of kinship, my analysis relies on a practical approach. Marked by the work of David Schneider (1968), by *New kinship studies*, or in France by the work of Florence Weber (2013), this approach consists in examining kinship not as 'being' but as 'doing' (Carsten, 2000). Florence Weber defines practical kinship as 'the set of obligations and feelings that make official kinship ties effective or that create other ties' (Weber, 2013). Thus, kinship ties are not described as the fixed consequences of filiation and alliance, but as relationships developed daily, through co-residence, care work, or even the sharing of a common cause (Carsten, 1995; Gollac, 2003; Weber, 2013). This conceptualization of kinship is particularly illuminating for Kiriwina, where work is central for the bonds and obligations between relatives (Protar, 2020).

The term 'family', which I use as a descriptive concept prior to my analysis, actually covers several family groups responding to different kinship logics. I would like to illustrate this idea by presenting an ethnographic case: Giyo's family, with whom I lived during my fieldwork in Vanubesa.

The smallest family unit, which I will call a 'household', is made up of the married couple and their children. Once married, men and women live, eat, and work together. Daily parenting work is shared, albeit unequally, between father and mother. Cultivating their gardens is above all a matter for the couple.

The household of Giyo and his wife, Mona, both in their early 30s and the parents of five children, was part of a larger residential group of four households. The group of houses comprised Giyo and Mona, Mona's parents (Tomwaya and Numwaya), Mona's younger sister and her husband (Mimi and Bobby), and Mona's adopted brother and his wife (Mokasai and Sogea). Each household occupied a house where they slept, but they shared a house-kitchen and a *bwema*, an open deck topped by an attic for yams, which was used as a common living space. Fire, wood, and water were shared. These elements allow saying that these combined households formed a domestic group, in the sense of a set of relatives with shared residence and production. Yet divisions existed: they were apparent in the movement of people between houses, during meal time, and in child care (for a visual representation, see below).

« The Family » (2018)

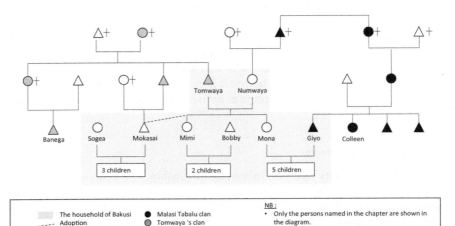

By observing the successive residential configurations between 2016 and 2018, I noticed that people moving houses and the circulation of children took place between Tomwaya and Numwaya, and their daughters. The adopted brother, Mokasai, his wife, and their children did not participate. This division was found during mealtimes. Numwaya and Mona cooked together for their two households. Sogea cooked separately for Mokasai and their three children. Likewise, daily child care revealed the existence of two subgroups. Tomwaya and Numwaya paid attention to all their grandchildren, but they only minded their daughters' children. Mona and her sister Mimi shared their children's upbringing. However, Giyo and Bobby, their husbands, did not even glance at the children of their wives' sisters. The intensity of the solidarity within the maternal line was evident here. It can be explained first by a strong sense of belonging, a result of the matrilineal conception of kinship. The *dala*, the clan identity, which is transmitted by mothers, appears implicitly here and is reinforced by daily solidarity. Nonetheless, members of the patrilineal line are also a source of support. Giyo and Bobby's parents were very involved with their grandchildren.

Thus, in the analysis, Giyo's 'family' can be decomposed into three types of family groups: the household, the co-resident group, and the matrilineal or patrilineal line. These different groups are activated differently depending on the context. When a new common cause arises (a newborn, an economic opportunity, guests, etc.), an extended household, in the sense of a provisional domestic group, is formed, mobilizing some of the family groups.

### Places and subjects of conflict

The analysis of family groups sheds light on the sources of conflicts within the family. As I went back over the quarrels that I was aware of within Giyo's family,

I realized that these tensions were at the intersection of family groups. I will focus my description on the conflicts involving Giyo, whose specificity is that he was torn between several households.

Giyo lived with his wife's family. This configuration is relatively rare in Kiriwinian society, where most couples settle in the village where the man was born.[7] It resulted from a land arrangement between Giyo's clan and Tomwaya's clan, relating to the right of occupation of the Bakusi hamlet.[8] The land in the hamlet belonged to Giyo's clan, the Malasi Tabalu, but had been entrusted to Tomwaya in the 1970s. Indeed, Tomwaya married Numwaya, the daughter of a younger brother of the Malasi Tabalu leaders. This was a long-term loan. To secure his presence there, Tomwaya arranged a marriage between his daughter Mona and one of the heirs of the Malasi Tabalu leaders, Giyo. For their part, the clan elders asked Giyo to settle in Bakusi to 'watch over' the land. This double strategy explains why Giyo and Mona lived with Tomwaya and Numwaya in Bakusi.

This context had an impact on the relationship between Giyo and Mona. One of the main areas of conflict between them was tending to the gardens. Giyo disliked such labour, and his lack of hard work was the subject of frequent gossip. Mona did most of the work, in the vegetable garden but also in the yam garden, whose harvest was allocated to Giyo's exchange obligations, the gifting of yams to certain relatives.[9] This situation weighed on her and she blamed him for it. The absences of Giyo, who regularly went 'for a spin' to the resort or town in search of entertainment and economic opportunities, gave rise to conflict, especially when Giyo hid his earnings. It is also likely that she suspected him of infidelity.

Based on conversations with some of the village women, I learned that infidelities and the sharing of the workload, both horticultural and domestic, are the two main reasons for marital quarrels. It is not uncommon for these arguments to result in physical violence. This violence is only denounced by women when it causes serious injury, requiring treatment at a health centre or hospital. In the case of Mona and Giyo, living with Mona's parents is likely to have limited the development of violent interactions within the couple. It is also possible that Mona felt pressure to stay married to Giyo, due to family stakes.

My observations do not allow me to be more precise about the extent of domestic violence in Kiriwina.[10] However, I found that women returned frequently and easily to their parents' families when they were having trouble with their husbands. Such fleeing has often been observed in matrilineal societies, where women retain strong ties to their families even after marriage.[11]

As one of Mona's sisters once put it, the Bakusi extended household had the specificity of bringing together 'two families in one family'. Indeed, in addition to allying with the Malasi Tabalu clan through his daughter's marriage, Tomwaya sought to strengthen his clan's presence in Bakusi by having his younger brother, four of his uterine nephews, and his adopted son, Mokasai, settle there over the years. Mokasai, the eldest son of Tomwaya's older brother, was adopted as a teenager. He lived near his adoptive father, worked the latter's land, and built a house for him: everything showed that he was the 'taker-over' of the family group. This term, coined by the sociologist Céline Bessière (2010) refers to the person who will take over as head of the family group. More than an 'heir', the expression shows that designating the taker-over is the subject of an active process and a socialization that begins in childhood. Bakusi therefore appeared as a household with two taker-overs, Mokasai and Giyo, each representing the interests of a different clan.

The tensions were palpable between the two men. They rarely spoke to each other, shared no meals or chores, and ignored each other's children. One of the areas of conflict between Giyo and Mokasai was the use of the land in the hamlet. When I arrived to the village, Mokasai refused to allow Giyo to build a new house to accommodate my companion and me. Our presence was a source of frustration for Mokasai, who probably envied the resources Giyo was gaining – or hoping to gain – from 'his *dimdims*', as whites are called in the region. To counter Mokasai's influence in Bakusi and increase his chances of taking over the use of the hamlet after Tomwaya's death, Giyo set out to ally himself with his neighbour Banega and his wife by entrusting them with his youngest son, when he was to be weaned.[12] Banega was the *kada* of Tomwaya, his uterine nephew, and therefore his rightful heir. He was a direct rival to Mokasai in the succession. Through this adoption, Giyo was acting in the interest of the Malasi Tabalu clan.

In addition to his nuclear family, his in-laws, and his clan, Giyo also had to deal with his birth family. Even though he did not live with them, Giyo was close to his father and mother, who lived in the nearby village. He visited them almost daily, repaired their house, etc. He helped his brothers harvest their garden and was affectionate with their children. Giyo's parents lived in the village of his father's clan, and Giyo displayed his belonging to the clan during funeral ceremonies but also as the captain of the football team in this village rather than in Bakusi, for example.

Giyo and his father shared ownership of a dinghy, a motor boat, which they bought with a government loan that they took out jointly. On market days in Losuia, the island's resort, they both ferried passengers. The sharing of the profits from this activity caused heated arguments between Giyo and his father. According to Colleen, Giyo's sister, he wasted the money earned from the dinghy, 'He used to use the money, eat the whole money'. The money was supposed to be kept in a bank account for the maintenance of the boat, but Giyo regularly tapped into this account to put money into his own bank account. When his father noticed this, he 'was cross and scolded him very badly'. The argument spread to the whole family, and Giyo and Mona did not visit Giyo's parents for several months. This was also one of the reasons why Giyo and Mona lived in Bakusi.

The relationship between Giyo's sister, Colleen, and Mona was particularly stormy. A few years before, during a *sagali*, a funeral ceremony that includes many rites of exchange, Colleen verbally assaulted Mona in front of the other family members, going so far as to call her a '*kodana*', that is to say good for nothing, a serious insult which led to a rift between the two families. Other female relatives of Giyo criticized Mona's miserliness, such as this aunt: 'But Giyo, you know the wife is peuh! [she smacks her lips with disdain], it's the hand like this [she shows me her closed hand], not like this [she shows me her open hand]'.

In fact, Mona was held responsible for Giyo's resource retention. According to Colleen, his sister, since Giyo was the oldest of the siblings, it was hard to blame him, even for their father. This was how the quarrels over dinghy money crystallized. Giyo dealt with dinghy money as he did with garden land, for example, by claiming his birthright. Probably because they had too much to lose, Giyo's parents did not directly put up resistance. They shifted their criticism to Mona, Giyo's wife, holding her responsible for their son's lack of generosity.

Thus, Giyo participated in several extended households: the one in Bakusi, the hamlet where he lived with his wife's family, structured around daily subsistence and child care, and his parents' place, united by the common ownership of the dinghy, among other things. In the quarrels I have reported, the subjects of conflict correspond to each extended household's common cause: the division of horticultural labour between Mona and Giyo, the use of the hamlet's land in Bakusi, and the management of the earnings from the dinghy.

Thus, understanding the magnitude of the 'family' in Kiriwina and the dynamics of the kinship relationships help to shed light on the spaces where conflicts can arise. Not all family quarrels lead to violence. Conflictuality seems to be expressed more often through slander, symbolic gestures (going to eat at another house, changing football teams, etc.), and more or less aggressive verbal exchanges than through blows.

In contrast to these family quarrels, another category of interactions materializes through physical aggression: the corporal punishment inflicted on children. Such punishment is not considered violence in Kiriwina.

## Hitting one's children: violence or education?

### A frequent practice

Living in Vanubesa for several months, I saw relatives slapping children on a daily basis. The frequency and extent of this corporal punishment varied with the children's ages. Before they were able to walk, babies received false slaps during games. Mothers in particular mimicked an exaggerated blow to the buttocks, followed by gestures of tenderness. Young children, between 2 and 4 years old, received slaps several times a day that were sharp but not very hard to punish behaviour or to support an order. These bodily reprimands were administered by the children's main caregivers, fathers and mothers, and grandparents in the extended household where I lived, as a continuation of the usual acts associated with upbringing and care. I did not notice any difference between little boys and little girls. Older children, between 6 and 10 years old, were punished less frequently by blows, but when they were, it was more violent, with objects (sticks or machete handles). This gradation has also been reported for Tonga (Kavapalu, 1993). Whenever I observed it, the reason for the punishment was the refusal to do a chore assigned by a relative. Parental control eased in adolescence, especially for boys (Lepani, 2012). Blows became very rare, even though a few unmarried young adults who lived with their parents reported being beaten.

Interestingly, while I estimated that educational violence was very common, and sometimes acute, in Vanubesa, other observers had not. For example, at the start of the 20th century, anthropologist Bronislaw Malinowski noted the great freedom enjoyed by the children of the Trobriand Islands, who were never punished by adults. Barbara and Gunther Senft's fieldwork, carried out in the 1980s on Kaileuna Island, led them to confirm Malinowski's assertion that 'the idea of definite retribution, or of coercive punishment is not only foreign, but distinctly repugnant to the native' (Malinowski, 1932 [1929], 44f; quoted by Senft & Senft, 2018, p. 130). According to them, children who disobeyed were rarely punished. Several factors may explain the discrepancy between my assessment of corporal punishment in Kiriwina and that of the anthropologists who preceded me. The first hypothesis is a variation in educational standards between different regions of Kiriwina. The second is that parental behaviour changed over the century, becoming more repressive. There is a lack of data that would allow ruling out or fully supporting these explanations. It is more likely that the scale of comparison of observers has changed. In Europe, tolerance towards educational violence has greatly diminished since the 19th century, when Malinowski was growing up. This shift in the social perception of corporal punishment has become more pronounced in recent decades. As I was born ten years after the Senfts' stays in Kaileuna, it is likely that my generation's educational standards explain why I perceived corporal punishment in Vanubesa as pervasive and violent.

### And a legitimate one

Vanubesa villagers viewed beatings as a perfectly legitimate educational tool, as shown by the following anecdote. One day, the youngest girl in the family, who was about 3 years old, fell from the *kaukweda*, the deck adjoining the house, and hit her head on the rocky ground. She was crying and her father immediately hugged her. He told her, 'Bodesi one, bodesi two', which means 'Enough one, enough two'. As the child did not stop crying at the end of the countdown, her mother grabbed her and slapped her on the head several times, which made her cry even harder. Gradually, the child stopped sobbing. She stayed on her mother's lap for a long time. A few hours later, I asked the girl's aunt about this event. My question ('Why do you hit children when they cry?') made her burst out laughing. She then gave me the following reason: 'Sena valam!' ('Too much crying'), before explaining in English: 'When too much crying, we get angry so we have to punch them so they stop crying'.

The practice of hitting children who are crying so that they stop makes sense with respect to the educational principles in Kiriwina. Exercising physical violence on others is rarely socially sanctioned. Children who are punched by their peers are encouraged by the adults present to retaliate, and laughed at if they cry. Controlling the expression of pain is imperative, for children as well as for adult men and women, who show great stoicism in the face of injuries, illness, or pain in childbirth. Learning to control one's negative emotions (frustration, pain, anger, sadness, etc.) is one of the major stages in children's socialization (Senft & Senft, 2018, pp. 100–110, 118–120).

Thus, parents beat children to punish some of their behaviour and to force them to contain the manifestation of their emotions. Physical assault is central to disciplinary action, which is often performed without words. The gesture is not only intended to be demonstrative or humiliating but also meant to inflict pain on children's bodies. This is not a deviant or stigmatized act. On the contrary, the previous evidence shows that, from the emic point of view, pain has an educational virtue. However, in some cases, corporal punishment retains the characteristics of a violent interaction. I saw children hit by women who seemed to have lost control of their anger. This was also noted by Gunter and Barbara Senft (Senft & Senft, 2018, p. 130). This expression of maternal frustration through beating their children suggests that child abuse also serves as an outlet. This might concern women more particularly, since their position in the family offers little outlet for negative emotions. However, this is an analytical distinction. Whether it is a controlled and educational act, or a spontaneous and emotional one, hitting children remains socially accepted. Nonetheless, children do not take the blows placidly. They scream, cry, and try to run away, and they may even throw stones in return. In the extended household where I lived, the children who considered that they were beaten too often or unfairly would go stay for a while with their paternal grandparents.

While violence against children is a canonical form of intrafamily violence in the literature, corporal punishment has an ambiguous status in Kiriwina. Although the physical aggression is unquestionable, the strong asymmetry of status between adults and children, as well as the educational and socializing aim of the blows, contributes to making this type of interaction completely legitimate from an emic point of view. Corporal punishment is part of the continuity of the care and education relationship that bonds children to their caregivers. Such punishment is integrated into the social relations between relatives and children.

While corporal punishment was not talked about in the village, rumours and worried conversations led me to pay attention to an unexpected form of domestic violence: magical attacks between relatives.

## Magical attacks: kinship threat and control

### *Analysing magical attacks as intrafamily violence*

Magical attacks have rarely been analysed as intrafamily violence. The supernatural nature of the interaction, from an etic standpoint, has often led anthropologists to analyse this form of aggression separately from other forms of violence. Another obstacle has been that anthropologists rarely witness the bewitching, only its consequences. Magical violence can only be grasped through the narratives that relate it (Dousset, 2016; Taylor, 2015; Taylor & Araújo, 2016), a roundabout means that is common in studies of violence (Dentan, 2008). Incorporating magical attacks into the study of domestic violence is doubly relevant for Kiriwina: first, because Kiriwinians deeply fear this form of aggression, a threat to relationships between relatives; second, because bewitchment narratives allow establishing a connection between conflict and violence.

Magic (*megwa* in Kilivila, also translated as 'witchcraft', 'sorcery', or 'black power' in English) has many uses in Kiriwina (Senft, 1986). It is used to become more attractive, to seduce (Lepani, 2012), to grow yams in the garden, to ensure good fishing, etc. Yet magic can also be used to harm, to make someone sick, or to kill.

On several occasions during my fieldwork, deaths or illnesses were attributed to spells. Certain relatives of the deceased were suspected, and accused in hushed tones of having resorted to magic to take revenge for spoliation, an affront, or out of jealousy. These attacks fit my definition of domestic violence: a malicious interaction between relatives. This is an abstract aggression, but one that interferes with bodily integrity. Indeed, while the aggression in itself is not physical, since the bewitching is done remotely, through a spell, and often through the mediation of an object, it aims at injuring the victim's body. From the point of view of Kiriwinians, there is no difference in nature between casting a spell or a stone, but rather a difference in power. The two modes of action can even be combined, or can respond to each other.

### Bagidou's assassination: accusation and jealousy

I heard of several cases of magical violence in which the alleged perpetrator was a relative of the victim. One story caught my attention because it concerned Giyo's maternal uncle, his *kada*: Bagidou. Based on this case of bewitchment, I will develop the idea that fear and the suspicion of witchcraft are one of the channels through which conflictuality is expressed within the families of Kiriwina.

Four women told me about Bagidou's death, separately, in taped interviews: his widow, his two daughters, and a more distant relative. These women's accounts, as well as various comments that I was able to collect from other relatives of Giyo, concurred on the following: Bagidou died in 2010, when he was still young (between 45 and 55 years old, according to my estimates) and in good health. The death of this man, who had an exceptional personality, was unanimously explained by a malicious intentional magical act: 'They make magic against him'.

According to Bagidou's daughter, the assassin, who was never named, proceeded as follows:

> He sort of make his magic and then he made it with the betel nut and then . . . you know . . . they already magic it and then talk with that magic and then they give it to poison it and give it to someone and he went and give to him. And not knowing, he didn't know that that was the magic so as soon [she whispers] as he got the betel nut he just chewed.

This modus operandi has already been described elsewhere in the literature (Patterson, 1974): the murderer says a magic spell over a betel nut, which 'poisons' it. The nut is then taken by an intermediary to the person targeted, who is not suspicious of it and chews it. The victim falls ill and dies. The gifting of betel nuts,[13] an essential social interaction in Kiriwina, is thus perverted.

My interlocutors were unanimous as to the motive for this assassination: jealousy. Indeed, Bagidou had been designated as the future village chief by the leaders of the Malasi Tabalu clan, who owned Vanubesa. The rules of succession made him the legitimate heir ('He's next to the King', his daughter said), and he had the makings of a leader ('He had the leadership qualities', one of his nieces told me). Several elements in his daughter's account show that Bagidou had been brought up to lead: 'My father knew all those clans and most of the land they're giving my father'. Bagidou's brothers, who were the leaders at the time, had passed on the history of the land to him. In Kiriwina today, the power of the clan and village leaders rests mainly on their role as custodians of the village land and the horticultural land. The land is owned by the clan, who distributes the use of it to its members, or to members of other clans, for varying periods of time. Knowing the history of this distribution and the various current arrangements is crucial, because, in the event of a land conflict, it is the leader who decides.

In addition to the land power that he was gaining, Bagidou was also an excellent gardener: 'When he makes garden, he makes so big heap of yams!' that is, he had very bountiful harvests. In Kiriwina, yams are stacked and displayed in the gardens after the harvest, sometimes even for competitions. Being a good gardener (*tokwaybagula*) is the main source of prestige for a man. Bagidou also had several betel palm trees and numerous pigs, both highly coveted goods that are markers of wealth and influence ('He makes big party for people!'). Finally, his skills as a carpenter were also extraordinary: the house he built at the time was still the largest in the village. This accumulation of benefits, power, and influence appears in the discourse of Bagidou's relatives, as a legitimate reason for jealousy: 'They are jealous', they repeated.

Who does 'they' refer to? As is often the case in the discourse on witchcraft, the alleged perpetrator of the act of witchcraft is not clearly identified (Rio, 2002). However, the four women directed their accusations towards the same people: some of Bagidou's 'brothers', members of the Malasi Tabalu clan but 'from a different mother'. They were referring here to the *dala*, the matrilineal clan. The members of the *dala* are considered to be made of the same substance. Kiriwinians say 'they are the same'. Marriage between members of the same *dala* is prohibited. Bagidou's family therefore suspected a specific category of relatives: those of the same lineage ('by blood', as is said in the West) but not from the same nuclear or extended household. They implicated men, Bagidou's competitors in gaining access to the position of clan and village leader, who were feared in the village because 'they know about magic'.

### The paradox of magical violence between relatives

The recounting of Bagidou's death thus allows one to grasp several characteristic features of magical attacks between relatives in Kiriwina. Accusations of witchcraft are levelled following a death or an illness by the victim's closest relatives, or by those who see themselves as such, at more distant relatives. There are even spells to 'wake up the dead' and make them identify their murderer. The accusations made by the relatives are then spread through rumours in the village. It is therefore the voices of families which (1) detect a human action behind the death of their loved one, (2) implicate one or more alleged culprits, and (3) construct hypotheses as to the reason for the discord. Witches always seem to act out of jealousy, an emic category that includes sexual jealousy, coveting a possession, and competition for prestige and power, as in the case of Bagidou. His assassination was presented by his relatives as inevitable because this man accumulated talents, wealth, and allies. The attitude of the Vanubesa villagers towards magical attacks is paradoxical. On the one hand, they fear them and denounce them. Suspicions of bewitchment introduce a disruption in everyday life and cause very strong emotions. On the other hand, magical violence appears as a social sanction. It punishes those whose pursuit of individual interests keeps away from their obligations of solidarity and sharing. The threat of magical attacks acts as a guardian of the kinship order.

## Conclusion

In Kiriwina, as elsewhere, insults, screams, blows, and spells are exchanged between relatives. However, ethnographic analysis raises the question of whether the notion of 'intrafamily violence' is a relevant indicator of power relations within the family.

Indeed, the family quarrels, corporal punishment, and magical attacks that I have gathered here under the etic category of 'intrafamily violence' are not thought of conjointly by Kiriwinians. It is the sociologist's eye that gives density to a phenomenon that does not exist in the emic discourse. However, the idea of domestic violence is marked by a normative weight, which makes it difficult to export to the Kiriwinian context.

First, the definition of violence as physical assault is based on a negative perception of pain and of the use of physical force, which does not apply to Kiriwina society.

Second, speaking of 'domestic violence' suggests that violence in the family is different in nature from other violence, as if the family were a closed sphere that is separate from other areas of social life. On the contrary, the study of the organization of kinship in Kiriwina reveals the importance of economic and political stakes in family relationships, as well as the permeability of different social scenes to kinship relationships.

In my opinion, resorting to the notion of intrafamily violence involves the risk of obscuring the logics of kinship and individual agency, which are formulated above all around the notions of reciprocity, generosity, and greediness. Understanding the tensions and conflicts between relatives involves taking into account the discourse on jealousy, and the diffuse and pervasive threat of magical attacks.

## Notes

1  Translated by Hélène Windish.
2  This is a pseudonym. In Kilivila, the language of Kiriwina, 'Vanubesa' means 'village'. All the names of the villages and people have been changed.
3  This study, which was carried out from August 2016 to April 2017, and then from May to July 2018, was the subject of a Ph.D.: Protar, L. (2020). *Produire le genre, fabriquer la parenté. Ethnographie du travail domestique et horticole à Kiriwina, Papouasie-Nouvelle-Guinée* (Doctoral dissertation). Université Panthéon-Sorbonne, Paris, France.
4  For a discussion of the definition of violence, see the introduction of the book.

5  There is abundant literature on kinship on the Trobriand Islands. See the works of Bronislaw Malinowski, Annette Weiner, Susan Montague, and, more recently, Mark Mosko and Katherine Lepani.

6  Kinship terms in quotation marks refer to the Kiriwinian conception of kinship. They include classificatory relatives and adoptive ones. Without quotation marks, the terms refer to the European conception of kinship.

7  Mimi, Mona's younger sister, also lived with their parents. Bobby, the father of Mimi's children, slept and ate most of his meals in Bakusi, but the two young people were not married, as the marriage talks were not over. Obviously, Mimi's father was delaying certain donations so that his daughter could stay in the family hamlet.

8  The story of this arrangement is detailed in Protar (2020, pp. 243–273).

9  My study of the Vanubesa gardens reveals that Kiriwina women are full-time gardeners but that their horticultural work, which has been minimized in the anthropological literature, is invisible in the emic discourse. While women work in the gardens as much as men, only the latter can derive glory and prestige from it. Protar (2020, pp. 298–233).

10  My position as a white foreigner dissuaded me from investigating violence within the couple, in a context where Papua New Guinea has frequently been singled out for its gender violence rates, and where these issues have been the subject of public action.

11  Katherine Lepani suggests that violence is less prevalent in Kiriwina than elsewhere in Papua New Guinea, due to matrilineage which protects women and to the sexual culture that is specific to this society. Lepani, K. (2016). Proclivity and prevalence: Accounting for the dynamics of sexual violence in the response to HIV in Papua New Guinea. In A. Biersack, M. Jolly, & M. Macintyre (eds.), *Gender violence & human rights* (pp. 159–196). Canberra: ANU Press. Also see Lawrence, S. E.-L. (2015). Witchcraft, sorcery, violence: Matrilineal and decolonial reflections. In *Talking it through: Responses to sorcery and witchcraft beliefs and practices in Melanesia* (pp. 55–73). Canberra: ANU Press.

12  Adoption is an important kinship institution in Kiriwina. In Kilivila, the verb -*vakalova* means 'to adopt' and 'to wean'. When a woman says, 'I have "vakalova" this child', it means that she has welcomed them into her home when they were a baby so that they would stop feeding at their mother's breast. This period creates a bond between the child and the adoptive mother that lasts even after the child has returned to his or her birth parents. Thus, even if the placement of the child is temporary, the filiation created is permanent.

13  Kiriwinians are fond of betel nuts, also called areca nuts, or *buva* in Kilivila. They chew this nut by mixing it with lime (calcium oxide) obtained from corals, *pwaka*, and leaves or stems called 'mustard', *mwaya*. The mixture is a stimulant that colours the mouth red.

# References

Bessière, C. (2010). *De génération en génération: Arrangements de famille dans les entreprises viticoles de Cognac*. Paris: Raisons d'agir.

Carsten, J. (1995). The substance of kinship and the heat of the hearth: Feeding, personhood, and relatedness among Malays in Pulau Langkawi. *American Ethnologist, 22*(2), 223–241.

Carsten, J. (2000). *Cultures of relatedness: New approaches to the study of kinship*. Cambridge: Cambridge University Press.

Dentan, R. K. (2008). Recent studies on violence: What's in and what's out. *Reviews in Anthropology, 37*(1), 41–67.

Dousset, L. (2016). La sorcellerie en Mélanésie: Élicitation de l'inacceptable. *L Homme, 218*, 85–115.

Gollac, S. (2003). Maisonnée et cause commune: Une prise en charge familiale. In F. Weber, S. Gojard, & A. Gramain (eds.), *Charges de famille* (pp. 274–311). Paris: La Découverte.

Kavapalu, H. (1993). Dealing with the dark side in the ethnography of childhood: Child punishment in Tonga. *Oceania, 63*(4), 313–329.

Lawrence, S. E.-L. (2015). Witchcraft, sorcery, violence: Matrilineal and decolonial reflections. In *Talking it through: Responses to sorcery and witchcraft beliefs and practices in Melanesia* (pp. 55–73). Canberra: ANU Press.

Lepani, K. (2012). *Islands of love, islands of risk: Culture and HIV in the Trobriands.* Nashville, TN: Vanderbilt University Press.

Lepani, K. (2016). Proclivity and prevalence: Accounting for the dynamics of sexual violence in the response to HIV in Papua New Guinea. In A. Biersack, M. Jolly, & M. Macintyre (eds.), *Gender violence & human rights* (pp. 156–196). Canberra: ANU Press.

Malinowski, B. (1932 [1929]). *The sexual life of savages in North Western Melanesia.* London: George Routledge & Sons.

Patterson, M. (1974). Sorcery and witchcraft in Melanesia. *Oceania, 45*(2), 132–160.

Protar, L. (2020). *Produire le genre, fabriquer la parenté. Ethnographie du travail domestique et horticole à Kiriwina, Papouasie-Nouvelle-Guinée* (Doctoral dissertation). Université Panthéon-Sorbonne, Paris, France.

Rio, K. (2002). The sorcerer as an absented third person: Formations of fear and anger in Vanuatu. *Social Analysis: The International Journal of Social and Cultural Practice, 46*(3), 129–154.

Schneider, D. M. (1968). *American Kinship: A Cultural Account.* University of Chicago Press.

Senft, B., & Senft, G. (2018). *Growing up on the Trobriand Islands in Papua New Guinea: Childhood and educational ideologies in Tauwema.* Amsterdam: John Benjamins Publishing Company.

Senft, G. (1986). *Kilivila: The language of the Trobriand Islanders.* Berlin: Mouton de Gruyter.

Taylor, J. P. (2015). Sorcery and the moral economy of agency: An ethnographic account. *Oceania, 85*(1), 38–50.

Taylor, J. P., & Araújo, N. G. (2016). Sorcery talk, gender violence and the law in Vanuatu. In A. Biersack, M. Jolly, & M. Macintyre (eds.), *Gender violence & human rights* (pp. 197–228). Canberra: ANU Press.

Weber, F. (2013). *Penser la parenté aujourd'hui. La force du quotidien.* Paris: Éditions Rue d'Ulm.

# 11 Contexts and levels of community violence in highlands Papua New Guinea

*Pamela J. Stewart and Andrew J. Strathern*[1]

## Introduction

Gendered violence has emerged as a major field of concern in a number of contexts among Pacific Island societies. We argue that patterns of violence at the domestic or family level are inflected by macro-level factors, such as historical circumstances of change in kinship and marriage practices, and national governmental and legal institutions that may embody ideological assumptions not shared by communities. Our focus is on the Highlands societies of Papua New Guinea (PNG), with a long history of the evolution of social practices based on clanship and networks of relations in arenas of exchange and alliance, as well as hostility. (See Strathern & Stewart, 2011, for a conspectus of materials, including numerous comparative references.) Women play important parts in these networks through the marriages that link groups together, but conflicts can also arise over control of wealth, and especially pigs. Women raise pigs but men claim control over them and over the land that produces sweet potatoes, a staple food for people and pigs. In the developing urban contexts, these issues transform into arguments about money, alcohol abuse, and sexuality that easily lead to violence. Frustrations over the exigencies of urban life conduce to violence, mostly by men but also on the part of women, and to the mistreatment of children. In the rural areas, however, intergroup violence over land leads to hardship for women, as well as the male fighters themselves, and this is compounded further by concerns over sorcery, environmental disasters, and most recently by fears over the spread of the COVID-19 virus.[2]

## Domestic violence in Papua New Guinea, and the borders of legitimacy

### The triangle of violence

Legitimacy of Action in Highlands Societies of PNG[3] depends on many circumstances, including basic ideas of individuality in relation to collectives; obligations to kin groups; adherence to religious and ritual belief systems, including 'witchcraft' and 'sorcery' ideas; and the place of wealth used in compensation payments for violent acts (see, e.g. Stewart & Strathern, 1999, 2004; Strathern & Stewart,

DOI: 10.4324/9781003146667-12

2004a, 2005a). Circumstances regarding these issues vary considerably and bring changes over time, especially with urbanization; shifting monetization of relationships; separation of persons from their wider kin groups; impacts of environmental disasters (e.g. the recent 2018 earthquake in PNG); disillusionment in terms of life's precarity; substance abuse (with a lack of treatment being offered); and the impact of language loss and associated culturally bound ethical mores. All of these factors lead to a disturbance of balance in systems that can mediate disputes and thus lead to an increase in the incidence of domestic conflict and violence.

In earlier publications, we have explored a model of violence which we called the 'triangle of violence'. Building on the discussion of violence by David Riches (1986) as a relationship between perpetrators, victims, and witnesses, we laid especial stress on the crucial roles of the witness in determining the legitimacy or lack of legitimacy of the acts involved (Stewart & Strathern, 2002a; Strathern & Stewart, 2005b). Riches was concerned primarily with overt physical violence and its consequences. The problems start with the question of what we mean by violence. The word itself in the English language evokes a sense of a lack of legitimacy, a crossing over from the normative to the excessive. The term *force* is more neutral sounding and raises the question of the degree of force that may be considered legitimate, or justified, in a given case.

### Witnesses

The triangle of violence model had the merit that it illustrated the point that the legitimacy of an act depends on the viewpoint of those involved. The perpetrators of an act may consider the act to be legitimate if, for example, it is carried out as an act of punishment or revenge. The victim is less likely to see the justification as correct unless they consider themselves to be guilty in some way. The victim, in fact, may be dead. At this point, the viewpoint of the witness becomes important. The witness may be an individual, a group, or the wider society. The same act can therefore be subject to different evaluations by different witnesses. Some may have more power than others. In any case, what we have called 'the borders of legitimacy' will vary in the eyes of different witnesses.

Here, we include in the category of witnesses anyone cognizant of the event or versions of the event. These considerations are most obviously important in circumstances of historical change when variations in the views of witnesses are most likely to emerge and will inevitably influence the further consequences of action. Further complications arise if we shift our viewpoint to collective rather than individual acts. Here, the perpetrators may be members of a whole group, and the victims are also perpetrators when revenge is at work. In this case, the designations of perpetrator and victim would conceal the ongoing negative reciprocity between the parties involved. The witness's role also becomes less clear, because the immediate actors are both perpetrators and victims in a chain of agency

Social media play a part in further complicating these categories. Many people see acts of violence that are displayed on the Internet, mobile phones, etc. And social media can be a source of psychological violence perpetrated against victims.

Actions of revenge within an ongoing context of conflict between groups are therefore not amenable to analysis in terms of a simple perpetrator-victim-witness schema. A closer look at the relationships involved is more complicated than a simple triangle.

It is important to distinguish between witnesses as observers and witnesses as sufferers from the results of an act. If a person has been wounded or killed as 'collateral damage' in a sequence of killings, that person is surely a victim whether or not they are identified as a member of a group involved in ongoing conflict with collective responsibility. The model also applies when we shift from visible physical harm to the emotional and mental effects of acts. Bullying, threatening, psychological harassment, malicious theft – these are all acts of illegitimate violence that impinge on the well-being of those acted on. Family members suffer if one of their kin is made to suffer in any way, and this in turn adversely affects their abilities to function.

### Terror and witchcraft

A sense of terror or extreme fright and dread may arise in persons (see, e.g. Strathern & Stewart, 2006). Questions of psychological damage and the further conflict that may emerge from it are most relevant for contemporary settings in which dysfunctional relations emerge between people. In our discussion, we include both physical and psychological violence and their consequences in social life. In the ongoing concerns and issues to do with gendered and domestic violence in Papua New Guinea today, questions of this kind come to the fore. Development, jobs, and a rise in income do not necessarily lead to reduced levels of violence because so many other processes impinge on people's lives. It is in this context also that we can understand the persistent resurfacing of fears and tensions between people in relation to ideas of witchcraft and sorcery (Stewart & Strathern, 2004). Such ideas have proved tenacious in the face of changes and admonishments to discard them. Indeed, fears of this kind are themselves intimately bound up with processes of so-called modernity.

These ideas breed and multiply in the shadows of development and its hidden results. Some churches that preach against the power of Satan may indirectly give support to beliefs in witchcraft and sorcery because they take their ideas seriously and grant to them a reality that they then offer to fight by prayer. This is particularly true of some Pentecostal and charismatic-style churches whose ritual experts preach about evils that need to be confronted and overcome. These churches have been around for a generation or so now in PNG, but they are still considered to be 'new' by contrast with other established ones, such as Lutheran, Catholic, and, to a lesser extent, perhaps Methodist and Seventh Day Adventist (SDA) churches. The canonical idea of speaking in tongues also gives credence to the idea of possession by spirits or spiritual powers. Pentecostal rituals deny validity to pre-Christian ideas as 'evil' while reincorporating the basic schemata back into their own forms of ritual communication. Identifying and combating the evils of witchcraft and sorcery goes hand in hand with an increase in the beliefs held by some churchgoers, as well as others.

### The importance of rumour

In an earlier work (Stewart & Strathern, 2004) we put forward a model of how social tensions and conflicts may get entangled with notions of witchcraft and sorcery through community-based or free-floating rumour and gossip sequences (for more on gossip, see Stewart & Strathern, 2020). The utility of this model lies in its processual character. It helps to explain how gossip about a suspected witch or sorcerer can lead up to an actual accusation made against them, and subsequently perhaps the killing of a person or a suspect. In other words, social processes inform us how an accusation is actually made.

The next important point is that suspicion frequently falls on women, especially those who are in some way peripheralized or disempowered in the community. Gossip works more strongly when it is directed against persons who are 'different', perhaps secretive, also certainly afraid, and who are without influential persons to speak for them. Accusations may be compounded by larger-scale rumours circulating, such as that a strange animal has been seen near the grave of a recently buried person, perhaps a prominent male leader in the community.

### The case of the Duna

We can take the case of the Duna people of Hela Province in PNG, an area also marked by persistent intergroup fighting (see Stewart & Strathern, 2002b; Strathern & Stewart, 2004b). Among the Duna, a minority of men who hold status in the male line within the parish are at the centre of the membership of their group, accompanied by a set of people tied to this group core by various bilateral links. Some marriages take place with distantly related or unrelated women. In the past, the further away from which such women came, the more likely it was that at some point they would fall under suspicion of being witches, *tsuwake kono* in the Duna language. If so, nothing much would happen as long as everyone in the group was well, but if a child or the child's mother fell sick and the illness did not get better, men would call upon the operator of a divining stick, *ndele rowa*, and this expert would carry the stick through the village area; the stick was said to pull the operator to the house door of a guilty woman. She might then be confronted, and her own kin could offer payment to the kin of the deceased, or they would allow her to take her own life by hanging or by jumping into a pool of water and drowning. From the viewpoint of a contemporary outside observer, such an outcome would seem unjustified, but it would appear to be a judicial act to the accused person being punished by the divining stick.

From the accounts we have, such an outcome was not the only possible one. An alternative was for the accused person to flee and seek refuge in a distant corner where she had relatives, perhaps outside of her language area. Today, this older pattern is returning, with women secretly going to stay in a town. We have been informed that there are many women from Hela Province who have found hiding places in other areas of PNG, such as the Hagen area in the Western Highlands, or even in Port Moresby (the national capital) located on the southern coast.

In one infamous case that reached the news media, a woman from a far western part of PNG's Enga Province came to Mt Hagen to hide in this way but was found and burnt to death, with the idea that the only way to get rid of her witchcraft was by killing her in such a dramatic way.

We do not wish to dwell on these kinds of phenomena as typical, but they do indicate how hard it is to eradicate the idea of witchcraft itself. The same holds for sorcery, the use of magical materials to bring about the death of someone.

### Social factors

Other factors are also at work, loosening the social fabric and making the emergence of various kinds of violence more likely. The most egregious factors are also the most obvious ones. They include the stressful circumstances of living in squatter settlements, mixed-up groups, lacking proper services, such as clean water or electricity or sanitation or access to health care. Urban settlements often include large numbers of unemployed migrants from rural areas who are dependent on theft from outsiders and help from kin for their survival.

Some men may have brought wives from their home place into these unfavourable habitats or may have taken a wife while there, exchanging little or no bridewealth. It is anticipated that co-wives will fight, and this pattern is exacerbated in urban contexts. In Mt Hagen, as for a longer time in Port Moresby, an underclass of impoverished people haunt the city's rubbish dump, they raise pigs and children, and they sometimes get into trouble with police or fight among themselves with little interference from outsiders or concerned insiders. Communities without an operative social structure are the places where gendered and domestic violence easily develop and are hard to control.

The aftermath of locally resurgent ideas about witchcraft can be seen in the emergence of remnant communities of women, some centred on the SDA church, who have left their home places under threat to their lives and have been given shelter by the church. In one case, we know of in Hela Province, among Duna speakers, the SDA pastor had a wall built around his station in order to help keep vulnerable women safer. Such informal methods of trying to help seem to work better than formal government operations. In some other cases, women who have taken refuge have also been dispersed further by the effects of the massive earthquake, 7.2 on the Richter Scale, that shook the whole island of PNG from north to south early in 2018. Environmental disasters and fears of climate change heighten people's feelings of insecurity.

More subtle kinds of change also have their effects. There is a growing incidence of interethnic marriages, as people move about at work or school. Such marriages mean the married couples do not share a common vernacular language. They will converse either in English or in the lingua franca *Tok Pisin*, which is easy to learn. Their children in turn will not learn either vernacular language. Correspondingly, they will not learn in any detail the customs and cultural meanings encapsulated in a local language. This in turn impacts the child's sense of identity, and perhaps the values they come to internalize. When it comes to gender and family relations, this situation will have multiple effects, and it must be a growing pattern. Here, local churches try to step in to fill such a gap in socialization. The loss of vernacular language means a corresponding loss of values coming from the past.

## Residence changes

A material factor that goes with all this loss is simply found in the ill effects of changes in residence forms and housing. Gender-based rules in traditional rural communities were buttressed by the spatial disposal of people and rules about their accepted forms of movement. Moral behaviour depended on location. The separation of genders in everyday life was an expression of order, not one of hostility. Urban buildings and spaces destroy this kind of order. They put spatial pressures on people and cause emotional tensions. Study of the effects of urban spaces on people and on tendencies to violence could be useful in this regard.

With the overall advance of business activities, political changes, education, and the march of changes in relations, there is a marked growth in the involvement of women in the economy at large. However, it is possible that barriers still exist. In terms of the larger question of gendered violence found in the midst of all the developments that are taking place, observers are wont to stress the importance of making available creative roles not only for women in particular but also for urban male advancement. Humans need creative outlets for their energy, and it is urban contexts that most need to be developed to enable this energy to flow rather than be blocked.

## Intergroup violence in the highlands of Papua New Guinea

Accounts of pre-colonial warfare indicate that crops and houses might be destroyed or damaged, livestock lost, warriors wounded or killed, and subsequently some people might be driven out of their territories and forced to take refuge with kin elsewhere or to flee to distant parts. Women and children might not be immediate targets of violence, but they were not necessarily protected, and they could be raped or abducted if they were unable to find refuge with allies.

Commonly, domestic relations were disrupted, and family members had to reconstitute their living spaces and raise pigs to be used in any peacemaking rituals between the groups involved. The patterns of hostility were modified by ties of kinship emerging from marriages between groups and the concomitant exchanges of wealth that accompanied such arrangements and continued over time with ongoing life cycle and intergroup political exchanges. Order and disorder in social relations were thus formed by the intersection of descent-based group identities and marriage-based networks. Gender-based roles were in turn shaped by this intersection of frameworks.

Phases of violence continue to alternate in relations between groups, in which pre-colonial patterns repeat themselves with modern weapons such as powerful guns.

## Wider frameworks

What we may call domestic relations were accordingly not separated out from these wider frameworks of relationships. Marriages set up households, whose members made a living together and had their separate settlements, but much social life was spent in contexts outside of the home, and domestic relations were set into the context of the ties of alliance and enmity between groups.

We have orchestrated our discussion with this standard sketch because these frameworks are still in many ways operative, albeit in changed or changing contexts and alongside other, introduced frameworks, such as political electorates, local government councils, business enterprises, coffee plantations, and small holdings, and the flows of state-based money forms in a multitude of transactions.

## Violence and compensation

We can ask how these different frameworks and processes interrelate in contemporary circumstances. Where violence has caused a death, the situation is basically clear: responsibility is involved, and responsibility brings with it an obligation to pay compensation to the kin of the person or persons killed. This circumstance holds whether the death has occurred in fighting or is a killing within the group, including violence between a husband and wife. Violence may also result in a wound, for example, a blow on the head that elicits blood or the chopping off of a hand or leg. In these cases, the victim's kin will also claim compensation, and delay in giving this, or refusal to give it, escalates the conflict.

## The Huli case and intergroup marriages

In Hela Province in the Highlands of PNG among the Huli people, a further element was traditionally invoked. In a circumstance of fighting between spouses, an injury would be remembered for many years, and if it was cited later as a reason for a person's death, compensation could still be claimed. A custom of this kind would be likely to inhibit a ready display of aggression. In general, the extent to which ideas about the body and injuries to it carry ongoing significance would be very important to examine in seeking to understand patterns of conflict.

A modern consequence of the interrelations among different groups in PNG, as noted earlier in this chapter, is that a wife and husband may come from very different cultural backgrounds, so constraints on behaviour may apply very differently between them. Different ideas about marriage payments and exchanges would provide an example where conflict could arise. Pressures of contemporary life also come into play. Christian churches would disapprove of actions of physical violence as a way to obtain redress for wrongdoing. One partner may be Christian and the other may not be, so there might be no common moral standpoint between them. A coastal man employed in the Highlands whose son has had a relationship with a Highlands girl may feel oppressed by constant demands for bride-wealth from the girl's kin.

These intensify if the girl becomes pregnant. Demands can erupt into violence if they are not met. A comparable scenario emerges on a bigger scale if there is a killing or accidental death that is not met by compensation payments. In city contexts, these problems are exacerbated when people are not surrounded by supporting kinsfolk.

### Village courts

Introduced institutions of governance attempt to fill the gaps in social control. One context in which this is brought into play is the village courts system, run by elected magistrates in local government council areas, both rural and urban. Village courts have limited powers, for example, they cannot try cases of killings, but they are well adapted to hearing dispute cases in families, for example, where a husband is said to have abandoned his wife or a wife to have run away from a husband. Moreover, children and other relatives are often caught up in such dispute cases.

Village courts were introduced in order to bring dispute settlement into the informal sectors of the community outside of criminal justice institutions. There are many problems in their operation, including accusations of bribery and political bias. They remain, however, a valuable resource in handling disputes that can, or do, lead to violence. Magistrates are local and know the local ways. Disputants understand the processes involved. Village courts should be strengthened to enable them to enhance their work further.

### Contemporary problems

Initial pacification of the Highlands was undertaken from the 1930s onward and was intensified in the 1950s and 1960s, as the Australian colonial administration gradually moved the people towards self-government and independence in 1975. This steady progression of political forms has not been accompanied by long-term solutions to problems of intergroup conflict. Serious fighting and killings between groups have come and gone in waves after independence.

Such fighting leaves long-term traces on the landscape. In some cases, people are driven out and the land remains unoccupied for years, until compensation rituals are agreed on and eventuate. Especial complications surround contemporary disputes over the ownership and exploitation of large coffee plantations formerly owned by expatriate individuals or companies. In one case, we know of fighting over a large plantation led in 2019 to the killing of two women who had brought food to their men who were involved in the conflict and who may also have been acting as warning scouts. They may have used mobile phones to warn their kin of approaching enemies. The fighting continued off and on in 2020 while we were staying in the nearby area for our own research.

Generally, fighting is a matter for men, but women can become targets also. In a much more severe case, which gained international media attention, the killing of 23 women and children in a sudden attack by enemy men on a village site in

Hela Province in 2019 caused an outcry of concern from many quarters in PNG because of the unusual scale of the killings, the manner of killing by the use of machetes, and also because the event took place in the electorate of James Marape, the recently elected prime minister of PNG (2020).

These killings were part of a payback or revenge killing sequence, enacted when the village men were hiding in the bush, and killing women in this way brought to light the way in which such violence, however based in custom, has become repugnant to many people in PNG today. The new prime minister vowed to see that the killers were found and punished, but sometimes police find it hard to arrest criminals because the criminals have very powerful guns. This killing has so far not set a precedent, but it is not known to us whether the killers have been caught or peacemaking negotiations entered into.

### The ethos of warriorhood

Does tribal fighting reflect a general male ethos of warriorhood that entails also a dominating or aggressive attitude towards women? Guns may have caused such attitudes to intensify and, as we have noted, non-combatants such as women could be subject to violence in the past and still can be today. In contemporary contexts, outside of tribal fighting, the greater patterns of violence occur in urban contexts in low-income or squatter settlements where unrelated people are brought together without local leadership, or norms of behaviour, without adequate services, and with many sources of tensions and disputes among them. In both urban and rural sites, alcohol and drug consumption exacerbate violent activity, and this plays out in domestic contexts of disputes over money, sexual behaviour, access to resources, and response to police raids in search of criminals. Peri-urban settlements, with their heterogeneous inhabitants living in various degrees of precarity, are surely the breeding grounds for interpersonal violence, including gendered violence, as well as for gang-related behaviour. It is in those contexts, rather than in relatively ordered rural communities, that we would be inclined to see the biggest problems of gendered and family violence in emergence. In both urban and rural contexts, church congregations can play a crucial role in addressing social problems and ameliorating the effects of changes on people's lives.

### TV programmes

The prevalence of violence-related problems has led to some media productions on TV in PNG oriented towards dealing with scenarios of causes of problems. The programmes take the form of short dramas and are performed in the lingua franca *Tok Pisin* rather than in English, with the aim of making their message accessible to as wide a range of viewers as possible. The dramas run through typical problems and also tackle issues that often are not discussed. In one piece, an older cousin shows his younger male relative sexually explicit pictures and also makes sexual advances towards him. When the pattern of his behaviour comes to light, he is admonished by further relatives. In another, an uncle sexually abuses his niece, who is deeply embarrassed and finally speaks about it to a teacher. The abuser is confronted, and he is required to leave the household where he has been a guest. In another story, a man acquires a well-paying urban job but starts to get drunk and date women at his workplace even though he has a wife. Again, his behaviour is discovered, and he is shamed into reforming himself. It is notable how in these narratives, self-help and community action, as against the use of formal courts, are portrayed as the way to settle conflicts. Such patterns obviously fit with a general community ethos and a background of Christian ideas.

These cases derive from scripted TV programmes, but they clearly reflect real, contemporary problems brought on by urbanization, migration, and the impacts of new ideas on people's lives. It is to urban contexts that we must look in tracing the effects of social changes on individual lives and how cultural mores can be disrupted by a breakdown in patterns of residential separation and the intrusion of new media into popular consciousness.

### The Enga case

A different front of action can be seen in the context of education and women's advancement. It is interesting to consider some materials published in 1989 in a well-known edited work by Margaret Jolly and Martha Macintyre, published by Cambridge University Press (1989). Chapters in this volume cover a range of topics, with some emphasis on the roles of Christian missions in changing domestic patterns of life, especially in relation to ideas of gender roles. One chapter is by Mervyn Meggitt, on the Central Enga people, and he attempts to assess changes among these people and how women have been affected by them. Meggitt studied this population, the Mae Enga, numbering some 30,000 people, over a period of years and wrote his essay on change among them in 1982. The Mae were like other Highlands people, being horticulturalists dependent on sweet potatoes as a staple crop, raising pigs, and belonging to largely patrilineal clans holding separate lands but linked together by a dense mesh of exchange relations.

Meggitt notes that women's 'labour and skill' among the Mae (p. 136) were essential for both gardening and pig rearing, as well as for bearing children for the clan. There was some separation between men and women because men tended to live and sleep in men's houses while women and their young children lived in separate women's houses nearby. This separation of men and women in residence was maintained, Meggitt says, because of male fears of the dangers of female menstruation. Meggitt also says (p. 137) that men could exact severe punishment on women who were 'errant'. Divorce was also 'infrequent' (ibid.).

After the early days of pacification, the Australians began to institute health care around primary forms of education. From 1963 onward, they set up local government councils, partly with the idea of giving openings to women for work or business. Women also had some opportunities to market their garden produce to public servants. Expatriate missions sometimes gave shelter to maltreated widows.

Over time, as people moved around more and alcohol consumption began, Meggitt argues that there was a rise in 'marital violence, divorce, extra-marital unions, and illegitimate children' (p. 141). Education for girls was provided for in government policy, particularly after independence in 1975, but the proportions of female students enrolled in high schools continued to be low. Public servants remained mostly male. When provincial governments were set up, similar patterns of gender imbalance held. Meggitt remarks (p. 143) that the Village Economic Development Fund helped to set up numerous business groups, each with its own management committee. In 57 such groups, there were a total of 281 men and just 3 women. Many of these start-ups also failed owing to misuse of money.

Women were involved in tending and harvesting coffee beans for sale in season, but 'men kept the greatly increased incomes of these months to buy motor vehicles, beer, pigs, and other valuables to meet their obligations in clan prestations' (p. 147). Few women stood for elections and even fewer were elected. In marital disputes, male litigants most often were favoured. Of 528 village court magistrates, only one was a woman.

Peace officers who attended to the courts were not very active in chasing husbands to face cases in the village courts, either (p. 151). All the same, these courts provided the only avenues easily accessible to women, and there was room for a woman's own kin to intervene on her behalf in the informal moots that often took place outside the court building as preliminary to a case being heard and decided inside – at least in the Hagen area.

Meggitt concluded his discussion by further pointing out that with the localization of offices among the Lutheran churches, there was less emphasis on social services, including those for women, and more emphasis on evangelization among less changed populations in the west.

It is interesting to take Meggitt's account as a snapshot in time. How different are things today? Not so different as one might imagine. Women are undoubtedly much involved in the marketing of produce, and in educational levels of activity. Yet they do not appear to have significantly higher political status or more influence in local disputes.

### The effects of COVID-19

We suggest that this is the context in which we need to consider the incidence of gendered violence, above all in urban as opposed to rural contexts.

The coronavirus disease 2019, COVID-19, has impacted people's lives by transforming patterns of behaviour and temporal routines. In situations where husbands and wives have been forced to spend more time together, due to 'shelter in place' (stay-at-home) orders during the pandemic of 2020, an increase in domestic violence has been noted in PNG as well as other parts of the Pacific, as noted in the national PNG media. Epidemiological challenges are just one example of the forces of the globalized world upon the peoples of the Pacific.

## Conclusion

We have pointed to numerous forces and contexts of change in the lives of people here. In rural contexts, tribal fighting has the most obviously negative effects. In urban contexts, normative practices become disrupted and the influence of senior kin is reduced. Village courts attempt to provide relief from these factors, and in general informal methods of handling disputes and transgressions work best. Violent gang activities, added to the circumstances discussed here, make social control harder to achieve and also tend to violate kinship-derived norms of behaviour. The use of shaming as a means of handling incorrect behaviour holds a crucial key to the containment of problems in the future.

## Notes

1  Pamela J. Stewart (Strathern) and Andrew J. Strathern are a wife-and-husband research team who are based in the Department of Anthropology, University of Pittsburgh, and co-direct the Cromie Burn Research Unit. They are frequently invited to give international lectures and have worked with a number of museums to assist them with their collections. Stewart and Strathern have published over 50 books, over 80 prefaces to influential books, and over 200 articles, book chapters, and essays on their research in the Pacific (mainly Papua New Guinea, primarily the Mount Hagen, Duna, and Wiru areas) and the South-West Pacific region (e.g. Samoa, Cook Islands, and Fiji); Asia (mainly Taiwan, and also including Mainland China and Inner Mongolia, and Japan); Europe (primarily Scotland, Ireland, Germany, and the European Union countries in general); and New Zealand and Australia. One of their strengths is that, unlike some others working in Mount Hagen among the Hagen people, they learned the language, Melpa, and used it to understand the lives of the local people. Their most recent co-authored books include Witchcraft, Sorcery, Rumors, and Gossip (Cambridge University Press, 2004); Kinship in Action: Self and Group (Prentice Hall, 2011); Peace-Making and the Imagination: Papua New Guinea Perspectives (University of Queensland Press with Penguin Australia, 2011); Ritual: Key Concepts in Religion (Bloomsbury Academic Publications, 2014); Working in the Field: Anthropological Experiences Across the World (Palgrave Macmillan, 2014); Breaking the Frames: Anthropological Conundrums (Palgrave Macmillan, 2017); Sacred Revenge in Oceania (Cambridge University Press, 2019); Sustainability, Conservation, and Creativity: Ethnographic Learning from Small-scale Practices. (Routledge Publishing, 2019); and Language and Culture in Dialogue (Bloomsbury Academic Publishing, 2019). Their recent co-edited books include Research Companion to Anthropology (Routledge Publishing, 2016, originally published in 2015); Exchange and Sacrifice (Carolina Academic Press, 2008); and Religious and Ritual Change: Cosmologies and Histories (Carolina Academic Press, 2009), along with the updated and revised Chinese version (Taipei, Taiwan: Linking Publishing, 2010). Stewart and Strathern's current research topics include Eco-Cosmological Landscapes; Ritual Studies; Political Peacemaking; Comparative Anthropological Studies of Disasters and Climatic Change; Language, Culture and Cognitive Science; and Scottish and Irish Studies. For many years, they served as Associate Editor and General Editor (respectively) for the Association for Social Anthropology in Oceania book series, and they are co-series editors for the Anthropology and Cultural History in Asia and the Indo-Pacific book series. They also currently serve as co-editors of four book series: Ritual Studies, Medical Anthropology, European Anthropology, and Disaster Anthropology, and they are the long-standing co-editors of the Journal of Ritual Studies (on Facebook: at facebook.com/ritualstudies). Their webpages, which list publications and other scholarly activities, are: www.pitt.edu/~strather/ and www.StewartStrathern.pitt.edu/.

2 COVID-19, coronavirus disease 2019, is one type of a coronavirus that comprises a group of related RNA (ribonucleic acid is a nucleic acid present in all living cells) viruses that can cause disease in mammals and birds that may have outcomes ranging from mild illness to death.
3 We have worked in Papua New Guinea for many decades – collectively, over 50 years.

## References

Jolly, M., & Macintyre, M. (Eds.). (1989). *Family and gender in the Pacific: Domestic contradictions and the colonial impact*. Cambridge: Cambridge University Press.

Riches, D. (1986). *The anthropology of violence*. Oxford, UK: Blackwell Publishing.

Stewart, P. J., & Strathern, A. (1999). "Feasting on my enemy": Images of violence and change in the New Guinea Highlands. *Ethnohistory, 46*(4), 645–669.

Stewart, P. J., & Strathern, A. (2002a). *Violence: Theory and ethnography*. London and New York: Continuum Publishing.

Stewart, P. J., & Strathern, A. (2002b). *Remaking the world: Myth, mining and ritual change among the Duna of Papua New Guinea*. Smithsonian Series in Ethnographic Inquiry. Washington, DC: Smithsonian Institution Press.

Stewart, P. J., & Strathern, A. (2004). *Witchcraft, sorcery, rumors, and gossip*. Cambridge: Cambridge University Press.

Stewart (Strathern), P. J., & Strathern, A. (2020, January/February). Gossip: A thing humans do. *Anthropology News*, pp. 18–21.

Strathern, A., & Stewart, P. J. (2004a). Afterword: Substances, powers, cosmos, and history. In N. L. Whitehead & R. Wright (eds.), *The anthropology of assault sorcery and witchcraft in Amazonia* (pp. 314–320). Durham, NC: Duke University Press.

Strathern, A., & Stewart, P. J. (2004b). *Empowering the past, confronting the future, the Duna people of Papua New Guinea*. Contemporary Anthropology of Religion Series. New York: Palgrave Macmillan.

Strathern, A., & Stewart, P. J. (2005a). Witchcraft, sorcery, rumors, and gossip: Terror and the imagination–a state of lethal play. *The Central States Anthropological Society Bulletin, 40*(1), 8–14.

Strathern, A., & Stewart, P. J. (2005b). Violence. Conceptual themes and the evaluation of actions [Special issue]. *Polylog*, 5 (2004). Retrieved from http://them.polylog.org/5/fss-en.htm (English); http://them.polylog.org/5/fss-es.htm (Spanish); http://them.polylog.org/5/fss-de.htm (German).

Strathern, A., & Stewart, P. J. (2006). Introduction: Terror, the imagination, and cosmology. In A. Strathern, P. J. Stewart, & N. L. Whitehead (eds.), *Terror and violence: Imagination and the unimaginable* (pp. 1–39). Anthropology, Culture, and Society Series. London and Ann Arbor, MI: Pluto Press.

Strathern, A., & Stewart, P. J. (2011). *Peace-making and the imagination: Papua New Guinea perspectives*. Brisbane: University of Queensland Press.

# Postface – analysing violence

## Lessons from a collective reflection[1]

*Michel Wieviorka*

The humanities and social sciences are never as useful as when they shed light on a problem by approaching it with a double concern: that of a theoretical demand, and that of a deep knowledge of the facts. Abstraction remote from empirical work too often leads to ideology or to the project of forcefully squeezing the facts into a theory, whereas absence of conceptualization prevents any deep analysis.

We must therefore praise the effort that is at both the origin and the heart of this volume. It obviously places its various contributions into an intellectually demanding, concrete, and factual space: one of violence in situations which are not those of the North, or the Centre, since it concerns the Pacific Islands. These situations do not come from some Global North or Global South – they come from both at the same time, from their encounter.

Everything here is an invitation to think about complexity and ambivalence, just like Georg Simmel and Norbert Elias suggested in their days, and Robert Merton a bit later (Tabboni, 2007). To put it briefly, this volume invites the reader to envisage the necessity of eventually renewing in some depth the available conceptions of universalism and universal values, starting with reason.

### Violence and family in situations of hybridity

The situations analysed here are always sociologically and historically hybrid. The words and categories that are used have to be considered on the basis of an experience combining, on the one hand, a culture and a history predating the domination from Europe or the United States of America, and, on the other hand, a Western presence which is more or less strong, sometimes giving the image of modernization – a word that we will leave aside, only reminding the reader that it has a long history and its concept is today much more criticized than it was in the times of evolutionist thinking, such as that by Daniel Lerner (1958) or Walt Whitman Rostow (1990), whose aim was to conceive of the triumphal march of modernity, actually an American one, in the 1950s and the beginning of the 1960s.

Let us consider more specifically the two keywords of this book: family and violence. How can we properly conceptualize what does not pertain exclusively to either world – precolonial societies and history, and the Western presence? How can we, on the one hand, avoid relativism, which would plead for the impossibility

DOI: 10.4324/9781003146667-13

of understanding unless we dwell fully inside the societies at stake, without trying to think of what would go beyond their experience? How, on the other hand, can we avoid ethnocentrism, which would symmetrically propose categories claiming to be universal, whereas they correspond first and foremost to the Western world-view and often imply the domination of men over women, of White over non-White peoples, of the colonizer over the colonized, etc., as many have shown over the years in the postcolonial literature, from Edward Saïd (1995) to, for example, Achille Mbembe (2016)?

## The end of a certain division of labour

As they appeared in the humanities and in the social sciences – which have been for too long unaware of their ethnocentrism or locked into their 'methodological nationalism', as Ulrich Beck (2006) put it – the notions of 'violence' and 'family' are, in themselves, not obvious. The 'family', if only in the West, corresponds to different models, and certainly not to the sole variant called 'nuclear'. These models have a relative importance that varies in time.

In France, for example, demographers such as Louis Roussel (1989) and sociologists such as François de Singly (2007) have proposed, since the 1980s, studying the 'democratic' family, whereas others suggested studying the 'single-parent' family. The recent cultural, scientific, and medical evolutions, particularly in relation to procreation, led to the appearance or reinforcement of types of families that were previously inexistent or rare. Descent, genealogy, alliance, and adoption – all terms referring to meanings and practices that differ from one experience to another – are being transformed, and so is the law. They also transform the humanities and social sciences, as well as activist engagement, which by and large are more frequently referring to gender (e.g. gender studies) than to the family, which has started to become a slightly obsolete category.

For their part, anthropologists have for a long time focused on kinship, being more interested in it than in the family models it can shape in non-Western societies. But contemporary realities do not allow this kind of dichotomy anymore, as if 'family' were a category having to give way to 'kinship' in the study of non-Western societies, this category being itself somewhat threatened by the rise of 'gender' in the United States and Europe. Already challenged by migrations in Western societies, these oppositions are for the most part, as this book shows, if not inappropriate then at least questioned when it comes to hybridization, the mixing of models which characterizes the insular situations in the Pacific that are examined here. We must be sociologists in Africa, Asia, or in the Pacific Islands, just as we must be anthropologists in the United States or in Europe.

Let us add the fact, which is often neglected, that the cultures called 'vernacular', as they are described today, are only the last state of local cultures before the encounter with Western modernity. They might have evolved considerably in the centuries preceding this encounter. They have never been an immutable, immobile given. They at least have a past if not a history.

## Subjectivity and objectivity of violence

As Loïs Bastide and Denis Regnier recall in the introduction to this volume, violence is both subjective and objective. It is highly subjective, since its definition changes from one person to another, from one group or society to another, and it also varies in time for a person, a group, or a society. It is also what is or is not tolerated according to societies and to historical moments. Until recently, in Western societies, many institutions could allow some of their members to practice sexual, paedophilic, or racist violence, or other forms of violence, without the culprits being bothered, in schools, boarding schools, or in the Catholic Church. The family, too, as an institution, could also harbour violence that was not treated socially, that was ignored by the law and the police, and therefore not recognized as such. For the public, such violence did not really exist.

In general, within these societies, since the 1970s a powerful trend has been at work to make this institutional violence visible and public, and therefore also liable to prosecution. This amounts to taking into consideration the subjectivity of the victims, and in certain cases this is a product of their collective fight, for example, in the case of the women's rights movement. But to get to the law, violence must be objectified and designated as such in an incontestable manner. If the phenomenon is lacking a certain objectivity, then it is not possible to treat it legally or intellectually, or scientifically, which is the first preoccupation in this book. How, and why, could we try to explain something that is entirely subjective? But how is it possible not to take it into account? And how can we deal with this if a 'vernacular' culture wants to see, as this book illustrates, certain forms of violence as something completely different from what Western norms say they are today, for example, a principle of education if children are at stake, or, in a case of violence against a woman, a question of structural tradition, inscribed in the family, and not a question of gender.

## The universal and the particular: can we save the project of conceptualizing violence?

This is a problem that the humanities and social sciences have never really managed to solve, and one which is particularly serious in the situations studied in the book. We need to square it not just with one culture and one principal history, which are hegemonic or at least dominant, but with two. Each of them can authorize differently an attempt at articulating the objective and the subjective, and each of them is also at risk of leading to incomprehension and the absence of the possibility of communicating with the other.

In any case, the best we can imagine, it seems to me, is a circulation, a permanent testing, which would allow us to universalize relativism, if we can say this, and relativize universalism. This is not the case when cultures cohabit without really mixing with each other, and the categories or definitions, the meaning of words, do not communicate much. This is in a way what Maurice Merleau-Ponty (2001) recommended in his time, speaking of an 'incessant testing of oneself by the other and of the other by oneself'. But he was thinking about 'his' French society, explaining that he was feeding on anthropological knowledge, whereas we need to fully dwell at the core of the situations where the issues are decisive.

Is this type of effort to save a concept of 'violence' not the hallmark of a modernization, which is brought about by well-defined actors, and which would impose norms from abroad, in particular norms coming from Western countries, onto cultures that do not conceive of 'violence' as such, or at least do so in very different terms? Or is this effort not abolishing itself via the irresistible progress of Western modernity? Is 'violence' not a contribution from a modernization which is less a hybridization than a domination and progressive elimination – by norms, words, and also by law – of the local ways of living and thinking?

Most studies collected in this book suggest that we need to propose modes of action and thinking that are respectful of the two registers, the Western and the vernacular. This is the case when, instead of deciding too quickly, we go back and forth to describe and understand the same problem, the murder of a woman, for example, between the idea that it is a case of gender violence targeting a woman as such specifically – a feminicide – and the idea that it is a case of intrafamily violence grounded in a culture. A violence between persons or a structural violence.

Our reasoning does not lead us to reject this or that classical approach to violence. It leads us to see that we need to know how to combine them by sticking to the facts, of course, and also by noting that the necessarily hybrid character of the society at stake obliges us to hesitate and switch between approaches where we will privilege one over the other, depending on whether we are being more or less sensitive to the domination imposing its norms or the resistance of vernacular culture. Let us repeat that this implies that researchers must have the capacity to think of the relationship to their object.

## Conclusion

The question appearing here, which is indeed very present in this volume, is that of the possibility of freeing the category of 'violence' from accusations of ethnocentrism and domination to make it a scientifically applicable category, in order to objectify the phenomena under consideration without denying the relevance – or even simply the existence – of norms, values, and culture-specific meanings that modernization would be eradicating. To put it differently, it should not be impossible to invent, thanks to the study of societies like those of the Pacific Islands, a concept of violence which is really or at least more universalizable, neither perverted nor doomed once and for all because of its Western origins. In addition, we can envisage in return the possibility that a conceptual opening and transformation comes from these Pacific Islands to irrigate and enrich the Western, dominant, arrogant, falsely scientific, and objectifying conceptions of a phenomenon such as violence.

These are questions that this volume inaugurates or invites to formulate. If they are not posed and sorted out by a reflection of the researchers wondering about their relation to their object and the fabrication of the concepts they use, then these researchers are at high risk, it is signalled in this book, of becoming a vector of the domination of the Western dominant cultures, a domination that is also intellectual, and of missing the meaning and the loss of meaning implied in violence.

A conclusion is emerging from this volume: 'violence' is better understood when we consider societies in their specificity. Here, both the domination coming from elsewhere and the weight of vernacular culture exert an influence which is not necessarily one way, unequivocal, unidimensional. Their encounter, in addition, also contributes to shaping violence. And to understand the facts, the concrete phenomena – for example, the fact that violence can be stronger than elsewhere in the family context but at the same time less strong in the larger context of collective life – one needs to invent notions and concepts that are themselves hybrid, or at least engage in approaches circulating between universalism and relativism, without breaking with the horizon of universality that founds all scientific approaches and without ignoring the local, vernacular categories.

## Note

1  Translated by Denis Regnier.

## References

Beck, U. (2006). *The cosmopolitan vision*. Cambridge: Polity Press.

Lerner, D. (1958). *The passing of traditional society: Modernizing the Middle East*. New York, NY: Free Press.

Mbembe, A. (2016). *Politiques de l'inimitié*. Paris: La Découverte.

Merleau-Ponty, M. (2001). De Mauss à Claude Lévi-Strauss. In *Signes*. Paris: Gallimard (Original work published 1960).

Rostow, W. W. (1990). *The stages of economic growth: A non-communist manifesto*, Cambridge: Cambridge University Press (Original work published 1960).

Roussel, L. (1989). *La Famille incertaine*. Paris: Odile Jacob.

Saïd, E. (1995). *Orientalism*. London: Penguin Classics (Original work published 1972).

Singly, F. de (2007). *Sociologie de la famille contemporaine*. Malakoff, France: Armand Colin.

Tabboni, S. (2007). De l'ambivalence sociale à l'ambivalence Culturelle. *Cahiers internationaux de sociologie*, *2*(123), 269–288.

# Index

Note: Page numbers followed by "n" indicate a note on the corresponding page.

Amnesty International 97
Amokura Family Violence Prevention Strategy 28
Aotearoa New Zealand, violence in 20–33; case studies 28–32; E Tū Whānau 29–30; healing whānau, addressing violence 27–28; historical record of 23–25; historical solutions, continual harm 25–26; movements of change 26–27; whānau violence 22–23; *see also* settler violence in Aotearoa New Zealand
Association of Hawaiian Civic Clubs (AHCC) 46

Bambridge, Tamatoa 55
Banfield, Edward C. 135
Bastide, Loïs 6, 13, 16, 180
Beck, Ulrich 179
Boudon, Raymond 17
Bourdieu, Pierre 56
Bourgois, Philippe 21–22, 133

Chamoux, Marie-Noëlle 16–17
children, violence against 3; child transfer and family violence 61–63; hitting 157–159
Christian Care Centre (CCC) 95–96
cognitive sociology and violence 16–17
Collins, Randal 16, 54–55
colonial violence 21
Committee on the Elimination of Discrimination Against Women (CEDAW) 97
conflict, places and subjects of 154–157
Convention on the Elimination of All Forms of Discrimination against Women (CEDAW) 83

Cook, Len 24
corporal punishment 159
COVID-19 effects 175, 177n2
Cram, F. 23, 29
culture-based counselling at domestic violence shelter 95–106; *see also* Solomon Islands
Cunneen, C. 20

demanding/seizing money 87–88
de Monléon, Jean-Vital 60
de Singly, François 4, 54, 57, 58, 179
Dilmaç, Julie Alev 135
domestic violence: as a foreign concept 99–100; shelter, culture-based counselling at 95–106; *see also* Solomon Islands
domestic violence in Papua New Guinea 165–170; case of the Duna 168–169; residence changes 170; rumour in, importance 168; social factors 169–170; social media in 166; terror and witchcraft 167; triangle of violence 165–166; witnesses 166–167; *see also* Papua New Guinea (PNG), Highlands societies of
dubal marit (double marriage) 93n6
Durkheim, Émile 4

economic control violence 84–87; gender-defined duties 86; household income management 84; independent income management 84; in Papua New Guinea 84–87; spending and decision-making control 84–85; women prevented from generating income 85–87
economic exploitation 84, 87–90; demanding/seizing money 87–88;

men's refusal to contribute to household
88–90
economic violence 8; in Papua New
Guinea 84; physical violence and 9
Elias, Norbert 178
E Tū Whānau 29–31
Eves, Richard 8

fa'a'amura'a (transfer of children between
parental households) 7; adaptations of
52–64; as a social institution 59–61
faetem (hit) 141–142, 146
faet (fight) 11, 141–143
family 2–4; anthropological and sociological
perspectives 2–4; family-based society
152–153; Family First Prevention
Services Act 47; Family Protection Act
97; 'family universes' 6; relations, in
French Polynesia 57–59
family violence 1, 151–152; in Aotearoa
New Zealand 20–33; defining 116–117;
factors of 10–12; (post)colonial
adoption and customary fosterage 4–7;
see also Kiriwina, family violence in
Farmer, Paul 126
Fassin, Didier 10, 125, 131, 132
Federal Child Abuse Prevention and
Treatment Act (CAPTA) 44
female economic success 115–116
feminicides 70–72
feti'i model of family relations 56–57
'fictive kinship' 3
French Polynesia, family violence in
7, 52–64; child transfer and family
violence 61–63; conceptual note 53–56;
Fa'a'amura'a as a social institution
59–61; family 55–56; from feti'i
model to practical kinship 56–57;
methodology 53–56; mobility, family,
and vulnerability 59–63; social capital
and 57–59; spatial mobility and 57–59;
transferred children and 52–64
French Polynesia today 124–136; four
portraits 127–131; from interpersonal to
structural violence 125–127; perpetrators'
experiences in 124–136; from structural
violence to family violence 124–136

Galtung, Johan 126, 136
gender-based family violence: identifying
factors 113–117; in Solomon Islands
97–98; Western human rights discourse
114–115

Gender Inequality Index (GII), 2018 83
genocide 21
Goody, Jack 4
Gorodé, Déwé 72–73, 78
Grennell, Di 29
gross human rights abuse 21

hānaī (traditionally fostered children)
38–46, 48
Hawaiian children 37–49; see also native
Hawaiian children, fostering
'Hawai'i Assures Nurturing And
Involvement' (HANAI) 42
Hawaii's Story by Hawaii's Queen 39
healing 28
Herzfeld, Michael 135
historical trauma theory 28, 33n17
homicides 22
Honolulu Advertiser 40
'Horizontals' 2, 4
Huli case and intergroup marriages
171–172
hybridity, violence and family in situations
of 178–179

Indian Child Welfare Act (ICWA),
1978 38
indigénat regime 76
Intergroup violence in Papua New Guinea
highlands 170–175
International Law and Justice 29
international organizations 14
interwoven family groups 153–154
'intimate partner violence' 3
intrafamily violence 68, 159–160
iwi (tribe) 33n14
Ixéco, Eliane 73

Jolly, Margaret 4, 113, 115, 163n11, 174

Kahukura (leaders of change within iwi,
hapū, and whānau) 31
kanaka maoli (Native Hawaiians) 41
Kanaks 68–69; Kanak feminism 77; Kanak
Métis 68–69
kastom (culture) 9, 113–117, 122n2
Ka Wai Ola 44, 48
Kede, Anne-Marie 67
keiki hānai 41
kilim (hit) 11
kilim nogud (hitting hard) 141, 144
kilim smol (hitting soft) 141, 144, 146–147
kin-making social practices 3

kinship relations 106n5, 153, 179; in French Polynesia 56–57; threat and control 159–162, 163n6

Kiriwina, family violence in 151–162; conflict, places and subjects of 154–157; corporal punishment 159; definitions 151–157; family-based society 152–153; hitting one's children 157–159; interwoven family groups 153–154; intrafamily violence 158–160; kinship threat and control 159–162; magical attacks 159–162; physical assault 159; quarrels 151–162; re-examining material through prism of violence 151–152

Kraemer, D. 9, 14

Kruger, T. 27

'labour' concept 17

lateral violence 21

law of the Republic versus law of the family 11

Lepani, Katherine 163n11

Le Play, Frédéric 4

Lerner, Daniel 178

Lévi-Strauss, Claude 2

local understandings 10–12

Loyauté Islands 75–76

Macintyre, Martha 120, 174

macro-structural level violence 21

magical attacks 159–162

mana, defining 33n15

Māori, Kaupapa 33n16

Māori problem 23, 33nn7, 10; children 33n5; family violence 23–25; men 33n11; women 33n3

Mbembe, Achille 179

McIntosh, T. 5, 16

Meggitt, Mervyn 174–175

Merleau-Ponty, Maurice 180

Merry, Sally Engle 138

metaphorization 16

micro-structural level violence 21

Miguel-Lorenzo, Xandra 9

missionary influence, head-on criticism of 77

mobility in transferred children 59–63

Mongrel mob 33n19

moral economies 10–12, 131–135

moral entrepreneurs 14–15

morality, violence and 15–16

Naepels, Michel 16, 125

*Nānā I Ke Kumu* 39

National Certificate of Educational Achievement (NCEA) 22

National Policy on Violence against Women 97

'nationhood' (*lāhui*) 6

native Hawaiian children, fostering 37–49; in an American state 37–49; background 38–40; child's place, determining 40–44; Native Hawaiian Child Welfare Act 45–47; relationships, political and cultural 44–45

nativist conservatism 76–78

nativist familialism 74–76

New Caledonian families, violence in 67–78; conjugal ties, dissolving 74; feminicides 70–72; multi-ethnic context 69; political responses 72–74; religious and nativist conservatisms 76–78; settlement colony 68; in women 69–70

*New kinship studies* 153

Nixon, R. 20

non-governmental organizations (NGOs) 14, 53, 114, 138

*'ohana* (Native Hawaiian extended family) 5

*'ōpū feti'i* kinship structure 56–57

*'ōpū ho'e* kinship structure 56–57

Oranga Tamariki Report 24

Pacific Islands 1–17

Paia, M. 10, 16

Papua New Guinea (PNG), economic violence in 83–84; economic control 84–87; economic exploitation 84, 87–90; *see also* economic control violence; economic exploitation

Papua New Guinea (PNG), Highlands societies of 165–176; community violence in, contexts and levels 165–176; contemporary problems 172–173; COVID-19 effects 175; domestic violence in 165–170; Enga case 174–175; ethos of warriorhood 173; Huli case and intergroup marriages 171–172; intergroup violence in 170–175; TV programmes 173–174; village courts 172; violence and compensation 171; wider frameworks 171; *see also* domestic violence in Papua New Guinea

Passa, Jone 74

physical abuse in Vanuatu school 138–148; abusive interactions

143–145; acceptability of blows, relational construction of 145–147; *kilim nogud* 141; *kilim smol* 141; naming and reacting to 138–148; in an underprivileged neighbourhood 139–140
physical abuse/violence 9, 91, 140–143
political responses to violence 72–74
polygynous marriages 9
polygyny 90, 93n6
Porter, A. 20
Port Vila, Vanuatu, women-only households in 110–121; female economic success 115–116; gender-based family violence, identifying factors 113–117; a gendered place 111–113; *kastom* reinterpretation 113–117; life before and after moving into 117–119; sites of social resistance 119; socio-cultural factors 116; Western human rights discourse 114–115
power struggles 14–15
Protar, L. 11, 13, 17
Protection Safety Notes (PSNs) 97
public sociology, violence and 15–16

quarrels 151–162

Regional Assistance Mission to Solomon Islands (RAMSI) 99
Regnier, Denis 13, 180
*Relais, Le* 73
'relatedness' 3
religious conservatism 76–78
Riches, David 166
Rostow, Walt Whitman 178
Roussel, Louis 179
rumour, in domestic violence in Papua New Guinea 168

Saïd, Edward 179
Salaün, M. 10, 16
Salomon, Christine 7, 15
Scale of Economic Abuse 82
Schachter, Judith 5–7
Scheper-Hughes, N. 21–22
Schneiderm, David 153
school as place of abusive interactions 143–145
Servy, A. 11, 13, 17
settlement colony (*colonie de peuplement*) 68, 79n

settler violence in Aotearoa New Zealand 20–33; *see also* Aotearoa New Zealand, violence in
Simmel, Georg 178
'single-parent' family 179
slow violence 20
Smith, C. 28
social capital and French Polynesia 57–59
social change and violent behaviours 12–14
social factors, in domestic violence in Papua New Guinea 169–170
social relations, restoring 103–104
social resistance sites 110–121
Solomon Islands 95–106; culture-based counselling 101–102; domestic violence as a foreign concept 99–100; gender violence in 97–98; *Kastom* 95–99, 103–104; no police 100–101; Sisters of the Anglican Church of Melanesia, culture-based counselling of 95–106; sisters' neutrality 104–105; social relations, restoring 103–104; Solomon Islands Family Health and Safety Study 97; Solomon Islands gender-based violence referral network (SAFENET) 99; Solomon Islands High Court 97; violence against women 98–99; women's house 102–103
spatial mobility and French Polynesia 57–59
Speed, Shannon 21
Stewart, Pamela J. 12, 176n1
Strathern, Andrew J. 12, 176n1
structural violence to family violence 21, 124–136; from interpersonal to structural violence 125–127; moral economy cast in mould of violence 131–135
symbolic violence 21
systemic violence 21

Taerea, Yasmina 62
Tai Tokerau Iwi Chief Executives Consortium 28
Tamariki, Oranga 26
Taonui, Rawiri 23
'Tensions, The' 97
terror, in domestic violence in Papua New Guinea 167
Thémereau, Marie-Noelle 72
transformation 13
*tribus* (tribes) 75

*vaelens* (violence) 11, 138–148, 141
Vanuatu school 138–148; *see also* physical
  abuse in Vanuatu school
Vernaudon, J. 10, 16
'Verticals' 2, 4
'Vila' 111
village courts 172
violence/violent behaviours 2–7, 12–14;
  cognitive sociology and 16–17;
  compensation and 171; deconstruction
  of 16–17; defining 116–117; emerging
  forms of 12–14; on and within families
  4–7; moral entrepreneurs and power
  struggles 14–15; naming 82–92; new
  conceptions of 12–14; public sociology
  and morality in 15–16; research context
  83; semantic *analogon* to 17; social
  change and 12–14; subjectivity and
  objectivity of 180; *see also* women,
  violence to
vulnerability of transferred children 59–63

Wardlow, H. 117
Weber, Florence 56
*whānau* (extended families) 5, 16

whānau violence in Aotearoa New Zealand
  20–33, 33n2; *see also* Aotearoa New
  Zealand
*Whāngai* (customary adoption) 5
Windish, Hélène 162n1
Wirihana, R. 28
witchcraft, in domestic violence in Papua
  New Guinea 167
witnesses of domestic violence in Papua
  New Guinea 166–167
women, violence to 69–70; definition
  7–10; economic control violence 85–87;
  economic violence 8; feminicides
  70–72; institutional feminism 8;
  mitigation 7–10; nativist familialism
  74–76; non-homogenous category
  in 69–70; polygynous marriages 9;
  resistance 7–10
women-only households 110–121;
  life before and after moving into
  117–119; sites of social resistance
  119; *see also* Port Vila, Vanuatu,
  women-only households in

Zimmer-Tamakoshi, L. 117

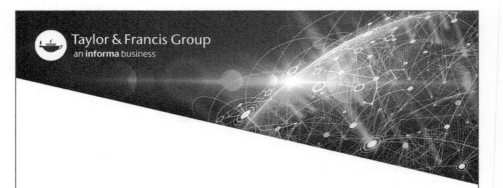